A First Hand Account of Discrimination in Civil Service (1997-2007)

Glass Ceilings for the disabled in Federal Civil Service

by

Dan McGrew

authorHOUSE®

AuthorHouse™
1663 Liberty Drive, Suite 200
Bloomington, IN 47403
www.authorhouse.com
Phone: 1-800-839-8640

First published by AuthorHouse 3/13/2008

ISBN: 978-1-4343-6183-7 (sc)

Printed in the United States of America
Bloomington, Indiana

This book is printed on acid-free paper.

"Thanks to GOD and all my good friends (Avionics, Elen, and Crew Chiefs) for helping me get through more than 10 years in civil service."

March 1996

A few weeks after my 30th birthday, I was riding my bicycle very slowly up Old Orangeburg road in Jedburg, South Carolina. There were three little girls behind me. Their ages were 4, 6, & 7. My wife Linda was riding behind them. We had designed a plan to sandwich the girls so that we keep a better eye on them. Eva, the middle daughter was excited and had just tried to overtake and pass me. Her objective was to show me that she could pedal faster than the rest of us. Linda saw her and made her get back into line and off the road. As a youth, 12 to 15 years old, I had ridden my bicycle up and down that road a million times.

We were riding directly in front of the Tri-County Baptist church's first leg of their horse shoe driveway. I don't know if any of them had seen the truck. I don't remember seeing it. Actually, I don't remember anything except what I've been told for over six months after that. I remember waking up on a fold-out bed at my Mom's house. I was going outside to smoke a cigarette. Wait a minute, I don't smoke. Why would I want a cigarette? I had a whole pack in my hand. I still wanted it, so I went outside and smoked it.

My wife came out of the house and I asked her what we doing at my mother's house. She started explaining to me that I had been hit and killed by an Isuzu pickup truck driving on Old Orangeburg road. I don't remember any of that. She told me that I had spent 3 days in ICU after that.

My memory is still rather patchy for the next six months after that. From what I've been told I up, around, walking, and talking but I don't remember any of it.

I asked her why I was smoking. She said that in the hospital after I was moved from ICU and had finally awakened I had asked for a cigarette. She said that I became angry when she told me that I didn't smoke. She called the doctor and he told her to give me a cigarette. She said that I had been smoking since then. I sighed and said, "Now I'm going to have to quit all over again." The first time was no piece of cake either.

I spoke with my mother when she arrived at her house. She gave me some information. She told me the name of the man (Mr. Cassidy – 70+ years old) who had hit me with his truck. I had known that man since I was a little boy. When I was 14 years old I had been the boyfriend to his adopted daughter (Hope Cassidy – Older than I was) and biological granddaughter (Faith Cassidy – Younger than I was), who were actually beautiful biological sisters. We had moved to Texas with my Dad when I was 15 and then back to South Carolina when I was 29, because Dad had terminal brain cancer. Now, over 15 years later my ancient girlfriends' Dad had hit and killed me with his Isuzu pickup truck. I've never been angry about it. I do forgive him, if there is anything to forgive. I really don't think he ever saw me.

Therefore, these 9 months worth of memories have been modified by input from others including my wife, mother, grandpa-grandpa, the children, and friends. I do remember that I had been working as a nurse in a nursing home in Summerville. They had fired me because I didn't show up for work. I had also been a United States Air Force Reservist and had missed a few UTAs. They did call me and Col. Bradley (The Wing King) came to visit me at my house, possibly twice, but all I can remember are pieces of one visit. I remember fragments of working at Charleston AFB base. I remember pieces of Col. Bradley's retirement ceremony, but it's like a dream, when I try to focus on the pieces they scatter away. My memory did start getting a little better. That's where all the little green books came into play. I started writing in them, what I did, where I went, and other things as I would get a chance to write them down. Everyone mentioned in this diary watched me write the little green books. I didn't wait, when someone started talking to me, if I felt it needed to be recorded or that I might forget it later I would write it down.

I began looking for work on bulletin boards. I found a place called 'FedWorld' and discovered that they had a list of federal jobs that were open. I downloaded the list and studied it. I read the FAQs and started applying for the jobs. I got a phone call and it was Altus AFB, OK. They asked me when I would be able to report for duty. I told them. I don't remember how I got the money. I don't remember packing my clothes or that last night in Pinehille Acres. I remember a little piece of driving my El Camino down the interstate to get to Oklahoma.

Friday, September 26, 1997 (Altus AFB, OK)

I first got to Altus AFB, Oklahoma in September 1997. I slept in my car (El Camino), by the payphone, by the Burger King the first night in Altus, Oklahoma. That's where the truckers park. The next day I started looking for Building 52. I found building 52 and checked in. The woman there told me to go to hanger 285 and check in. I went to the hanger and checked in, the assigned someone to in-process me. Showing his infiniteness once again GOD led me to be in processed by John, who had also been hit by a truck while riding a bicycle. This was amazing; I had never met another person who had been hit by a truck. We talked about the aftermath of our similar event for a while before he handed me an in-processing checklist.

Friday 17Oct97

**Life support crew (the people who put food on the A/C, and empty the rest rooms) told me that there is a regulation. It says that people are not supposed to use the rest rooms, while the A/C is on the ground.

0200 - Assist launch.

8087 - Assist R2 hydr. Line L main & assist launch.

Monday 20Oct97

*Boots - When I first got here, they gave me a pair of new boots. I got to pick them out. They didn't have my size, but said that they would get them in again, eventually. They gave me size 11, I wear size 12.

0146 - #2 UHF inop %. Assist launch. *Was told to w/u #2 engine throttle lever for engine troops, and call w/u into center, by Glenda. She stated, "You should know that, you've been here long enough." BTW, I still do not have a trainer, and no one showed me how to do that.

0263 - Removed L wing oval panel, sat with crew and elen during pressure regulator valve replacement.

Tuesday 21Oct97

0146 - #2 UHF works again. HF #1 & 2 couplers are in TNB. R2 HF #2 connector @ 85ft. TDR'd both HF foam flex lines. Did danger tags, so other maintenance. personnel could apply power. Swapped RT & Control boxes for HF. Same errors.

Wednesday 22Oct97

0146 - Went to GO-81 class, 'till 12 O'clock. Changed #1 HF coupler with dayshift comm/nav crew. R2 #2 HF coupler. #2 HF still has a coupler fault light at certain frequencies.

0161 - Helped change light bulb under L wing. Helped R2 #4 engine drain, due to a crack. Came in 1 hr early to work on GO-81. Helped open #4 engine cowling doors. Helped with engine run. Navigator had radar in TEST position when people were walking in front of the a/c.

Thursday 23Oct97

0200 - Sat with a/c in fog, waiting for clearance from ground control. Finally got clearance. Towed a/c to last parking spot. Next trip for 0200, is to the bone yard.

Friday 24Oct97

087 - Changed R main taxi light & #3 hydraulic system pressure switch. Both checked good. Launch.

Assisted recovery of two a/c.

Monday 27Oct97

0610 - Assist refuel & pre-flight. Launch.

0629 - Ops check UHF #1 & #2, VHF #2 (Comm Only)

0161 - Recovery & Tow

Tuesday 28Oct97

0263 - TACAN (MX Adapter) #1 %, Ops checked good. R2 TACAN #1 MX adapter. Did not fix problem. Ordered navigators HSI. Assisted recovery of a/c. Ed wanted me on 0263 to learn how to do a pre-flight. He missed me due to the fact that I was in the L main, looking at the hydraulic pump wiring. When I came out, the maintenance. crew told me that Ed was looking for me. So, I waited in front of the a/c. He came and picked me up, and took me to a/c 0263. Read pre-flight work cards.

0141 - #1 UHF w/n rec/trans. Discovered that pilot's KY-58 RCU was in the cypher position. Placed RCU in the plain position and the UHF checked good. Did radio check with ground control, frequency 275.8.

4

Wednesday 29Oct97

0243 - Recovered. Wrote up #4 engine oil leak. Assisted #1 TACAN Ops check. Went back out and used TACAN test set to check bearing and DME accuracy. Swapped TACAN RT, control boxes, MX adapters, NO help. Swapped HSIs. It would appear that the connectors needed to be reseated. Because the TACAN system worked fine after we reconnected them. Ops checked good.

Thursday 30Oct97

0161 - Sat right seat during engine run. Ran up all four engines to 100%. Assist launch.

0629 - Helped remove center deck plate in center cargo bay.

Friday 31Oct97

087 - Recovery. Checked engine oil. Fixed jump, push to test, light on right rear cargo door. (SPR) Refuel. Assist launch.

Monday, November 03, 1997

8087 - TACAN control box channel display cover cracked. Ordered TACAN control box. R2 TACAN control box. Ops checked good.

æ½¼ - I was advised by the union to write a 'memo for record' and give it to my supervisor. The 'memo for record' below is the one that I handed to my supervisor.

Memo   For Record

    to: Glenda McCarty
    cc: Randy Greenwood
    from: Daniel Leroy McGrew
    re: AFIN Training
    date: November 3, 1997
    My resume is accurate. I have worked on VHF, ADF, UHF, GPS, Radar, HF, TACAN, IFF, KY equipment, the KIT1C. I have worked these pieces of equipment when configured for C-141, C-5, and C-17 aircraft.

However, I have no experience with AFIN equipment. I have no formal education and/or on the job training with INS, Auto-pilot, FSAS, or cockpit voice/data recording systems (flight-line or shop).

I hereby request that I be given formal education and on the job training, concerning this equipment. This education and training will enable me to completely perform the job that I was hired to do.

I have accepted your request to move to dayshift until my training (including formal education) was completed. I have remained on dayshift for four months awaiting formal training. I have received no formal training at all, in the AFIN career field.

I have ventured up my chain of command to Colonel Sparks, our logistics commander. He has assured me that no formal avionics training has been planned for Altus AFB at all. "I have 1.3 million dollars budgeted for training, here at Altus, over the next 3 years. I have every intention of training my most essential career fields first. They are - engines, hydraulics, and electrics", said Colonel Sparks.

Tuesday, November 4, 1997

0610 - Marshaled plane, ran fuel panel, Flight engineer interphone, Ops checked good.

Wednesday, November 5, 1997

0223 - Rode truck. Recovered A/C.

Thursday, November 6, 1997

* Rode truck. Watch training slides, course #94.

** Glenda told Richter to tell me to stop wandering and let her know where I am and what I was up to. I can understand the reasoning. I told Mr. Richter that I would comply. I just wish that she had told me herself. She's not interested in why I was doing that. I am from the backshop. When I finish with a job, I go the next job. That's what I've always done. That's not the way that it works out here. Plus, the life support crew told me not to use the A/C restroom. They told me that a person could get a letter of counseling or a letter of reprimand, and I do not want one of those. So, I go to the shoe every now and again to use the restroom. Sometimes, I smoke a cigarette, or get a cup of coffee, and walk back to the A/C, when I know that a crew just arrived. Because, I know that they are going to take at least 30 mins. to an hour doing their pre-flights. So, I drink my coffee and/or smoke my cigarette on the way back to the A/C. I can understand why it's important to let someone know where you are. In case there is an emergency. So, I guess, now, I'll just have to hold it more.

Friday, November 7, 1997

Rode truck and recovered 2 A/C.

Monday, November 10, 1997

Rode truck. Did fuel panel for defuel. Recovered A/C. Volunteered to work 3 hours overtime to recover A/C at 2320 hours, chain, secure, cover intakes, and pitot tubes. Because swing shift did not work because of the Nov. 11 holiday. Glenda said, that I could work overtime with everybody else, but I'd "better not be wandering around". Of course, I stopped doing that a week ago, when Ricter told me that she didn't like it, but she keeps holding it over my head, and reminding me.

Tuesday, November 11, 1997

Veteran's Day. Holiday.

Wednesday, November 12, 1997

Rode truck.

0203 - Towed. Walked left wing.

0223 - Moved radar control head, at request of crew, to navigator position. Glenda showed up and started fussing at us about not doing a thru-flight. There were three civilians on the A/C, including myself. Marvin explained to her that none of us were qualified to do a thru-flight, much less sign one off. She had two GI s join us on the A/C. One of them was qualified on thru-flights and he signed it off. But, he was a little concerned about the air crew having already done their pre-flight checks. Marvin launched. I pulled the right main landing locking pin and removed the chocks. Then, we pushed the power cart out of the way.

Thursday, November 13, 1997

0223 - Checked GPWS system. Ops checked good. Assisted launch.

0161 - Pilot's stated that they had a radar problem. They said that the radar would not test. True enough, there was no test pattern, when the radar control panel was placed in test mode. R2 radar (APS-133) RT. Fixed the problem, but the radar returns were now pink. So, we tried to swap the control panel to the navigator's position. Problem with this is that, the connector was seated improperly. The reason why, someone connected the connector improperly and bent two of the pins together. When, I separated the pins, the radar worked fine, and the control panel worked fine in both positions (Navigator's and Center Console). Radar system Ops checked good. Assisted launch.

** Glenda told me that there were some classes available for us to take. She said that she has signed me up for all of comm/nav classes, some AFIN classes, and some APG classes. I sure do appreciate that. But she doesn't know where the classes will be at, or when. Oh, well, guess I'll just have to live with that.

Friday, November 14, 1997

*** AFGE Union - I went to the Union today. I talked to them, about Glenda skipping me and going straight to Ricter about my supposed wandering. They said that they would fix that. I told them that what I wanted was to have the regulation fixed, not Glenda. Because, I don't want to offend anyone. I really do like my job here. I really want to fix stuff; I just wish that I knew a lot more about how. I'm trying to fix that. Oh, well, guess I'll have to live with that too.

0146 - Assisted with pre-flight, chained and covered A/C.

087 - Assisted towing A/C from hanger. Snow began, and snowed for about three hours, then stopped. The snow did not stick; it melted when it hit the ground.

* Chained and covered two more A/C.

**æ½¼_ I ordered some books from Hastings. The books were Thomas Jefferson's notes on the state of Virginia, a book on the Bill of Rights, and a book about the Constitution. I wanted pamphlets on these items, but have been unable to obtain them.

Monday, November 17, 1997

204 - Got on the truck at the shoe, got off at the hanger that 204 was in. Pushed two stands, helped an older fellow push one stand, and pushed an engine cart out of the way. Then while we waited for the other guys to get the door working again, I pushed the power cart out of the way. At this point I walked out to fifty feet and waited with seven other people for the doors to start working again. Then Mr. Greenwood pulled up, Ssgt. Partain picked this time to tell Mr. Greenwood that I was reading my book on the "Bill of Rights", instead of helping them. He hadn't even given Mr. Greenwood a chance to get out of his truck. Of course, this was not the case. (At least, Mr. Greenwood acted like a man, he didn't go behind my back, not talk to me at all, and tell the shift supervisor, Mr. Richter.) Also, I could have said the same thing about Ssgt. Partain, last week. That is, three times, when I was present, the truck driver asked him to get off the truck, and he told the truck driver to "kiss my a - - , I'm reading my PFE manual!". So, this is obviously a case of the pot calling the kettle Black!

204 - Anyway, we towed the A/C from the hanger with QA watching us. I walked the right wing.

*X1 - Checked out TACAN system. Ordered new TACAN RT and new TACAN (in-line) test unit.

Tuesday, November 18, 1997

*Four men sitting at the round table, at the shoe. Greenwood and Glenda drive up. Glenda says, "whatsamatter McGrew, Nutin' to do." I explained to her that all five of us were waiting for the "10" truck to pick us up, so we could go tow a plane. Glenda said, "Oh!". I was sitting at the square picnic table, the farthest from the group. Why me? * I was on the truck, but "TEX" told me & Wert to get off, because it was full. He said, he would come back and get us. I have to admit. At least this time, she did it like a man. She asked me herself, instead of going around behind my back. There is a first time for everything.*

203 - I washed windows. Told a Ssgt on the flight crew what our radio freq was - 148.125. Helped SrA Holland with the aircraft. SrA Holland and SrA Odom taught me about the 3 step emergency landing gear equipment, and how it worked. Also, what the four hydraulic systems are for. Then I stood SPR, and we air started the engines and launched the plane.

0161 - Recovered A/C. Checked oil. #2 engine needed 6 quarts in the main, and one quart in the CSD. Worked panel for refuel, until mid-shift relief arrived.

Wednesday, November 19, 1997

*Billy is driving the truck tonight. Normally, Allen Crewnut drives the "10" truck. I got on the truck, but they told me to get off, it was full. I asked Billy, what he wanted me to do. He said,"Just hang out for now, Dan!". So I hung out with 8 civilians and 9 GIS.

204 - Helped close #3 engine cowling doors, & prepared to tow.

146 - Glenda moved me to this A/C for comm/nav training, on APS-133 color weather radar. By the time the truck got me there, they were finished and were putting stuff up. Then, we waited for a fuel truck. 9 people hanging out in the cockpit for two hours. Helped with an APU wash. Fuel truck arrives, can't have too many people on A/C while refueling. Some of us had to leave the area.

204 - Got on truck. Got dropped off at A/C. Towed A/C to hanger 435. I was the hydraulic hand pump operator. Got A/C into hanger. All crew chiefs went to lunch. That left 5 comm/nav and one AFIN troop. None of us were qualified to pump up the A/C struts or jack up the A/C. So, we all stood around for 2 hours and waited for some crew chiefs and a nitrogen cart.

* Got picked up and taken to be a fire guard for the people at the LOX/LIN farm.

263 - Went to sign off write up for VHF antenna. Someone wrote up the wrong antenna. They wrote up the UHF antenna instead. Oh well. I just ops checked them both. They worked fine. So, I signed them off, and asked Billy to please call Center and tell them that the antenna write up was complete.

Thursday, November 20, 1997

Went to pollution prevention class, from 1500 to 1700.
087 - Refuel, launch.

0161 - Tow.

** Randy Greenwood, picks this time to have his discussion with me. He tells me that the other guys are complaining about me not wanting to help them out. (Well, I can only do what Glenda and/or the truck driver tell me to do. They are the ones who decide what the priorities are, and what A/C to put me on.)I explained to him that I was practically sitting in the middle of seven people (who were just standing in a circle, talking about nothing [also known as shooting the breeze], and doing nothing), while reading my book. I also explained to him, that 70% of the people who graduate our schools today, cannot freakin' read and/or write. I saw a danger sign on a flammable storage locker, it read, "Danger! No Smoken!" Wow, this was written by active duty military. It was inspected by his/her supervisor, then inspected by Air Force environmental people, and people from the state and federal sections of the EPA. Gee, that says something. So, why can't I read a book? I told him that I would do better, I would not bring a book again, and I won't. I wouldn't want to appear to be, more intelligent than Glenda, Randy, or Ricter's drinkin' buddies.

223 - Tow to hanger 435

Friday, November 21, 1997

263 - Jump seat (Instructor pilot's seat) comm cord inop. Hold for down time. Refueled, worked fuel panel.

243 - Chained down A/C, refueled (stood SPR).

Sunday, November 23, 1997

Volunteered to work today. The brown shirts sent a list around at roll call last week. I signed up for Sunday, that way I could have Thursday, Friday, Saturday, and Sunday off Next weekend.

**** My wife and children arrived at 1900 hours. It's going to be an interminable 5 hours until time to get off work and go home to see them.

Monday, November 24, 1997

0161 - R2 radar control head, dummy plug connector. APS-133 color weather radar system ops checked good.

Tuesday, November 25, 1997

219 - Assisted Doug and Marvin with a pre-flight. I checked exterior skin condition, tire pressure (#1 nose tire pressure was low & #6 main landing gear tire pressure was low - I let Doug know about it, he said that he would write it up), brakes, landing gear hydraulic lines for leaks at the swivel valves, amount of oxygen (front & aft), and hydraulic fluid levels.

243 - Assisted Marvin with a pre-flight. I checked the exterior skin condition, walked across the tops of the wings with Marvin (had one in-board formation light bad on top of left wing), tire pressure checked good, brakes looked good, hydraulic fluid looked good, O2 looked good (fore & aft).

Wednesday, November 26, 1997

203 - Covered, secured, and tied down A/C.

219 - Stood ground to assist engine run.

161 - Closed doors, and secured A/C.

146 - Recovered A/C, refueled, covered, secured, and tied down.

Thursday thru Sunday --- Thanksgiving Holidays

Monday, December 01, 1997

8087 - Did thru-flight, launch. A/D companion had a fuel leak right wing. Recovered A/C.

8087 - Launch A/C, Recovered A/C.

Tuesday, December 02, 1997

Went to 781 forms class at 0730 this morning. I'm going to have to find out a little more about this letting a person off early, for classes the next day. I got off work at the regular time 2400 hours. A few people told me that I should have left 2 hours earlier, but Glenda did not say that. She handed me the paper telling me to go to class today. She gave me that paper yesterday at 1500 hours. I reminded her at the end of the shift briefing, at about 1520 hours that I had a class today. She said, "OK, I know". Oh, well, another one of those humanitarian things that the union people were telling me about. You know, about being allowed to use the bathroom, eight hours of sleep, stuff like that. Wish I was allowed all of that stuff. Guess, you have to be a shop steward or something to get those things, or have a male boss, or be a female employee.

Wednesday, December 03, 1997

087 - Crew discovered that A/C popped a circuit breaker on the co-pilot's side. This is connected with the flood lights. I started looking around and found the co-pilot's map light wire to be extremely frayed to the point that the conductive portion of the wires were wrapped around one another. This was causing a rather direct short. I re-spliced the wires and re-taped the wire bundle and the lights worked and the circuit breaker stopped popping. Fell up crew boarding ladder, fell on right hand and left leg. Told Randy Greenwood, as Glenda and Richter were absent (sick or something, I guess). I remember that Richter told us to fill out a form if we are injured at work, but I forgot what it was. He didn't spend a lot of time explaining all that stuff to us, one night, about 10 to 20 minutes. Oh, well. I'd just have to find that stuff again, and with moving and all, I'd probably never be able to find it.

Launched A/C.

0269 - Recovered A/C. A/C aborted for fuel leak spotted on right wing during flight. Went to lunch at 2100 hours.

Thursday, December 4, 1997

161 - Changed 40 light bulbs in the cargo area. Repaired one light fixture in cargo area, at the back of the a/c, near the cargo bay doors, on the right

side of the a/c. A real distressing point is the fact that I couldn't take time for any of these fixes. It appears that the a/crew must write them up first. A person cannot just go off and start fixing stuff, until a flight crew writes it up. So, I have to attack this problem from a different perspective. That is, from now on, I'll just try to get the flight crew to write up all the light bulbs for me, so I can fix them. They are supposed to write them up anyway, its part of their pre-flight, but they never do. As a result, I've replaced as many as 50 light bulbs on some a/craft. These are all interior lights, so no one appears to care about that much. The a/c ground aborted, due to stressful factors that affected flying. For example, the co-pilot side, O2 regulator, was making a gurgling noise. Come to find out, it had water in it. So, we fixed it. But, the a/c was scheduled to fly an air drop, so it was to be a partner a/c, and had to fly with at least two other a/c. This couldn't be done, because one of its partners had a fuel leak on the left side of the a/c, in the a/c armpit.

0200 - Went to the North ramp and installed the lower strobe light, on the a/c.

0243 - Helped Brian the electrician repair a connector for the spoiler defeat switch, and helped him to ops check it. Spoiler system ops checked good.

Friday, December 5, 1997

161 - Wiped down right main landing gear. Assisted launch.

146 - Tow.

243 - Chained down, secured, closed up for the weekend.

8087 - Towed to the fuel barn.

I have yet to bring another book to work. Even though I see lots of goofing off. I just find a quite place to sit and wait for these 5 to 15 co-workers, and sometimes 1 to 3 supervisors to get motivated and then we can all get back to work. Of course sometimes this takes a few hours, not including lunch. I do like my job. I just wish that I could do more.

Monday, December 8, 1997

219 - R2 and ops checked right cargo jump door interphone cord. Ops checked good. Sat with engine and electric troops while they ran engines. Refueled a/craft.

Tuesday, December 9, 1997

0219 - Towed to hanger 435.

8087 - Waited on a/craft for to tow. a/craft 263 was running engines. As soon as he shut them down, we got clearance from the tower to tow to spot 26,

* Got on truck, went to lunch at 2030 hours.

7946 - New a/craft, from a different base. Recovered it, checked it's oil, and towed it to hanger 509.

Wednesday, December 10, 1997

* Put in my suggestion to save thousands of trees and thousands of Air Force dollars today. I gave the idea to Glenda Odem. She said that she would check into this for me. I just suggested that the Air Force make everyone use their double sided printing features, or go back to using the old US printing company contractor.

* Rode truck.

219 - Recovered, pushed a/craft back into parking spot, checked oil.

610 - helped re-install upper outboard flap panel and lower outboard flap panel. Flaps ops checked good.

223 - Recovered, checked oil (need 11 quarts).

203 - Recovered, checked oil on left side only (needed 13 quarts), pushed back into parking position.

Thursday, December 11, 1997

8087 - Recovered, checked oil, thru-flight, launch.

223 - Stood ground during engine run.

* - No Comm/Nav trainer yet.

* - Lost Allen Crunut, the "10" truck driver. He and Glenda did not see eye to eye on something. I believe that it had something to do with him letting the active duty military people go home a little early. "Tex", let them go home at 2030 hours for a week. They are swing shift, helping us. They

arrive at 1500 hours, get an hour lunch, and are supposed to go home at 2400 hours. Of course, "Tex" is a cool name and seems like a pretty cool dude. I guess Glenda likes the way he looks a little more. Anyway, Allen Crunut quit his job as the "10" truck driver. He had had enough.

* - Can't get flight-line drivers license yet. I have to talk to MOCC before 1500 hours. I work 3 to 12. I have to get permission to come in early, because they have to let me go home early. They have to plan all that stuff. I understand that. Mr. Ricter gave us all 30 days to get a license, but did not give us permission to come in early and get it done. I told Mr. Greenwood that there was a problem with this. He told me that he would fix it.

* - Billy (crew chief), Wert (AFIN), and Dennis Scott (AFIN) are the closest people I have to trainers here so far. They don't know much about Comm/Nav stuff, but like Ms. Glenda they can sing off any red X write-up. Whether they know anything/everything about that system or not.

Friday, December 12, 1997

8087 - Got new power unit for a/craft. Helped Dennis Scott and Marvin Leverett use the APS-133 radar RT, control head, navigator's MFD for trouble-shooting. I put it all back together and ops checked it all. The radar system ops checked good.

*8087 - A key element in this is the morale. Marvin and Dennis complained that Glenda met them halfway across the flight-line to the target a/craft, we were trouble-shooting and told them, "if you want to keep your jobs for a little longer, you won't pull a stunt like this again.". Marvin was upset the whole night. He is retired military, and has more experience with everything than Glenda does. He told me that, "no one has ever threatened me or my job before.".

243 - Recovered, checked oil, chain and cover.

Monday, December 15, 1997

æ½¼ - Glenda gave a spirited little speech, about talking bad about other shifts.

8087 - Refuel, thru-flight.

7946 - Tow, push-back. FE told me that right extended range tank gauge was off by 1500 lbs. I swapped the gauges and ran the boost pumps for 2 mins. The tank gauge showed that the tank was draining. It dropped down to 500 lbs. #3 aux tank went up 1000 lbs. I was about to sign it off, when they came and told me that my wife had called and I needed to call home. So, I got on the truck with "Tex", went to the shoe, and called my wife. 'twas a minor emergency at home. The FE didn't write up the fuel gauge.

60203 - SPR - defuel, and tow to the north ramp.

Tuesday, December 16, 1997

0243 - Assisted Jeff Swoboda fixing left lower landing light. Found 3 bad splices and one bad ground.

** Fixed interphone cannon plug wiring, on a/craft right main landing gear pylon. It had a bad splice.

60161 - Got pulled off fixing 0243 before I could finish the job. "Tex" said that he needed us now, for a redball tow. I told him that I wasn't done yet, I had wires hanging out and tools still laying out on the a/craft. He said, "get on the truck, let's go." I got on the truck.

0243 - Went back to interphone job. Finished splicing, and taping wires. Cleaned up area and put tools away. Landing light and interphone cord wiring ops checked good.

*Boots - Still no boots that fit. My second toe on the left foot is tore up a little. The end of it has a permanent blister on it. It's been there for about 2½ months. I sprained my left ankle on an a/craft ladder. I blame that on the boots. I have three blisters on the top of my right foot. Have had since I got these boots. This clothing thing is ridiculous. They were supposed to give me some uniforms. I have torn up five pairs of pants that I know the government will never replace. They gave me one coat, which I appreciate. But they didn't give me any long johns, or any other winter stuff to combat the -20 degree temperatures, when the Oklahoma wind blows. I have what I bought and brought with me, to keep me warm. I wear three coats, two that I bought, two pairs of long johns, two pairs of socks, and stuff that my dad gave me when he was civil service. Like a cold weather hat. I also wear a pair of gloves that I got on active duty 10 years ago. That's what I have to keep me warm. There was a nice pair of insulated cover-alls. But, the CTK room here gave all those to the people on dayshift, and to people in offices. Being on swing shift, I would really appreciate a pair of those once the sun goes down on my shift. Oh, well, I've asked all my supervisors for cold weather stuff. That's how I found out about the insulated cover-alls. They know that we're cold. Maybe they just cannot do anything about it. Of course, they sit in offices and ride around in trucks and watch us shiver. Glenda said that we should go and buy cold weather stuff at Wal-Mart. Easy for her to say. Being a brown shirt (a boss) they did just happen to give her some free cold weather stuff. She really needs that stuff too. A person like her could freeze her butt off in that truck, with the heater turned up.

Wednesday, December 17, 1997

*Came in at 1400 hours (2 hours early) to get my flight-line drivers license stamped. This allowed me to get off work at 2200 hours, because civil service is almost violently opposed to paying overtime. At least not to everyday ordinary people like me.

0223 - Sat with spare a/craft to keep it ready to go.

Thursday, December 18, 1997

50243 - Checked oil, pushed back.

40629 - Spare. Assisted with pre-flight. Fixed mount for left upper main landing gear light. Replaced left nose landing gear spin brake. Called in flight engineer's, crew entrance door interphone door interphone write up. He said, that the wrong interphone box is installed. I am still researching that.

* - Actually, the flight engineer was correct. The tech data states that an:

> Intercommunications set control
>
> ID #: C-3942(B)
>
> NSN: 5831-00-061-1577
>
> Part #: A81-52

belongs in the cargo area's three PA/Interphone stations. The set controls have a two position wafer switch on them. One position is "PA", the other is "Interphone".

The set control that is being installed in every aircraft position is the seven position wafer switch version. It's identifying numbers follow:

> Intercommunications set control

ID #: C3942(P)

NSN: 5831-00-523-5328

Part #: A81-91

This version has seven transmit key lines inside. Therefore, a person at the a/craft pilot and/or co-pilot positions can transmit on a/craft radios. To install the two position version is both costly and useless. The seven position version can only transmit in three locations on the a/craft. There are 7 to 9 locations on an a/craft (c-141, c-5, and c-17). At any rate the supply data notes that a technician can substitute either set control in any a/craft position. Both set controls cost the same. Approx. $5983.65 each. Since the two position version is missing 5 key lines and all the associated circuitry involved, it should be much cheaper. However, it is not. That is because they are the exact same box but each one has a different cover. They could've made them a huge amount cheaper if they just made one with only two positions.

0610 - worked with Kim Cough on the a/craft flap panels. We ordered a light-all and installed the bottom flap panels and got up on a stand and watched as the flaps and speedbrakes were worked through a few times. This way we make certain that the problem with the jack-screw was fixed.

Friday, December 19, 1997

0610 - Negotiated #3 aux fuel tank with flight crew and fuel shop. Dayshift said not to use the #3 aux fuel tank at all. The flight crew said that their training included putting at least 3500 lbs into the #3 aux tank. The fuel shop said that as long as they didn't put over 5000 lbs into the #3 aux tank, it would be ok. The crew said that they could take the a/craft that way. Repaired instructor pilot's seat. Put new locking feet on it. Hooked up air cart, assisted launch.

60144 - helped chain and cover.

0263 - a/craft in hanger 510. Assisted installation of rain removal duct, with Allen CRUNUT and Claud.

670946 - Recovered a/craft. SPR (refuel), chain and cover.

æ½¼ - Allen Crunut told me that he would be gone for good in two days. He and his wife are going back to Chicago. He has been here about 8 years. He said that he was very glad to be going. Of course, the two best places on Earth are the place that you are leaving and the place that you are going to. Old military philosophy. Hope he's going to be happy in Chicago. He was a really nice fellow. A crew chief and expeditor. He really helped me a lot with workings of Altus, and how to stay out of the petty politics of the brown shirts. I hope it works for me.

* - I did discover that there are no classes any longer. That is, I talked to the training people and they showed me a list and told me that there are no CNAD or AFIN classes for 141s. So I guess they just don't believe in training people to help them learn to do a better job. Oh, well. I'll give them the benefit of the doubt. Maybe they'll come up with some more classes, in the future.

æ½¼ - Still no uniforms, no cold weather gear, no correct sized boots, no trainers, and/or no training classes available for us swing-shift CNAD people.

Monday, December 22, 1997

0144 - Checked tire pressure for tow from hanger.

0263 - Tow a/craft from hanger to wash rack. Rode brakes.

66172 - Write up states that pilot cannot xmit on VHF. Against my better judgment Marvin tells me that he is going to order a pilot's yoke interphone switch. I told him that at Charleston I had repaired hundreds of yokes in the shop. We should just order a yoke. But he insisted, and told me that Tammy Ramero had taught him how to order a switch and replace it on the flight line. I told him that switches were shop replaceable units and yokes were line replaceable units. He still insisted and went over my head to Glenda and got us a switch. While replacing the switch he broke the wire and we wound up ordering a whole yoke anyway. The bad part is it just had a bad solder joint on the old wire. Marvin kept telling me a bunch of old C-130 yoke stories. I told him that these are not C-130s. These are C-141s. I've worked on C-141, C-5, and C-17 parts. Yokes that is. Anyway, he also insisted upon replacing an upper strobe light. Come to find out, if he had just checked the K's he would have noticed that the upper strobe light had been disabled due to a TCTO. So, he didn't need to buy that. We could have fixed that yoke wire and saved a lot of money. But you cannot do extensive shop work on the flight line. Repair wire, "Yes". Replace microswitches, "Probably Not". Anyway, he says that he will try to fix the next one the same way. He wasted at least $12,000.00 worth of government time and money trying to do what Tammy Ramero showed him. He admitted to me that he didn't have any soldering classes under his belt. I wish that he wouldn't do shop stuff on the flight-line, since he's never been in the shop. He's not even qualified to solder, and I'll bet my bottom dollar that he'd die before he'd let anyone teach him, because he knows everything.

Tuesday, December 23, 1997

144 - Write up is, #2 TACAN (Co-pilots) is inop. Both TACAN systems ops checked fine. However, the pilots HSI DME flag pulled when TACAN is placed in Rec. mode. Of course that's wrong, just to be certain, I went over the problem with Dennis Scott. He is an AFIN expert. I also swapped the HSI just to be sure. It did the same thing in the co-pilot's position. So, I ordered an HSI. In came in and I swapped them out. Now, both TACAN systems ops check good. The co-pilots BDHI has a mechanical problem. It's needles will only rotate clock-wise. Ordered a new BDHI. This part did not come in, and I was told that it probably would not. Because, there are several other a/craft that have BDHI s on order. They went back-order, and have not arrived.

Wednesday, December 24, 1997

172 - Chain & cover...

Monday, December 29, 1997

263 - Towed a/craft. I walked right wing for the tow.

0161 - Helped Kim & Martin install a L main landing gear down lock grease fitting. Serviced R nose tire with nitrogen. Helped with pre-flight.

`- A religious conversation was boiling on the "10" truck. _____ asked me what I thought about prostitution. He asked me what I thought about Jesus defending a prostitute. He said, "Where in the Bible does it say that prostitution is wrong?". I told him that I didn't know. I told him what I did know. I told him that yes, as I remembered it, Jesus did defend a prostitute.

æ½¼ - At this point Marvin became mad at me. He started telling me that I did not know anything. He said prove that the Bible says that prostitution is OK. I did not say that prostitution was OK. He did not let me finish. But, he hopped off the truck mad before I could finish.

æ½¼ - Later, as I was sitting alone at the shoe. Marvin walked up and started pacing back and forth. He started talking to me. Marvin said, that "surely you know that _____ was unsaved." Marvin said, "so be careful what you say." He further stated, "if you make a mistake in scripture, it will be a terrible mistake." I asked him to help me then. I told him that I had a thorn in my side. The thorn is much like Paul's. I told Marvin that I have read many versions of the Bible. I have looked upon Greek, Latin, and Hebrew versions. I can read Greek and Latin. I understand the principles of Hebrew writing. I understand some of the Hebrew vocabulary. I asked Marvin to please keep reminding me that I did all that for the Glory of God. Then Marvin started talking about the difference between a person's mind and heart. I reminded him that the Bible says that a person should, "love God with all their hearts, all their souls, and all their strength." This is the old testament version of that. Mavin stated that the Bible said "Mind". I told him that a person's mind is a part of their flesh. I said that "mind" is not mentioned. However, it is. In the New International version of the Bible. But, only in the new testament and that part refers you to Duet. Ch.6 verse 5, which says strength.

æ½¼ - At this point Marvin gets really mad. He has been pointing his finger in my face for about twenty five minutes now. I told him that pointing is impolite. Musingly, I mention that pointing is probably illegal in some states (a joke of course) Now, he gets closer. He tells me that I am a stumbling block to him (not to God or the Holy Spirit or even to Jesus, but to him) Still pointing his finger in my face. He tells me, "Don't you ever bring up the Lord's name or Bible passages, in my presence, ever again." I agreed with him. I felt rather threatened. I did not, and do not want to fight anyone. Especially at work. I started saying, of course Marvin. Your always right Marvin. Attempting to cool Marvin down a little. Marvin cools somewhat. Marvin leaves.

¼ - At this point, I find and I tell Mr. Greenwood about the incident. I ask him to please ask Marvin to stop threatening me. The golden rule flashes in my mind at this point. I would not have done what Marvin did to me, to anyone. Mr. Greenwood comes back and tells me that Marvin states that he will not talk about Jesus with me anymore. This is not exactly what I had in mind. However, if he can't handle talking about Jesus, then this is probably best.... Although it hurts, that he would demand, so threatening, that I not talk about the love of my life. I have read, studied hard. I have learned a lot. For what. So that I could be, at least, as close to God, as people like Marvin. But, Marvin is a wolf in sheep's clothing. As described in 1st Timothy. He is not close to God at all. I will pray for him.

æ½¼ - Now, I go back out to work with Kim and _____. I tell them that I feel prostitution is wrong. I tell them that the only place that I can find supporting evidence for that is in the old testament. Exodus, chapter 19, verse 29 says, "Do not prostitute thy daughter, to cause her to be a whore; lest the land fall to whoredom, and the land become full of wickedness." Back to work.

Tuesday, December 30, 1997

0610 - Write ups are #1 UHF inop. and SKE bad as follower in Freq. B. Both RT on order. Went back order. UHF RT issued.

629 - swapped crew entry door (CED) interphone control box face plate.

60144 - Tow, walked right wing. Defuel, sat on top of fuel truck, watching fuel quantity.

o - Gave Mr. Greenwood my written version and opinion of what happened Monday night. Marvin should apologize for that, but I won't expect it. Not out here in the back woods of the military and civil service. Besides with Bill Clinton in office, respect, common courtesy, and religion have gone out the window. I guess that the Israelites where not the only people to live in the desert wilderness. At least I have my family. That is, until the government makes it so very profitable for someone to take them away.

Wednesday, December 31, 1997

223 - Helped remove the left wing, mid, leading edge. Helped to remove and replace a wing de-ice valve. The valve ops checked good, and we put the leading edge back on. I took all the top screws out and put them all back in. Then, I smoothed out the RTV for the top part.

Friday, January 2, 1998

* - Went to base retail sales for boots. I had my letter with me. The one that Mr. Bagg signed, so that I could finally get a pair of boots that fit. However, base retail sales tried to give me a pair of steel toed boots. But, I need the fiberglass toed boots, because I work with electricity. High voltages. So

base retail sales tells me that I need a special letter to those kinds of boots. They tell me that they only issue steel toed boots to civilian employees. All of my fellows avionic technician friends have fiberglass toed boots, as per Air Force regulation, dealing with high voltages. So I talk to Susie, Mr. Bagg, and Mr. Greenwood. They tell me to talk to Mr. Mobely. I went next door and left the letter with Mr. Mobely's secretary, because he was at lunch. She said that she would tell him and that he would take care of it.

223 - Tow, walked left wing.

æ½¼ - Emptied five small fuel bowser cans into a large fuel bowser with wheels.

0144 - Defuel (panel). Towed to hanger (rode brakes). Did one hour overtime.

Monday, January 5, 1998

6607946 - ops checked write up on jump seat interphone system. Ops checked good with & without hotmic. Also, had a write up for the wrong intercommunication set control installed at the crew entry door. Changed the face plates and wafer switch dial plates.

æ½¼ - Information to indicate that Intercommunication set control boxes are identical. TO 1C-141B-2-23FI-00-1-2, Sect. 23-40-00, pg. 5-9 and TO 1C-141B-2-23GS-00-1-2, Sect. 23-40-1, pg. 6-1, para. 6-2(b).

8087 - FE extra interphone cord inop. Re-soldered U-94A black wire, ops checked good.

Tuesday, January 6, 1998

æ½¼ - Talked to Mr. Mobely personally. Gave him the same information that I gave his secretary the first time. My name, bosses' name, duty phone number, and what section I work in. He told me that he would take care of the problem. I reminded him that I wear size 12, and I have 7 blisters from wearing these size 11 boots for three months. He reassured me that he would take care of the problem.

7946 - Took interphone control box face plates back to the shop.

** Rode truck. Joe is the driver now. Tex is going to the phase docs soon. So, sometimes Joe drives the "10" truck and sometimes Bruce drives the "10" truck.

8087 - Recovered. Did SPR position during refuel. Launch.

Wednesday, January 7, 1998

** New work phone number is X7896.

8087 - IFF mode IV audio inop. I checked all the test equipment out to do the job, but I was not on the list. So they couldn't give me the codes to do the Mode IV checks with. Someone who was on the list would have to get the codes for me and stay with me while I used them to trouble-shoot the a/craft. No one was available. The only people available to go with me are Eric Wert, and Dennis Scott. But, they had to work a/craft 223, because it was a flyer. 8087 can fly with the Mode IV bad. The troubleshooting and the ops check require two people.

æ½¼ - Marvin and Claude got their 90 day evaluations today. I've been here almost 120 days, I never got an evaluation. Glenda did give me a paper about me being raised to a step 2 in March sometime. But, it wasn't addressed to me, it was addressed to "suprv. of Daniel L. McGrew". So, I don't know why she gave it to me. Anyway, I went and asked Mr. Ricter about my 90 evaluation, too. He said, " Don't worry 'bout it."

0144 - Refuel (panel).

æ½¼ - I made a slight mistake here. Claud told me that he was changing an interphone control box face plate. Eric told me that he was taking Claud out to do the IFF. So when Claud went to lunch I took the interphone control box that he was going to turn in after lunch and started putting it together. He got rather upset and told me not to do his work for him again. I tried to explain what Eric had told me, and that I was just trying to help. I told him that if I put that one back together first, then we could all just get right to work on the IFF problem. He was still mad. He told Eric that he didn't want to be a part of his herd. He told Eric that he did not want to fix the IFF. He said that he didn't have anything to do, but he didn't want to help us. I still don't understand that.

8087 - Got back to work on the IFF problem. I checked out everything, I had Eric Wert with me, and we were getting started. We had the FI, the JG, the test set, tool boxes, and everything. We got up to the loading the codes part, and bang Glenda gets on the plane and tells Eric that she needs him on a/craft 223 to help the one AFIN and two Comm/Nav troops on that a/craft. It had an INS problem. So, I had to quite again. I put everything up. I gave turn-over to the mid-shift guy.

@ - I was sitting in the seat, in the "10" truck behind Joe, and in front of Claud. I heard someone making burping noises over the radio, on net one. Then, I heard Glenda's voice. She told them to stop. Then, someone came over the radio and said, "SHUTUP!!!" Glenda got mad and went around to everyone asking them if they had told her that over the radio. She also asked who had done it and if anyone had recognized the voice, at shift change.

Thursday, January 8, 1998

8087 - Pushed a/craft back into position. Checked #2 & #3 hydraulic reservoir. Both were a little low. Filled both with one quart of hydraulic fluid.

70022 - Check tires for two to the North ramp.

67946 - Checked tires for two. #2 NLG tire was low (150psi). Kim Cough, Jeff Swoboda, Myrac and I serviced it with nitrogen.

60161 - Towed (R wing).

243 - recovered, checked oil, changed KIT 1C batteries.

146 - Changed KIT 1C batteries.

7946 - Changed KIT 1C batteries, tow (R wing).

263 - recovered, checked oil, checked KIT 1C batteries. The date was 7/98, they did not need to be changed.

æ½¼ - I am still looking for the technical references for changing the KIT 1C batteries. They all need to be changed. I have asked all three brown shirts above me. I have asked the C-5 C/Nad and AFIN troops. I have asked all the C/Nad and AFIN 141 people, on all three shifts. I looked at the KY-58 batteries on 263 last night. They were last changed 4/95. These are going on three years old. They are lithium SO4 batteries. I did talk to one C-17 C/Nad troop, he said that they change their every three months, but they are good for six months. The shelf life date is one year. We'll see.

Friday, January 9, 1998

æ½¼ - I asked Mr. Greenwood if I could do some more quick checking on the batteries. I did get to work at 1400, just for that purpose. He said,

"Sure! Go!" So, I went over to the "MOCC" (Center), and asked them about the batteries. Then, I went over to the command post and asked them about the batteries. No one knows anything about these batteries. No one knows how to change them, no one has any technical references to change them. I did find one. It is in KAM 528B/TSEC, pg. 44. It is a warning not leave the batteries in the equipment for the purposes of storage, for more than 30 days. How to change the batteries can be found on the next page, pg. 45. But, I am apparently the only one who knows this, so far. Apparently batteries are only to be changed in the shop. I'll have to fix that with an AFTO 22.

7946 - Attempted launch. Elevator problem prevented take-off. Flight crew swapped to the spare a/craft.

263 - Launch.

7946 - Refuel (Supervisor). Attempted to fix the jump seat interphone cord. I had collected all the parts and tools that I needed. I was on the a/craft, ready to go. When bang, Joe pulled me off to help tow a/craft 243 instead.

243 - Towed to the South side of the hanger.

; - Still no letter for me to get boots. Mr. Mobely has not called. I will check again Monday, Lord willing.

Monday, January 12, 1998

0219 - VHF #1 will not TX/RX from jumpseat. INS batteries due cap check. Took old batteries to the battery shop, and put the new batteries into the a/craft. Ops checked the INS system, INS system ops checked good. VHF #1 ops checked good, from the jumpseat position.

50263 - Tow to fuel barn.

0146 - Tow to North ramp (R wing).

946 - Launch.

0141 - Launch.

0172 - Recover. After watching me recover two a/craft, Glenda asks me if I'm signed off to be a chief marshaller. I told her I didn't know, but I've been marshalling a/craft for a few months already. I sure hope that someone has signed me off.

946 - Recover. Mike and I fixed the engine cowling pressure seals. Launch.

æ½¼ - Randy Greenwood and Glenda McCarty appeared to be tailing me. Every time I launched or recovered an a/craft they were parked kinda' close by. Ha!

Tuesday, January 13, 1998

219 - Took over refuel job for dayshift. They had already put in one fuel truck (35,000 lbs). They went home. We (swings) called for another truck. When our truck arrived and we started fueling the a/craft, we noticed that #2 & #3 aux. fuel tanks were filling. After re-checking circuit breakers, we discovered that dayshift turned off the #3 generator switch. Those two gauges get their power through that circuit. Now, that they had power, they said that they were full to the point of bursting. We were supposed to fill our plane with 85,000 lbs. It was already filled to 109,000 lbs. So we had to defuel approx. 24,000 lbs of fuel. Launch.

610 - Recovered, down for bad emergency generator. Billy, Brian, and Charles removed the emergency generator. Billy installed the four mounting bolts for the new one. I safety wired and hooked up everything else for it. Emergency generator ops checked good. Glenda was present. She picked up the part, and came back and watched us work for about an hour. She kept saying that the dispatch girl at center had an attitude. She said, "I'm could just kill that bitch!" Pilots and air/crew did pack it in. They went home. They lost their tanker slot.

æ½¼ - Dawn (another comm/nav troop) asked our CTK people to please order us two MSDS sheets for the KY and KIT batteries.

æ½¼ - Talked to Capt. Shaun and base comm sec monitors about KY and KIT accountability. He told me that they just keep the keys. They insisted that supply was responsible for the equipment itself. They said that supply should have a special person for that job.

; - Talked to Mr. Mobely again. He said that he was still waiting for the base retail supply people to call him. I also asked him about my uniforms. He said that there was a breakdown in our uniform contract. I don't quite understand that. I just want some uniforms so that I don't have to keep tearing my own clothes. If I have to keep wearing my own clothes out at an alarming rate, I sure wish that civil service would do something to help me buy some more.

Wednesday, January 14, 1998

æ½¼ - Talked to Col. Sparks, QA, & supply. Col. Sparks appeared to be interested. QA is lost. Supply informs me that they are only accountable for the KY and KIT units that they have in supply and on hand. They do not know who is accountable for the a/craft KY and KIT units. KY and KIT units are coded "9" in supply. This means that they are not classified items, but are cryptographically controlled items. I cannot find any control.

946 - Glenda assigned me to 946, but Joe needed someone quick to recover a/craft 610.

610 - Recovered, checked oil, did oil samples and sent them to CTK to be sent to the oil lab. Joe taught me how to make up the paperwork to send to the lab with the oil samples.

æ½¼ - Dawn tells me that Mr. Praetor (C-5, dayshift) wants me to make up a list of security problems with the KY and KIT units. My personal concern is two-fold.

Î Anyone could just walk onto the flight-line & take some KY-58s and no one would ever know, because they are not inventoried. None of the a/craft have 781Ls.

Ï The mercury batteries will go bad, either here at Altus, or at Davis-Motham (the bone-yard) and will destroy the equipment that they are in and leak into the environment.

946 - a/craft had elevator problems. A/crew went the spare, 0223.

223 - APU bad. Started ground air cart. Got #1 engine started. Pilot tried to start #3 engine next. 50 ft. flames shot out of the back, he shut it down. Motored #3 for about 5 mins and started it up again. It started fine. Ground air cart would not shut off. Had to hit the emergency cut-off switch. A/craft departed straight from the wash-rack.

610 - Recovered. Pushed Kim around on the stand to check the oil.

** - Told Glenda that I might be late tomorrow. I explained that the Dr.'s office sprang my wife's MRI appointment on me. She said, "So what do you want?" I said, "My wife's appointment is at 0730 tomorrow." She said, "So, what do you want?" I said, "I may be late tommorrow, but I expect to be here on time." She said, "You better be." Personal note --- Some needs to have her dosage of sympathy medication increased about a hundred-fold. It's rather sad that a woman's most endearing quality is at roll call, when she tells people how "Fugly" (her expression for the girl is so ugly that you can't f- - - her) people's girl friends are. Of course her other endearing qualities, listening to her constantly say, "I could kill that Bitch", about the supply girls, and the dispatch girl at center. I'm certain that she has many more endearing qualities. I just don't want to know about them.

Thursday, January 15, 1998

æ½¼ - Mr. Greenwood had a talk with me, as soon as I came in. He was visibly upset. He told me that Col. Sparks blind-sided Mr. Hilley & Mr. Francis about the KYs and the KITs. He said that I needed to use my chain of command. He said that I needed to let them know what my intentions were. I did tell Glenda. I told Mr. Greenwood. I told Mr. Richter. Mr. Richter is the highest person I know of in my chain of command. I did tell them that I couldn't find anyone responsible for the KY s or for the KIT s. I told them that I have talked to people in the Command Post. I talked to the Base Comm/Sec monitor and her assistant. I talked to all the C-141 comm/nav and AFIN troops for swing shift, dayshift, and midshift. I talked to all the C-5 and the C-17 comm/nav and AFIN troops for swing shift. I didn't tell them that Alice and Dawn told me good luck, finding someone who gave a damn, because they had tried this before. Apparently, I found some people who want to chew my butt up for their mistakes. Besides, Mr. Richter never told me anything about this Hilley and/or Francis person. They are on dayshift anyway. I never see them. I don't even know what they look like. I don't know where their offices are. There are no names on any of the doors. No titles on office doors. Besides, I told my bosses that I was going to look for answers to my questions. I did this on dayshift, while I worked on swingshift. For two weeks I came in early to find answers. I talked to the base comm/sec, command post, and QA people on dayshift. Because they only have a dayshift. I would come in at about 12 O'Clock everyday and went looking for information. I didn't look in my hanger, because I thought that I had exhausted all of my information sources there. All the supervisors that I knew of told me that they didn't care. So, I met Col. Sparks over at the training building. I was there talking to QA. I asked the Col. what his degree was in, because I have two degrees. We got to talking. I mentioned that I worked for Mr. Bradley, when he was a Col. at Charleston AFB in South Carolina. I told him that I was at Colonel, now Mr. Bradley's retirement ceremony. We got to talking about the security stuff. I mentioned my concerns to him. He asked me to come into his office. He made a list of my concerns. He was the only person that I had found so far, who cared. Apparently he went and talked to Mr. Hilley and Mr. Francis. Mr. Greenwood told me, "Don't you ever go over and talk to those GI s again! They always blow things out of proportion. Use your chain of command. Tell them what your intentions are." I told him. I did use my chain of command. My intentions were/are to find answers, to protect AF people, AF materials, and AF equipment. They knew that. That's their job too.

610 - Went with Jeff Swoboda to test an a/craft APU. Got pulled off by Joe to work on 8087

8087 - Navigator's extra comm cord broken (intermittent). Crew said that they would like to fly with it that way for now. They said that I could fix it when they got back. So, I helped Eric Wert fix the AMI indicators. T-Shooting successful. The co-pilot's AMI was bad. So, we CANNed one from an a/craft going to the bone yard (It was sitting at the North Ramp), but that AMI was bad too. So, we CANNed another one. This one was good. Next, someone swapped the radar control head to the center console position, but they forgot to connect the cannon plug behind the navigator's panel. If you don't connect that cannon plug, the radar will not work. So, I connected the cannon plug, radar system ops checked good. Launch.

0223 - Helped take off the left mid, outer, leading edge. This time for a hydraulic leak. Accomplices are Mike Tays, Myrak, Charles, Billy, and the new electrics person (Charles).

Friday, January 16, 1998

æ½¼ - Talked to a person in the AFGE union office. This person identified himself as the Union Vice-president. I explained my predicament and gave him a copy of my aircraft history logbook. I thought that maybe he could help me a little. I signed a paper for him to be able to represent me. He told me that he would have to take at least a week to review all this information. I told him that it contained information that was of "Official use only", to the Air Force. I told him that he should keep it in a safe, just to be on the safe side, if he had one. He assured that he would take care of it. He asked me what I wanted him to make management do. I told him that I would just like to be able to go outside of my chain of command to find answers. Only if my chain of command did not have the answers. Without getting killed (fussed at) over the deal.

æ½¼ - Talked to Mr. Francis. I told him that I was sorry about Col. Sparks blind-siding him. I explained to him that I didn't know that he was in my chain of command. He asked me what I thought he did. I said that I thought that he was a supply management person. I told him because the doors were not marked, no names were anywhere.

æ½¼¼ - Talked to Mr. Greenwood. I asked Mr. Greenwood if he was still mad at me. He said, "No!" I told him a little more about what Mr. Francis and I talked about. I explained to him that I had never heard him or anyone else talk about Mr. Hilley or Mr. Francis. He said, "That's because we don't like 'em".

æ½¼¼ - Talked to Mr. Praetor. He asked me to just give him a summary of all the information that I have accumulated. I tried to do that. He asked me if I could get him a list of all the CCEs on the 141s. I said that work-load permitting I could. I explained to him, that I do not set the priorities. He said,"Yep! The priorities get screwed up around here sometimes." He said that he wished that I had my security clearance already. I told him that I would try. I asked Joe and he said that I could go to some of the a/craft and start on my list. I told him that if he needed me for anything just come and get me. I told him that I would stop at anytime he wanted me to do something else; all he had to do was just let me know.

946 - Push back (Right wing).

0172 - Inventoried CCE (Controlled Cryptographic Equipment). Refuel (Panel).

0223 - Inventoried CCE. Helped put left, mid, outer leading edge on B1 stand, so that we could attach it to the wing.

610 - Inventoried CCE. Chained and shut down a/craft for the weekend.

0144 - Inventoried CCE. Ordered intercommunication set control box.

h - I told Mr. Francis that someone would have to alert NSA (National Security Agency), because they are the ones who are responsible for all the Cryptographic equipment. I think that you have to file a 437 for security incidences like this one.

0144 - Chained and covered for the week-end.

Tuesday, January 20, 1998

æ½¼¼ - Talked to the base comm/sec manager and her assistant. I tried to give them my CCE inventory. They refused to take it.

æ½¼¼ - Bruce came by and told me that the boss wanted to see me. He was pointing to Glenda. He added that she was really, "Pissed!" I walked over and Glenda started fussing about a rumor that she heard. She heard from someone (she wouldn't say who), that I said that she taught me how to safety wire badly. Brian the electrician got a QA fail for some safety wire. She heard that I said that it was her fault, because she taught me how to safety wire. I did not say that. I told her that I didn't say that.

946 - Inventoried CCE. Refuel (SPR).

219 - Inventoried CCE and dumped FO. I was picking up the FO between the two a/craft. During the inventory Glenda walked up to cockpit and asked me what I was doing. I told her that I was dumping some FO off, looking at the a/craft forms, and checking some equipment. I left very quickly. Mainly because Bruce and Kim Kough were waiting for me.

æ½¼ - Handed my annual leave projection calendar to Mr. Richter. I used this time to talk to Mr. Richter about Glenda sneaking up on me in the cockpit of 219. I told him that in my nursing background, we didn't let things like that happen. Men and women were not left alone together, if they knew what was good for them. I told him that I didn't want it to happen again. I told him that it was her at the Roach Coach, and that she saw me getting on a/craft 219. She followed me there and climbed on the a/craft after me. About five minutes later, when I had returned to a/craft 946, Bruce and Kim were hanging around the fire bottle watching. Bruce said, "Hey! Now, she's following you. Huh?" That scared me a lot. I told Mr. Richter about all this.

8087 - Recovered.

0629 - Recovered.

æ½¼ - Asked Mr. Richter for permission to pursue the CCE thing. "I want to do some more investigating". I told him that we needed to remove the batteries from some of the CCE before they destroyed the CCEs they were in because the batteries were leaking. Most of the batteries are lithium, but some are mercury. He said, "Permission denied".

Wednesday, January 21, 1998

æ½¼ - A1C Bunse at 97th Comm is the alt. wing comm/sec manager. Msgt. Bruha is the primary wing comm/sec manager. Msgt. Wise is the base comm/sec manager. He suggests that I read AFI 31-401. A1C Bunse says that we can write "IAW KAM ***", in our 781s.

æ½¼ - I called and talked to a Mr. John Pavlov at NSA. He referred me to a Msgt. Stephanie Hornwell at Scott AFB. She is with AFSC. Her phone number is ###-###-####.

æ½¼ - I called and talked to the people from the EPA. I talked to a Tammy Johnson at Waste Management, at phone number ###-###-####. I told her about the leaking batteries.

263 - Moved the radar control head to the navigator's position, for the navigator. R2 NLG spin brakes. Launch (R wing).

æ½¼ - Did some more investigating at lunch time. Read through the 00-20-5, page 3-19, para. 3-21 "AFTO Form 781B, Communications Security (Comsec) Equipment Record" and 00-20-5 pg. 3-3, para. 3-8 "AFTO form 781L. Record of removal/installation of controlled cryptographic items (CCI)." and KAM-337A. I read these and made some copies for Mr. Richter. I took them to Mr. Richter, and placed them on his desk. Glenda was sitting there, beside him. She immediately asked me why I kept bringing this stuff to Mr. Richter. Mr. Richter concurred, and added that he had already read all of the material that I placed on his desk. I started to explain that I wanted to protect AF equipment and the environment. I told them about the break in accountability and the possibility of mercury leaking from the batteries at Davis-Motham. He said that he had already thought about that. Glenda said, "What do you want us to do about it?" I said, play by the rules. Obey the AFIs. Mr. Richter spoke up and said, "We are not in the Air Force. We are civilians, and we are not going to play comm/nav at Altus, like you played comm/nav at your last base." I took that as my cue to leave. I said, "yes sir!" and left.

Thursday, January 22, 1998

æ½¼ - Talked to Mr. Bradely. Gave him a copy of the papers that I was taking to the base comm/sec office. He asked me why I was doing this. I told him that when my boss told me to do a job, I needed the tech data available to do the job. I went through what I could find in my chain of command. Mr. Hilly and Mr. Francis were there. I also mentioned loyalty, duty, and the military oath that I took. He said, "But you're not in the military.", "You're not on duty 24hrs anymore." I just said my usual, "Yes Sir." Plus, he told me that he was late for a meeting. We were all in a hurry. I just handed his secretary the whole notebook.

æ½¼ - Mr. Hilly said that I was at work illegally. Since they are not paying me for being here, how can I be at work. Mr. Francis had disappeared. I did what Mr. Greenwood told me to do. I told them of my intentions. Mr. Bradly acted and told me that I was dropping a ball in his lap. He said that he needed time. I told him that I told Mr. Francis last week.

æ½¼ - I took my stuff over to the base comm/sec managers. Just like Mr. Plumber told me to.

0144 - Pilot's yoke interphone switch intermittent. Used contact cleaner on switch. ops checked good.

0161 - assisted pre-flight. Launch.

Friday, January 23, 1998

æ½¼ - Came into work early to check a tool box and get some coffee. Mr. Francis caught me at the CTK window. He said, "Follow me." We got into his office, he left the door open. He said, sit in my chair and pick up the phone." I did. I dialed the phone number that he told me to dial. I spoke with a Mr. Ply on the phone. He told to come over; he would like to speak with me. I asked him to speak with Mr. Francis about my missing roll call in order to talk to him. He said that he had already talked to Mr. Francis. I told him that Mr. Francis was my boss; he needed to talk to him. He said, "Okay." Mr. Francis and Mr. Ply talked for a few minutes, and Mr. Francis told me to go over to talk with Mr. Ply.

æ½¼ - I went over to see Mr. Ply. Mr. Ply (OSI) asked me about the Ky s. He also asked me if I knew how to make bombs. He asked me if I knew how to hide a bomb on an aircraft. He asked me if I had talked with anyone about these things. I told him that I did not talk about these kinds of things with anyone. I told him that I did not remember talking about these things with anyone. He said, "Do you remember talking about making land mines". I said, "Yes!" I talked about making land mines with Mr. Marvin Levitt. Mr. Levitt brought the subject up about making land mines. We had been talking about the Oklahoma city bombing and about the Waco siege. But, I told them that I never really thought about making bombs. I've studied things that blow up by accident, but not things that blow up on purpose. He just kept asking me if I could make a bomb. Finally, I told him that I would make, just as good bomb as he could, if you laid all the stuff to make one with in front of me. He said that he couldn't do that. I told him that without instructions, I couldn't either. I should have asked him what his degree was in. At one point he told me that he was asking me all these questions because I was the expert on secure equipment. I just kinda' rolled my eyes at this. I am rather young here. Everyone I work with is close to twenty years older than me. They never listen to anything I have to say. I don't care. I just do my job the best that I can. They think that I am a know-it-all or something, when I try to tell them anything. So, I have just stopped trying to tell them anything. I have always been, and will always try to be a bigger/better person. That is, if you want somebody to do something/anything. I can/will find a better way to do it. Once I've studied the problem. Rather intensely of course.

æ½¼ - I made an appointment with Lt. Col. Charles E. Ayers, he is the base IG. The appointment is at 1300 hrs, Monday (26 Jan), in the HQ Bldg. This is mainly because Tammy Ramero told me that I am protected under the whistler blower act until I go and talk to the IG. Tammy is a nice person, so is Dawn.

; - Mr. Ply informs me that Mr. Bradley has a copy of my a/craft diary. I did not give it to him. He was late for a meeting yesterday when I talked to him. I handed his secretary my folder, while I was talking to him. Instead of copying the loose stuff in the book, she must have copied everything in the book. The folder wasn't taken apart. I would think that you would have to take the folder apart to get to the stuff in the middle, to copy it. Oh well, I didn't count on that. Apparently he has an extremely effective secretary.

8087 - Launch.

7946 - Tow (L wing).

50219 - Towed to indoor washrack.

8087 - Recover, refuel (panel), chained and covered.

Monday, January 26, 1998

æ½¼ - Talked to 97th airlift IG, Lt. Col. Ayers. He had talked to the OSI, the base comm/sec people, and to Tammy Romero. He filled me in, and asked me if he had left anything out. I told him about Mr. Hilley saying that I was at work illegally. I told him about Mr. Greenwood telling me to drop the whole thing. I told him about Glenda asking me why the h- - - I kept bothering them about this stuff. I told him about Mr. Richter specifically ordering me not to pursue this avenue, not to seek answers to my questions.

æ½¼ - Mr. Richter gave me a message from a Lt. Apple. Mr. Richter said to call him at home. He told me to use the pay phone, it cost me $0.50. I made an appointment with him for tomorrow.

8087 - Filled out and installed danger tags for Chuck to change the upper hydraulic RMLG actuator. #1 TACAN test light comes on & remains on at the end of the test. Swapped RT-1159A, problem switched to #2 TACAN. I asked Glenda to please order a TACAN RT. She did. Refuel (Panel). Launch.

- Rode truck.

263 - Assisted recovery. Checked oil.

Tuesday, January 27, 1998

I - Met Lt. Apple of vehicle ops. He told me and showed me, all the stuff that I had given to the base comm/sec people, and to the OSI. He told me that he reported to the Transportation squadron commander. He said that he was picked as a person who knew nothing about the situation, to come in, and review it. He (like everyone else that I have talked to) assured me, first, that this had nothing to do with my job, aka that I would not be fired over this. That's good to know. He asked me to tell him what I thought about the KY stuff. I told him and mentioned that it should have been done right to start with and that was annoyed because I wasn't getting paid for any of this.

æ½¼ - Mr. Greenwood asked me to meet him at lunch to go over my 90 day initial evaluation, over 120 days after I'd been hired. I said, sure.

8087 - Refuel (panel). Glenda asked me look at two battery problems on this a/craft. They were listed for time changes. One was ELT battery, the other was the underwater acoustic battery. We could not find the replacement batteries in CTK; some of them were not marked properly in the CTK refrigerator. Mr. Eric Wert was my accomplis in this job.

?@Noæ½¼ - Met with Mr. Greenwood to discuss my 90-day evaluation, Mr. Richter was present. I got fours and fives out of possible nines, which I hear is about average. I asked him about a trainer, riding the truck, and the KY batteries. He said, "We told you to begin with that we do a kind of self training thing here.", "You are getting better about your wandering", and "I haven't heard anything about the batteries." hanswers are mentioned in the same order as the question, from left to right. I still don't understand the self-training stuff. I've never read about it anywhere before, I can't find anyone else who knows. At any rate I re-emphasized the fact that I needed more training in the AFIN department. I just find it absolutely amazing that I worked on comm/nav equipment in the backshop never stepping foot on a C-141 or C-5 before. Now, all of a sudden they put me on these aircraft and tell me to fix them. Thank GOD for books. Otherwise, I'd be 100% lost instead of a measly 95%.

629 - Taped up for wash-rack.

223 - Towed a/craft (R wing).

æ½¼ - Got uniforms. Mr. Mobley told me that civil service would send me $55.00 in the mail, so that I could go out and buy a pair of boots that fit. That's because, he said, that active duty would not give any civil service people electrician's boots.

Wednesday, January 28, 1998

æ½¼ - Dennis was hired here to be an AFIN instructor. That job was taken away and he was made a flight-line AFIN person. He admits that he didn't like that a lot. He didn't get promoted last time, he hated that too. He told me that he wouldn't train AFIN/COMM/NAV people anymore, because all the ones that he trained kept leaving. I try to stay away from him a little, he is somewhat unconventional, that is he says nasty things. I try to get along with everyone as much as possible.

Thursday, January 29, 1998

;Fiasco - Before shift change, I asked Dawn to tell me how to do an ELT battery change. We asked Joe (The truck driver - who we now refer to as the Extension) if we could talk for about 10 to 20 mins. He said, "Ok! The plane's not even down yet." Dawn finished explaining the possible dangers and complications of the job, and I left and went out to the flight-line. Glenda pulled over, in her little truck, and started fussing at me. She said, "They almost had to push your d- - - aircraft back, because you weren't there." I told her to go fuss at Joe. I told her that he knew where I was and what I was doing. I told her that I asked him first. She said that she going to go straighten Joe out.

æ½¼ - I got my personnel brief. Hey! This time it was sealed in an envelope and had a privacy act sticker on it, just like I suggested on that AF form 1000. I never did get an answer from that one. I guess that they are just like every other air force base I've ever been at. They want you to think up ideas and submit them, so that they can steal them, and they can get the credit for them.

8087 - Assisted pre-flight, launch.

æ½¼ - I told Joe that I would be glad to do an ELT battery change now. He said that he would try to let me do one tomorrow (Friday).

Friday, January 30, 1998

æ½¼ - There has been a change. Some new ingredients have been added to the soup. It happened Wednesday (1-28-98). Tuesday, Glenda gave the briefing at 1500 hrs as always. However, Wednesday & Thursday, Bruce & Joe did all the talking. Even today (Friday), Glenda is not here (which is normal); Mr. Greenwood normally gives the briefing. But today he just started it. Joe & Bruce finished it. Mr. Greenwood did read a letter, out loud, that he had received from the base IG. The letter talked about people being harassed in the 97th airlift group.

æ½¼ - I noticed that Dawn was rather unhappy today for some unknown reason. I didn't ask. I saw her husband today at the civilian personnel office. I was there talking to the reserve liaison.

243 - Chain and cover.

161 - Refuel (panel), tow (R wing).

æ½¼ - I noticed that Marvin is rather unusually angry. He usually says hi, or something when passing me. Today, he just ignored me completely. Of course, he appeared to ignore a few other people on the truck. I hope that he and Dawn get over whatever is troubling them.

Monday, February 2, 1998

æ½¼ - Met with Mr. Harold Church, the chief steward of the AFGE union. He talked about his past dealings with Glenda. I gave him one thing to do and three reasons. I told him that,

I wanted my 160 hours over-time, and that I would go down to 120, if they were hurtin' too bad about it. My reasons were:

    Î I was preserving the integrity of the air force security system.

    Ï I was attempting to save air force equipment.

    Đ I was attempting to help the air force comply with environmental standards.

263 - Baby sat air craft because it was a spare.

161 - Assisted Mr. Rick Carter with a pre-flight.

æ½¼ - Maria called to wish Eva a happy birthday. While we had her on the phone Linda talked to her. They talked about our visit this time and made the arrangement to meet. Maria is working at Motorola now. She is living with some friends of hers in a mobile home.

Tuesday, February 3, 1998

0172 - Push-back (rode brakes). This aircraft had two AFIN jobs when it landed. I wanted to work them with Dennis, so that I could learn AFIN stuff. But Joe (the truck driver - the extension of Mr. Ricter) said, "Don't go there!", "Dennis said that he didn't want to work with you!", "Dennis is funny that way!" I just told him OK, whatever. I would just as soon not work with a person who sings songs about having sex with his dog, and selling his sister to truck drivers for a dollar. And he sings them to everybody on the truck as loud as he can. I suppose that that is how he is going to express his displeasure with the system, by harassing everyone around him.

æ½¼ - CTK people (Larry Lee, Pablo, and the chief) asked why I told the EPA that they were throwing batteries in the trash. I told them, "That's bull!" I told the EPA that Altus AFB is sending lithium and mercury batteries to the bone yard at Davis Motham AFB. Then I asked them, "Who told you that I called the EPA?" Larry said, "Our dayshift boss came in and told us that you did!"

40645 - Aircraft from Andrews AFB (AFRC), parked in spot #1. Then do battery changes on the KY-58s at their base. They have KYV-5s instead of KY-75s for HF on their aircraft. Info. source:MSgt. Sneed, pilots, and other aircrew members. Launch.

263 - Emergency recovery at spot #1. Popping phase "C" circuit breakers.

; - Mr. Greenwood called me into his office at lunch. Mr. Richter and Glenda were present. He presented me with a paper (hereafter referred to as attachment #1) about the KY-58 and KY-75 batteries. He said that the batteries were no longer a time change item. He said that the -6 said so. I went and got a -6. True enough it was not in there. However, I told him that the -6 was a TO for the aircraft, not for individual pieces of equipment. I told him that I will go with the manufacturer's information in the KAM rather than the -6. The -6 only mentioned underwater acoustic batteries and ELT batteries. It did not mention the INS, KY, or KIT batteries. He said, "Well go ahead and sign the paper, all the other Comm/Nav and AFIN troops have." I told him that I would sign it if he made me, but that I didn't want to sign it, because it wasn't correct. He said, "Ok!" I signed the paper as ordered.

Wednesday, February 4, 1998

æ½¼ - AFGE, talked to Mr. Church.

æ½¼ - Talked to AFRES recruiter.

æ½¼ - Talked to Jennifer, at Civilian personnel office. I asked her for a copy of my DD214s. She gave me a copy, I gave it to the AFRes recruiter.

æ½¼ - Talked to the hospital people. I asked them for a copy of my medical records. They don't have them. I filled out a form to have them sent here to Altus AFB, from where ever they might be.

æ½¼ - Talked to Col. Ayers assistant. He kept our conversation focused on at least two things. "Was I out to get somebody?", "Was I trying to make some money out of this?" I repeatedly told him that I was obeying my military oath, and that I was obeying the orders of the officers who signed the books that I use to take care of all this AF equipment.

; - Personally I don't think that I want any of their help. I don't think that they really want to help me anyway. I'm not officially any kind of minority, so their not interested in helping me. The Union tells me that it can't really help, and will not represent me in some areas. The OSI is primarily interested in whether I can make bombs, and whether I can hide them on aircraft. The Inspector General's office is apparently interested in whether I have an ax to grind with someone. I haven't been here long enough, or on one shift long enough to know anyone well enough, to have an ax to grind with anyone. I'm just trying to do my job like the book says.

æ½¼ - Mr. Richter called me over the radio. He wanted to see me in his office. I went in & he and Mr. Greenwood started reading me stuff about the "Fair Labor Practices Act". Stuff like, "Come to work at 1500 hrs, not before, leave at 2400 hours, not before. I told them that I came in for a pair of boots. I told them that my union rep told me too go and get a pair of boots. They were mad at me because I came in at 1300 hours to get a pair of boots. My old ones were falling apart. I was walking barefooted on the flight-line, because the bottom had fallen off my left boot. For months I had been wearing a size 11 and a ½ on my size 13 foot. I told Mr. Greenwood that. Mr. Richter was mad at me because I did not tell him. Well, I will not come in early again.

æ½¼ - I did get a pair of boots. I told them that I was 20% electrician. My contract says so. I showed them. But they still will not give me a pair of electrician's boots (Hi-Tech boots) that will fit me. Everyone with a foot size under 12 has a pair.

Thursday, February 5, 1998

223 - Launch.

Friday, February 6, 1998

æ½¼ - Sat down and talked to my bosses and the union people. We talked about training, the CCIs, Dennis, and over-time. Hilly said to submit an AFTO 22 and an AF form 1000 for the batteries in the CCIs. I told them that Dennis did not want to train me. I told them what he said. That everyone he trained went off and left him. Mr. Greenwood told me that Dennis told him, that I did not want him to train me. He said, that I told Dennis that I already knew everything about the a/craft. I told them that Dennis lied to him. I never said anything like that. I mentioned Jennifer's name, but the meeting was breaking up at that point. Mr. Hilly had another meeting to go to.

946 - Assisted launch.

610 - Chain & cover.

172 - Sat right seat during an engine run. We had a fifty+ foot flame shoot out of #3 engine. It lasted a while. Looked pretty cool, bright yellow, lighting up the night and the surrounding hanger and a/craft. Chain & cover.

Tuesday, February 17, 1998

æ½¼ - Talked to Hilley, Greenwood, and Mr. Francis. They suggested that I go to dayshift, get my formal training, some OJT, and help Mr. Prater.

219 - R2 T-tale interphone box.

629 - D. Depew signed off a bunch of installations of KY-75 & KY-58 parts. She did write them up as requiring MOCs. For the installations & ops checks she cited a C-5A TO (1C-5A-2-8-1).

Wednesday, February 18, 1998

Î - Went to civilian personnel office with Desert Storm paperwork.

Ï - Went to hospital, got height and weight statement for Mr. Giles (reserve recruiter).

Đ - Went to AFGE president's office. Signed statement about what happened in Hilley's office.

946 - Refuel (spr). Spare. Launch.

8087 - Launch. Recover left wing.

æ½¼ - Painting contractors are out to paint the red lines. They painted the red lines on the back of the anti-terrorist barricades this time, instead of on the ground. They high-pressure washed up the old red lines that were left on the ground.

Thursday, February 19, 1998

946 - Refuel (spr). Helped Jeff Swoboda T-shot a landing gear handle light. R2 right wing taxi light. T-shot landing gear handle to the nose down-lock switch.

*** - Rode truck.

Friday, February 20, 1998

946 - Refuel (SPR). Helped Jeff Swoboda T-shot a landing gear handle light. R2 wing taxi light.

Monday, February 23, 1998

#7 - First day of day shift.

æ½¼ - Shift FOD walk.

0629 - Truck put me out here to work an IFF mode IV problem with Dawn and Tammy.

æ½¼ - Sat down & talked to Mr. Bagg & Mr. Don Obriter about formal training. I told them that I thought it was funny that Mr. Greenwood would wait almost 5 months to tell me that Dennis Scott didn't want to train me.

Tuesday, February 24, 1998

172 - T-shot problem. Towed a/craft. IFF RT%. R2 IFF RT.

610 - Learned more about the radar, DIUs, INS, & FSAS.

Wednesday, February 25, 1998

(- Lband SatCom class. I talked with the instructor, Mr. Leismister, at length about the KY problems. He told me that he was helping Mr. Prator. I told him that I was helping Mr. Prator also.

Thursday, February 26, 1998

219 - Has radar & TACAN problem. Got dropped off there by the "10" truck driver. I am learning from Theo this morning.

610 - Tammy needed help on a red streak, and called over to our a/craft for Theo to come and help her. Tammy had an appointment. Theo and I finished trouble shooting the a/craft.

æ½¼ - Don told me that he would sign off everything that I felt comfortable with. He signed it off as a third party certifier. I'm still not 100% certain that he can do that. He's not an AFIN or a CNAD troop.

Friday, February 27, 1998

223 - Worked with Tammy on SKE and interphone. She was teaching me about engine instruments.

æ½¼ - Talked with Mr. Don Obriter and Mr. Baggs about my 971 (personal information file = PIF). He said that he had to talk to Mr. Richter first and then we would talk about it some more on Monday. Don asked me to work some over-time on Sunday. I told him, "Sure". They reaffirmed their interest in training me as a crew chief. By re-stating that they would get me qualified for a lot of (what I consider to be specialized) crew chief tasks.

Sunday, March 1, 1998

0223 - Dropped off at a/craft with Mr. Darnell. Unchained and uncovered a/craft. Waited an hour for a power cart. Mr. Darnell tells me that he's been here a year and still hasn't gotten any training. He says that he came from a naval base that was shutting down. He is the fifth person to tell me that same story. We are apparently getting people from everywhere. Including from naval bases, who have never stepped foot on a C-141, C-5, or C-17, and we aren't giving them any training. Finally got power unit (GPU). GPU has bad idle control. Called for another one. Got another one. Stood ground for engine run.

0610 - Dropped off to help Dawn and to learn how to check and calibrate the pitot-static tubes and the instruments connected to them.

Monday, March 2, 1998

æ½¼ - Watched module #57. Did practical with Dawn. Module #57 is about how to drive a land-all (De-icing truck).

æ½¼ - Tammy had to go work on C-5s today. They have one CNAD troop on sick leave, and one on military leave.

æ½¼ - Finished De-Ice truck training. Went to lunch 1145. Checked on KAMs in co-ordination with the AFTO 22s that I'm trying to write.

æ½¼ - Mr. Prator wants me to sign some papers about my security clearance. He just can't seem to find the time.

æ½¼ - Dawn wants me to write a letter about the training that her, Tammy, Theo, and Mike are giving me. I asked her if an excerpt from my a/craft diary would do. She said, "Sure!" The training I've had on dayshift is very comparable to military training. That is the highest quality that I can think of. Even having been to college for years. (240 semester hours). Besides, I received no training at all on nightshift. I told my supervisors at least every other night that I needed a trainer. They keep telling me, even on dayshift, that they can't actually assign me, or anyone else, a trainer. Weird.

172 - Dropped off to work interphone.

æ½¼ - Discovered a paragraph in the KAM 528 that says leaving fill batteries in KY equipment can lead to personnel injury/death and damage/destruction to equipment. I told Mr. Richter, Mr. Bagg, and Mr. Obritor. They said that whatever I did, clear it with Mr. Prator. Don added that if I made any AFTO 22s, I should take them to a Mr. Weaver in QA.

Tuesday, March 3, 1998

172 - Assisted launch.

æ½¼ - Lunch at 1245.

æ½¼ - Talked to SATCOM instructor and QA people about the "Warning" that I found in the KAM 528.

æ½¼ - Went to base comm/sec office and talked to SrA Bunse. Looked at KAM 337A. It said that the c/c/a E-DTE was still classified "Confidential". I made certain that SrA Bunse was made aware of that and that he would tell his supervisor. This took 14 mins.

æ½¼ - Made up AFTO 22s at the QA office per Don's request. Don signed the AFTO 22s and I turned them into Mr. Weaver in QA.

0161 - Changed INS batteries, assisted Mike Gross with an INS ops check. Sat in a/craft during engine run.

141 - R2 EDC (Engine Data Converter) with Mike, Theo, and Dawn watching. Mike, Dawn, and Theo taught me how to ops check the N1 & N2, RPM, EGT, & FF indicators.

Wednesday, March 4, 1998

629 - FSAS screen (Mike Gross) "1" = binary yes, "0" = binary no.

7946 - Fuel flow indicator problem. FE said that the a/craft had no spray. Which means that the engines did not dump fuel when they were shut down. So, the engine was really not getting any fuel. Got that and an FF indicator problem, called fuel shop.

629 - INS training with Mike.

141 - Defuel (SPR), observation, Dawn Depew changing and calibrating a #1 aux. fuel gauge. Tammy reading the T.O. Mike Gross supervising.

Thursday, March 5, 1998

æ½¼ - Got base driver's license finished, through the transportation office.

æ½¼ - Got final copies of AFTO 22s from QA.

æ½¼ - Talked to Mr. Leismister about the CCIs. He gave me the item manager's phone numbers. I sat in his office and called him. He is at Kelly AFB. He said that NSA declassified the DTE-E c/c/a a while back, but forgot to tell anyone. I asked him to please send us a copy of that message. He said that he would send us a list of all declassified CCIs, with NSA's signature on it.

æ½¼ - Power was out in our hanger. I had to divert for lunch. No power for the microwave.

087 - Assisted recovery, checked oil, helped open cowling doors on #1 engine.

æ½¼ - Signed my PD today for Don Obritor.

Friday, March 6, 1998

223 - HSC (ISO) a/craft. HSC did not have enough CNAD people, so they sent Tammy, Dawn, & I over to troubleshoot an HF coupler fault write up. HSC crew discovered a wing crack right under an engine pylon. They came in and told us not to worry about the HF, the a/craft was going away.

8087 - Assisted recovery. Assisted opening engine cowling for #3 engine.

629 - Assisted launch.

æ½¼ - Talked to Mr. Church today (chief union steward). I gave him an amendment to the union statement that the Union president asked me to sign on 2-18-98.

0144 - Refuel (SPR).

Monday, March 9, 1998

263 - #2 ADF bad. assisted Dawn & Tammy trouble shooting the problem to the #2 sense antenna. It was very corroded.

Tuesday, March 10, 1998

263 – Assigned to aircraft in hanger with ADF problem. Cannot troubleshoot ADF in a metal hanger.

223 - Tow (hand brake)

172 - Assisted recovery & checked oil. Refuel (SPR). Got arms drenched in JP-8 jet fuel. Told Mr. Baggs & Don. Washed up and put on some hand lotion. I had to let the fuel dry on my clothes because I didn't have any new clothes to change into.

Wednesday, March 11, 1998

7946 - Towed (Brakes) to fuel barn, because it had a leak in its armpit.

629 - Towed (left wing) a/craft at a 50 degree angle for a flight crew picture.

7946 - Towed (right wing) it back from the fuel barn to spot 1.

629 - Towed a/craft back to its proper alignment.

Thursday, March 12, 1998

(- My birthday...)

263 - Went over the new HF ops check with Tammy.

æ½¼ - Told Don Obritor that I had to leave work at about 0900, because I had to get my civilian drivers license. I got back to work around 1000 hrs. They charged me about 2 hours of leave.

161 - Tow (Brakes).

610 - Tow (Left wing).

Friday, March 13, 1998

263 - Checked out SKE. Training with Tammy.

8087 - Tow (Brakes).

263 - Checked out the SKE system again. This SKE has an error code, 35 and 36.

æ½¼ - Got car door fixed for lunch. That took about 15 mins to take it to the Chevy dealer.

æ½¼ - Studied TO 1C-141B-2-34GS-00-1.

Monday, March 16, 1998

946 - Assisted launch.

æ½¼ - I asked Don and Carl (our truck driver) if I could go to the VA people (at the unemployment office in town - about 15 mins) and fill out some papers for them. Carl said that I could go around 1000 hrs. So I got on the truck and waited for him to tell me to go. I was sitting right behind him in the truck. At about 1015 we had an IFE (In Flight Emergency), come in for a landing. Carl decides to drop me off at the a/craft to tow it back. I reminded him that I had an appointment. He still decided to let me help tow the a/craft and leave three crew chiefs sitting in the back of the van (truck). Well, I guess I missed this VA appointment. I made absolutely certain that I told Carl and Don that the VA rep was only at the office in the early mornings. That is Monday mornings and half a day Wednesday. They let me go to lunch at 1145 hrs. I went to the VA office anyway. The VA representative left at 1000 hrs.

946 - Stood ground for engine run.

946 - Refuel (panel)

æ½¼ - Tammy was assigned to hang out with a Mark Fletcher (C-5s) and work Kys and instruments and stuff today.

Tuesday, March 17, 1998

8087 - Assisted launch. Re-did SKE test for navigator. He was getting an error code 35. We ran the test 2 more times and it ran without a fault.

946 - Push back (hand brake).

8087 - Assisted launch.

8087 - Recover.

Wednesday, March 18, 1998

æ½¼ - They gave me two people to sign off a ball

#1: Personal hand tools are prohibited on the flight-line.

#2: Workplace violence, including verbal abuse of fellow employees.

629 - Worked with Mike Gross on an AVVI problem.

629 - Assisted launch.

æ½¼ - Got VA package from Altus VA office (AKA - unemployment office).

8087 - Assisted recovery.

Thursday, March 19, 1998

946 - TPLC problem. Mike Gross was here. Can't be fixed yet. A/crew is taking the a/craft FAI (fly as is).

æ½¼ - Scott Johnson is taking over for Don Obriter for awhile. I was heading into the CTK for some new earplugs. He stopped me halfway there, and asked me where I was going. I told him. He replied, "Just making sure that you're not pulling a Houdini on me." This told me that these supervisors were telling each other that I was a bad egg.

946 - Assisted launch.

144 - #2 ADF inop, R2 #2 ADF Rx. It did not fix the problem.

8087 - Assisted recovery, debrief.

8087 - T-shot APS-133 radar problem, ordered radar RT.

Friday, March 20, 1998

144 - Moved radar control head to navigator's position for the navigator. Ordered a control panel for the #2 ADF.

144 - Assisted launch.

æ½¼ - Lunch time. Dawn and Tod O'Neil were sitting at a table talking. I sat down with them. At first it sounded as if they were talking shop (avionics). However, they were talking about some of Dawn's EEO complaints. I heard Mr. O'Neil telling Dawn that he had talked to the brown shirts and that her complaint was probably just going to disappear. I figured that I should leave about then.

æ½¼ - I went over to Mr. Leismister's office. Mr. Prator was there. I asked them if the item manager's at Kelly had sent us the list of declassified

CCI s. They said that the item manager's had not sent them anything. I re-emphasized what we all knew. They KY-58 are still classified until we get something from the classifying agency, NSA, telling us otherwise. They told me that they understood that, and were trying to fix that. I said, OK and left.

Monday, March 23, 1998

219 - Assisted R2 of the #3 hydraulic system pressure switch.

219 - Checked out a radar write up. Ordered an MFD.

æ½¼ - Carl came and picked me up for a tow job. He left two crew chiefs and one hydraulic troop listening to the "swap shop" on the a/craft ADF radio. I'm sure that they were way too busy to be bothered by working. So, Carl just took me.

243 - Dropped back off to check out the flight engineer's altimeter. The TTU-205F test set was shocking me. I told Dawn and she touched it and it shocked her too. She took apart the power cord and discovered that the wires had come loose and were shorted to the cannon plug. While she took the power cord back to the CTK to get it fixed, I used our tool box voltmeter to check out the ground wire. The ground wire was an open. Someone had crimped the connector with its insulation still intact. So we had an 115VAC, 400Hz, 3 phase short to ground. But we had no ground. So every time we touched the test set we became the grounds. It's a wonder it didn't kill us. If the ground had been a little wet it may have hurt one or both of us. Mr. Hilley and Mr. Francis drove by in their truck, and asked me and Mr. Testerman how it was going. Mr. Testerman was working on the #3 engine. I explained everything to Mr. Hilley and he took the ground cord from me and assured me that he understood the problem with the ground cord. He said that he would take the ground cord up to the CTK and talk to Dawn about the power cord. The shame of it is, we would have long fixed this problem, if we didn't have to spend 7 hours trouble-shooting our test equipment. Plus, we found out that the test set was shocking CNAD troops on swing shift on Sunday night. Namely Mr. Marvin Leveritt told Dawn and I that the test set was shocking him. However, he did not tell anyone. He just handed the test set over to the CTK people. That's very dangerous. Test set was cooked and had to go back to the shop to get fixed.

243 - R2 MFD, radar ops checked good.

NI - Dawn sent me an e-mail about her EEO thing...I have simply inserted it directly into my aircraft diary... as seen below...the *.txt file attachment was opened and has been included directly below her e-mail.

e-mail message #1 had said that she was giving our boss T.O. Hilley a memo. She asked me to keep my ears open at roll call for the next few days and to send her an email if they said anything about her temporary transfer to ISO. She said that she wished she could be there to see the reactions from her co-workers and to hear what they said afterwards, basically wishing to be a fly on the wall. She said that she felt that the politically correct restraints would off and it would Dawn trashing time by at least a few people.

The actual memo in the email said that it was a memo, at the top. It said that it was from Dawn an dto Mr Hilley. It cited the date as March 26th, 1998 and attested to being about her transfer to ISO. She said that she appreciate his concern and his desire to defuse the EEO problem. Furthermore she stated that she could understand why it would be easier to move one worker bee as opposed to moving two supervisors. However, she said that she was concerned that others might feel she had been moved because she had done something wrong. She said that she didn't feel like she had done anything wrong. All she had done was to stand up for what she felt was right. Now she felt that she was being moved as a form of retribution. She said that she had put up with a lot and had talked to everyone she knew in her chain of command with zero positive results. Therefore, she felt she had no doors left open but the EEO door.

She recanted her previous knowledge of similar problems and said that the troublemakers were always fired to another position. She was concerned that being fired to another position would make her look like a troublemaker to her co-workers. She asked Mr. Hilley to announce to the C-141 dayshift crew that she was being temporarily transferred over to ISO to defuse the situation and that she had every legal right to contact the EEO office. She felt that perhaps she might think too much of what her co-workers thought of her. She said that that was part of the reason why she had waited so long to do anything about the problem. She maintained that throughout the entire situation she had always been able to perform her work with the highest degree of effectiveness and efficiency. She felt like her professional reputation had been soiled by taking a stand with EEO. She just didn't want anyone else to be stopped from going to EEO because of what they were witnessing her go through. She was distressed by the fact that she had had such a wonderful AF career and had never had to utilize any of the Air Force's minority equalizing organizations to help her find solutions to a problem. How she stated that she had spoken with at least three of them, EEO, Social Actions, and the Inspector General (IG) before getting to dayshift. She signed it respectfully Dawn M. Depew... like the rest of us repressed EISMs... WG-2610-11, Step 5

Out of the memo she added that tomorrow she would be officially transferred to the ISO docks. She made certain to mention that it was against her wishes. She said that the decision was TO's and that he felt that it was what was best for everyone. She said that she felt that this was wrong, like putting a bandage on a severed arm or leg. She what they really needed was surgery. She said that she told TO that it was funny how it was easier to move the victim. She said he flinched at the word victim. She asked him if he were still going to rotate supervisors to different shifts. She said that he didn't want to talk about that. She explained to him that ISO was not her cup of tea. She said that she LOVEd troubleshooting, and everyone knows that you don't do much of that in ISO. She told him that this mess was going to drive her into a nervous breakdown. She was worried about adapting to all the other personalities in ISO, but she was still willing to move for what her boss thought was for the good of all. She felt that TO had won the battle but that he would not win the war. She prophesied that she would be vindicated.

She added a note that TO stated he was genuinely concerned about the 2610 and training dilemma. She said that TO had listened to Bob Bagg so much that he didn't have a clue what was going on. She reminded TO that they (Dawn & Tammy) had put together a training plan that addressed every issue affecting the EISMs and the ELENs. She repeated that Mr. Bagg had told them he could care less if any training was ever done... as long as the planes kept flying. She said that she kept bringing up the 10 and 20 percent thing, that was specified in all of our position descriptions. She didn't believe that her union witness, Jana Jarvis, was very helpful. She said that she reminded him about how Billy had quit over a training issue. We had had a lot of people quit over training issues. She said it appeared as if he didn't even realize that Billy had quit because he was an EISM and they were using him, and all of us, as a crew chief.

(The actual memo's and email's are much, much longer... they all had a lot of feelings about these situations)

Tuesday, March 24, 1998

172 - Assisted launch.

æ½¼ - Called MIS to change my GO-81 user ID and password. Left work early at 1510, don't worry they charged me an hour annual leave.

Wednesday, March 25, 1998

æ½¼ - Dropped off El' Camino at the Chevy dealer before going to work

0200 - CANN bird at the North ramp. Helped Tammy install a new pitot tube on the left side of the a/craft.

æ½¼ - Went to lunch at 1130 hours.

æ½¼ - Came back from lunch, Carl ('10' truck driver) told me to go to spot 37, to recover an a/craft. I told him that Tammy told me to meet her back on a/craft 0200 on the North ramp.

629 - Assisted recovery. Refuel (panel). Reseated #2 ADF, ops checked good.

æ½¼ - My wife picked me up at 1430 hours.

Thursday, march 26, 1998

æ½¼ - George's brother died. So, I gave Mr. Bagg a dollar for that and asked him to please express my condolences to George.

æ½¼ - Went to ER about getting shocked on Monday. Gave Don my ground mishap report and CA forms.

263 - SKE write up. SKE ops checked good. Still need to do an interplane check. Don stopped by and told me that Jeff (mid shift) found a broken antenna cable on the RT. Don said that Jeff already fixed it. He said that it just needed an interplane check.

8087 - Carl pulled me off 263, because we didn't have another CNAD troop to do an interplane check with me. Installed two comm cords in back cargo compartment (left & right troop jump doors).

263 - Finally enough people for an interplane check. Theo helped out, in a/craft 144. SKE RT %.

Friday, March 27, 1998

263 - Rechecked #2 ADF at the request of Don Obriter. Helped Mike trouble shoot some AWLS caution lights. Ops checked good. Assisted launch.

144 - Chain & cover.

263 - Assisted recover (B man). Refuel (panel).

Monday, March 30, 1998

629 - (a/crew training). Didn't need me on this a/craft.

æ½¼ - Kurt is going to a 16-wk APG school.

200 - Assisted Tammy with ops check of the pitot-static system.

219 - Assisted crew chiefs by running hydraulic pumps. co-ordinated over the radio.

æ½¼ - Carl did not take me back to the north ramp.

272 - Assisted recovery.

Tuesday, March 31, 1998

263 - ADI problem. Tammy is teaching me about flight director computers. Ordered & R2 flight director computer. Flight director system ops checks good.

** Rode truck.

263 - Recover (hand brake).

æ½¼ - At roll call a Colonel thanked the C-5 team for the great job they were doing. Apparently he does that sometimes. That makes the rest of us feel kinda' bad, because we don't have any military people to thanks us. Ah, it's probably just a psychological thing.

æ½¼ - Mr. Hilly briefed us on the appearance of an EEO (equal opportunity) complaint against the MEO.

Wednesday, April 1, 1998

263 - Worked on SKE write up. Changed coder/decoder. Did not fix the problem. Assisted launch.

æ½¼ - went to Ms. Margaret Malon (as per Mr. Bob Baggs suggestion) to talk about updating my personnel records. I explained to her secretary that I had been trying to get the education portion of my records updated for about five to six months now, with no success. I have two associate degrees and my educational records show me as not even graduating high school.

æ½¼ - I only got to talk to Ms. Malon's secretary. She gave me a form 172 and showed me how to fill it out. I explained to her that Debbie Shell at the civilian personnel office filled out the last one for me. That was four or five months ago. My records are still not updated.

Bldg. 517 - a/craft 629 - assisted putting up #3 & #4 engine cowling doors.

æ½¼ - Talked to a Mr. Swain (a wash rack brown shirt) about the washrack clothing and boots. They are worn and sweated in (because it's hot in the washrack) by different people all the time, and have been for months, without being washed and/or disinfected. I got him to call the bioenvironmental people and at least get some Lysol and stuff. He did, I sat by, while he made the call.

Thursday, April 2, 1998

263 - Found short in SKE RT connector. Tammy Lowe came out to the a/craft to lend us her expert knowledge. We found a short in the antennae pedestal connector. Fixed all shorts, SKE ops checked good.

Friday, April 3, 1998

272 - I wrote up the INS batteries because this a/craft came from McGuire AFB (I think) with no date stickers on one INS battery, and a cap check due (Nov 97) on the other one.

æ½¼ - Got a list of courses available from Jerry (97th Airlift Training manager). Most of the CNAD courses are in-shop courses.

263 - Assisted recovery.

Saturday, April 4, 1998

(- In-processing at Tinker, AFB. I am now a part of the 707th Comm. Flight (CF). Yet another secure comm. shop ran by a radio operator. I hope that this one isn't as bad as the last one (Donna Pruit - 924th Comm. squadron NCOIC at Bergstrom AFB, TX - 1992).

æ½¼ - Donna Pruitt had the Security police diked the 4 - position combination lock off our Track Van. That's because she was a radio operator, our NCOIC, and didn't have a need to know the combination. So, I didn't give it to her. After that she became a real pain in the butt. She started leaving a lot of disks and typewriter ribbons, that were marked 'secret' laying around on the tops of tables, in rooms, with the doors open. The assistant NCOIC told me to leave her alone. He told me not to file any security incidence forms. He also, was a radio operator. It is also interesting to note that she was going with us to an Army camp, close to Bergstrom AFB, and teaching the girls in our flight, under her supervision, how to drink mixed drinks that were named, 'BJ's (Short for Blow Jobs - she tells us) while being recorded on camera. Simultaneously, she is having a man in supply charged with sexual harassment against her.

Sunday, April 5, 1998

æ½¼ - Still in-processing. Maj. Collins asked me to go to Cannon AFB with them. The dates are 21 to 27 June. I said, "sure!" I also asked my supervisor if I could just do the whole two weeks there and get it over with. He said okay.

Monday, April 6, 1998

144 - #2 UHF inop. CND. Radar altimeter will not test. I don't have much experience with CARA, so Don called Mike Gross and Theo to help; I went into the shoe (CTK) to get the books (JG & FI) for the CARA system. Assisted launch.

æ½¼ - Asked QA guys about the difference between earplugs and headsets related to the proximity of operating jet engines. They said it had something to do with decibels, but that they weren't sure. They told me that they would find out and tell me later.

219 - Refuel (SPR).

Tuesday, April 7, 1998

610 - Assisted launch.

æ½¼ - Talked to Msgt. Brougha and got a copy of an unclassified page, from the AFKAM 1B, from TSgt. Cody, so that I could complete my AFTO 22s.

0629 - Helped close#2 engine cowling doors.

æ½¼ - Went to the QA office, talked to Mr. Weaver about my AFTO 22s. He looked in his book and they are now 4 days past their suspense date. He said that he would call them. I fixed their ProComm Plus program for them, and explained to them what a comma means in telecommunications talk (a pause). They had one too many commas in the phone number they were dialing. Take one comma out and their telecommunications program worked fine.

8087 - Removed SKE antenna for TCTO mod for ISO dock.

Wednesday, April 8, 1998

æ½¼ - Sent an E-mail to my senators and representatives about being dissatisfied with my annual appraisals.

8087 - Back to help with the installation of the SKE cable modification TCTO.

æ½¼ - I was having a cup of coffee (waiting for sheetmetal to take the air ducts out of the a/craft, so that I could finish the SKE mod) and talking to Mr. Vargus, when Mr. Baggs came up behind me and started hassling me. He asked who I was assigned to today, and what I was supposed to be doing. I told him what I was doing. (There were about 10 - 15 other techs standing around having coffee, taking their 15 mins. break - why me??) Bob said, "OK! Just making sure that you stay busy!" Don asks me at least 5 - 10 times a week, "Are you staying busy?" I always answer yes. I don't understand. Why do all the brown shirts, always ask me if I'm busy. Just my brown shirts. They kept asking me this on nightshift, and now on dayshift. Of course this all started happening after I reported the security thing. I've never been late for work, never left early unless given permission.

8087 - Came back from lunch. Left note for ISO brown shirt about my having hurt the right side, middle, of my back by pulling on the SKE cabling. The cabling kept getting stuck in the hole.

æ½¼ - Got a call from Msgt. Nichols. He said that I am going to get a visitor. It is to be a colonel. He didn't say about what.

æ½¼ - Went to the JCMH ER to have my back looked at. The ISO brown shirt sent me over to my brown shirt (Don Obriter) to get all the paperwork filled out. The ER doctor (Daniel) gave me some medicine, told me to put ice on it, and to take it easy.

Thursday, April 9, 1998

8087 - SKE cabling. Still waiting on cable clamps to get positioned correctly. Walked around with Tammy and Lawrence for a while. They were looking for some non-magnetic screws for the a/craft wingtip. We all talked, she knows I can't do anything until she fixes the clamps under the cargo bay floor panels. At least that's what she tells me. She's the expert on the SKE TCTO. She keeps saying that she needs some motivation. She keeps whining about being a single parent now. She is getting divorced. She talks about a person who turned her into the child protective services division. Something about her sleeping with a married man, and not paying enough attention to her child. Gee. Do you think that if I shot myself in the foot and complained about it all day, a lot of people would listen? It sucks; the children are always the losers, when mommy and daddy can't play nice anymore.

æ½¼ - I'm applying some characteristics of water to people. Some people are still waters and some people rage (spiritually - emotionally). Still waters are sponges. They soak up everything (wisdom - knowledge) - They fight for it. Raging waters are bricks - they can't soak up a drop of water.

Sometimes I rage, sometimes I am still.

Tammy Romero rages -she tells sexist jokes about dumb blondes to fit in. She wonders why women have to wear clothes, just because men cannot control themselves. She is very confident with her comm./nav knowledge.

Tammy Lowe is rages, of course. She whines incessantly about being a single parent and how inconvenient it is, but the sex was convenient.

Dennis Scott rages - He rages about training CNAD troops and then they leave him. He rages about being quoted. He rages about being hired here as an instructor and winding up fixing a/craft, like all the other AFIN technicians.

Billy (crew chief) is pretty calm. He has problems just like everybody else, but only shares them, when he feels he needs to. Like payment for acceptance. He talks of buying guitars. He talks of finding good doctors to help him, with his nasal problems. (I hope that he finds one)

Sometimes Dawn rages, sometimes she is calm. She is an obsessive-compulsive helper. She thrives on order. She feels and talks about being persecuted, by other AFIN troops, and by the brown shirts. I believe that she is correct about that because the brown shirts are crew chiefs (inexpensive and easy for civil service to hire) and we are specialists (expensive to hire, train, keep up to date, and even harder to hold on to).

æ½¼ - These are some of the many faces that my co-workers have shown me. I wonder if my face appears calm or raging to them? I wonder what they see in me.

' - Mr. Francis came by 8087 and told me that he was supposed to make an appointment with Colonel Sparks to see me. He said that this had to be voluntary. I told him that I did not need to see the Colonel if he thought that he could fix my problems at his level. He said that we should meet in his office at 1500 hours and talk about my problems to see if they could solve them. I said OK. He came and got me at 1500 hours, I accompanied him to his office and we talked about my concerns. I began by telling him that I had a list of things. Then, I asked him if he would mind me taking notes. He said, "NO! Just don't misquote me." I said, "Yes Sir!" The list:

Î QUESTION: Classified E-DTE cards in the KY-58s. I explained that I had talked to the item manager at Kelly. They told me that the KY-58 had been declassified by NSA. They told me that NSA just forgot to tell everybody. I asked them to FAX me proof. They said that they would. I told Mr. Francis that until they did, the E-DTE cards are still classified 'Confidential', according to the KAM-337A. I asked him to please get Mr. Leismister to bug the item managers about that FAX.

Î ANSWER: He said that he would look into it. He also said that if the item manager at Kelly AFB said that the CCI s were not classified, he would believe him. I told him that it was up to him.

Ï QUESTION: Fill battery AFTO 22 suspense date is 7 days past due. I told him this just for his information. I told him that QA was calling about it.

Ï ANSWER: Does not require an answer at the present time. He simply acknowledged the information.

Đ QUESTION: OJT at Altus AFB (perversion of OJT system). Crew chiefs, electrics, and C-5 troops getting lots of training. C-141 troops getting nothing.

Job description at Tinker AFB are either for AFIN or CNAD, not both, and they are getting paid more.

Active Duties obligation to training, according to General McPeak. Even fuel truck drivers get formal training.

I gave him a few analogies. First: I was a nurse. I have followed doctors around for years. Does that make me a doctor, just by watching them? Will you let me operate on you? I don't think so. Why? Because I lack about 12 years of formal education and many more years of training.

I told him that you can't just watch and/or listen to someone and suddenly know how to do their job.

Đ ANSWER: He told me that management is accessing the need for formal training.

He started talking, about having worked at Altus for a very long time. He talked about pulling old radios, that were on fire, out of a/craft. He said that he could do a CNAD person's job. He said that he could replace the radios; control heads, being able to ops check radios ect... I asked him if he could ops check the UHF HAVE QUICK system. He said, "Some things about radios are more complicated than others." I asked him if he could ops check the SKE system. He said that "..some systems are more complicated than others." Furthermore, he said, "Like the civilian crew chiefs, I can pull boxes." I said, "yep. But can you pull the right ones?" I told him, some people have formal knowledge. They can walk onto an a/craft and they know what's wrong, even before they go to get a book. Because, only certain parts produce certain signals. Only that part can have certain symptoms. I told him that I wanted to be that person. I still do.

He said that they (civil service) didn't want to waste training on people who didn't need it. He said that my supervisor was going to go over my training records with me soon. He explained that this would be part of their assessment.

He talked about who said they would train me and who said that they would not train me. Dennis Scott - w/not train me. For reasons mentioned earlier in the diary. It just upsets me that Mr. Greenwood waited five months to tell me that Mr. Scott did not want to train me. I told this to Mr. Francis.

Kevin Sherill - w/not train me, because he says that training others is not in his PD. Of course he spares no ends to seeing that Denise is trained, and that others (such as Mike Gross) train her also. Of course he'll get '6's on his appraisals, probably '7's.

Mike Gross - told me that he would love to help train me. He does train me every chance that he gets.

Theo - w/not train me. Says that it is not in his PD. (Mr. Francis did not go into more detail)

Tammy Romero - I brought up her name, but Mr. Francis would not talk to me about her. He would not tell me whether or not she would train me or anyone else. I told him that I respected her effort to learn and work AFIN stuff, but I thought that she might be a little too confident about her AFIN knowledge. I told Mr. Francis that it's really good, and sometimes necessary to be able to ask people questions.

Dawn Depew - Mr. Francis kept focusing on her as a trainer for me. I told him that she had already told me that she did not see herself as teacher material. He continued to focus on her as a trainer for me. She is CNAD also. He said, "Maybe she can teach you something, and maybe you can teach her something too." Finally, I told him that that sounds great.

Then, Mr. Francis began talking about how; we were the future of Altus AFB. He started asking me if I would mind going over to the C-5 side. I told him that I would do whatever they told me to do. He said, "No! It has to be voluntary." I said, "Sure! I'll go over to the C-5 side." He said, "OK! We've been thinking about sending you over there. Don't take that as being written in stone, though." I said, "Yes sir!"

Ñ QUESTION: Making up of your own MOIs that cite no Tech data and/or no AFIs and are not signed by anyone. I told him that the MOI that Mr. Greenwood made up had been put into my 971.

Ñ ANSWER: He said that he was unaware that the MOI had been put into my 971. He started explaining to me, what a 971 is. It is a tool for supervisors. I knew that, but out of politeness, I allowed him to finish. Then, he told me that nothing derogatory could be put into a 971 without the employee's knowledge and signature. I told him that I never signed that MOI, asked why it was put into my 971, and the remarks that Mr. Greenwood put on it where derogatory. He said that he hadn't read my 971.

Ò QUESTION: I told him that a person could not get to a computer in our building if their lives depended upon it. I explained to him that I wanted access to some of the computers so that I could fill out some AFTO 22s, for saving personnel and money. I explained to him that there is an AF instruction that prohibits over securing something to the point that it reduces efficiency and /or effectiveness. The fact that a person cannot get to a computer to look at AFEPL (for an AF instruction or publication) and/or Delrina FormFlow is a little over protective, in my opinion. I told him that I know that some people like to change stuff on their computers, but the brown shirts are doing that anyway.

Ò ANSWER: He said that this problem was being looked into. He mentioned some computers in an alternate location and said that they were looking into getting us access to them. He offered to let me use his computer, but declined his own offer, with a comment of, "but it doesn't have a printer connected to it." I told him that I could save the information on a disk, but that I would rather use the computers in the QA office, because Mr. Weaver had all the addresses and stuff. I didn't mention that, his computer being on the network could access a printer almost anywhere.

Ó QUESTION: I mentioned that it appeared to me that I found a security problem and reported it like the book said, and found myself with '4's on my appraisal. I told him that even people with no formal training at all had gotten '6's or better. Like Mr. Coup, Mike Gross, Dawn Depew, Tammy Romero, and Claud Miller, just to name a few.

I explained to him that Mr. Greenwood sat down with me for my appraisal and asked me if I had any friends.

I told Mr. Francis that my records stated that I was a high school graduate and a disabled veteran. That's all they say. I told him that Mr. Greenwood did not know me. He didn't even know if I had any friends or my education level. I told him that it wasn't fair that he should write an appraisal on me.

Ô ANSWER: He stated that getting '4's on an initial appraisal was not that bad. He said that it was not career ending or anything. He kept offering to show me his initial appraisal. I said sure I'll look at it; he never did show it to me.

He said that he would have told Mr. Greenwood that he didn't have any friends. He said that a new annual appraisal was in the works for me, even as we were speaking.

Ô QUESION: I talked to Mr. Francis about getting paid '8 hours' of 'injury admin' leave for taking 1 hour to go to the ER. I said that it didn't sound fair, because I still came back and worked those other seven hours. I told him that somewhere someone's statistics about how much a work injury was costing the American public was sky-rocketing. Now, I know why...

Ô ANSWER: He said the same thing that Don Obriter said. They both said that 'injury admin' leave, must be like 'military leave'. It only pays out by the day, not by the hour. But, I still had to work, even as the government was telling the American people that I was staying at home because I was injured.

Friday, April 10, 1998

272 - Sat on a/craft for 30 mins, then Carl picked me up to sit right seat on an engine run, with Boss Hogg and John Aspinwall.

144 - Sat right seat during engine run. Assisted closing #1 engine cowling doors.

7946 - Chained & covered.

æ½¼ - On '10' truck, people are complaining about 'Denise (a/craft electrician). That would be Lawrence, George, Carl, Brian, et Bob. They told Carl that he needed to separate the "love birds" (Kevin & Denise). Because, when they are together they do not work well. The refuse to do crew chief serviceing, when they are together. From what I have seen and experienced, I concur.

272 - Assisted recovery. Checked oil, pushed back onto spot (right wing), refuel (panel). #1 VHF bad. Swapped control panel, swapped RT s, still bad. Turned over to Claud Miller.

Monday, April 13, 1998

219 - Assisted Roy (New hydraulic troop) & Leonard (Crew chief) in timing drips from a swivel valve (pressurized & unpressurized).

æ½¼ - I stopped Mr. Francis' truck on the flight-line and asked him about my meeting with Col. Sparks. He said that Col. Sparks was off.

æ½¼ - Talked to Leonard & (CTK) Tammy about public schools, police, ect..Tammy said that it made her mad that a policeman that she knew, had two of his cars repossessed, because he wasn't paying for them. Yet he drove around in a police car, and used it as his family car. Tammy was having some kind of truck problem with a friend of hers. That's why she brought the whole thing up.

æ½¼ - Asked Don about going over my training records with me. He said he was too busy.

0243 - Tow (right wing).

æ½¼ - Denise reminds me of something that I learned about in psychology class. It is a Freudian philosophy. It is called "P- - - - Envy".

æ½¼ - Told Lt. Julie Birt (airfield management) about the grounding points on the flight-line being filled up with dirt & being corroded. She said that she would fill out a hazard report on it. She said, "We wouldn't want a spark, would we?" I said, "No!"

æ½¼ - walked over to 7946 for a minute. Talked to Dawn Depew about what Mr. Francis said. She said that she would train anyone that they told her too.

0243 - Engine run. Assisted Leonard on ground. Helped with the power unit and stuff.

50272 - Assisted recovery. TACAN #2 inop. - CND. Refuel (Panel).

æ½¼ - Turned in an EGT gauge for Carl.

Tuesday, April 14, 1998

60172 - Pilot's ADI problem. Bank steering bar would not center during test. I asked George to call '7' and ask for an AFIN troop. He did. Kevin Sherill and Denise showed up. We ops checked the flight director computer and ordered a new one. I installed it, while Denise paced and kept telling me to hurry up. I told her that I was checking pins. She said, "You don't have to check the pins. Just put it in." I ignored her and checked my pins first. Pilot's ADI ops checked good. Assisted launch.

æ½¼ - Don Obritor - Still no time to go over my training records.

629 - Refuel (SPR).

172 - Recovery refuel (panel).

æ½¼ - Did not see Mr. Francis today at all.

æ½¼ - Talked to Carl about training. He said that he was only 85% qualified & he's been here for over a year and half. He said that he did not like Denise, because she is a know-it-all, and has a better-than-thou attitude.

æ½¼ - Talked to our unit training person. I told him that they are evaluating us improperly. I pointed out that crew chief tasks are broken down, but avionics tasks are grouped together in tasks of threes or fours. He said, "I did write the training records." So, that was a bust.

æ½¼ - John Aspinwall tells me that Tammy Lowe told him that she was forced to go to ISO, because she was sleeping with the boss. She was KC-135 avionics before.

æ½¼ - Did FOD walk for spots #21 & #22. The fuel people are done, they have given us those spots back.

' - Our Security Managers are: Î Bob Harris Ext. 7315 and Ï Jerry Caldwell Ext. 7530

/ - Questions about 781Ls and/or 781Bs, call Ext. 5754.

Wednesday, April 15, 1998

æ½¼ - I use to ask Don if I could go to QA to fill out an AFTO 22 or to do this or that. He would say, "Go ask Carl." This time, I asked Carl and he said, "Go ask Don." I said, "He says to go ask you." Carl said, "Have you asked him lately? Have you asked him today?" I said, "Never mind, Carl." I got off the '10 truck' at a/craft 629 and asked Don. Don said, "We'll talk about it later." I find this all rather confusing. So I go to talk to Mr. Bagg. He says that Don is the person that I should tell and he will radio Carl. So, he says, "I will talk to Don for you and straighten this out." I say, "Thanks a lot Mr. Bagg."

0200 - Went to the North Ramp to help Tammy and Mr. Praetor take out some KY stuff and annotate the 781s. He said that this was the first time that he had taken KY stuff out of an a/craft. This tells me that the previous KY stuff, with its mercury batteries, went to Davis-Motham, and they don't know it. I did tell them about that a few months ago. I called the EPA and told them. They said that they would get back with me about it. They never did call me back.

40629 - Tow (right wing).

æ½¼ - According to MSgt. Nichols, the IG's assistant, I was to see a Col. Lendowsky. However, Mr. Francis found out and I was re-routed to Col. Sparks. Later discovered that Col. Ayers had told Col. Lendowsky, who had told Col. Sparks, who had told Mr.Hilley, who had told Mr. Francis, Who had told Mr. Baggs and Mr. Obriter. Gee, I guess, they just had to tell everyone that I went to see the IG. That's a little intimidating.

æ½¼ - Meeting with Col. Sparks. Went over the same stuff that Mr. Francis and I went over, last week, with a few extra items on the menu. Also, discussed Denise & Kevin . I suggested acquiring an avionics supervisor. (Col. Sparks appeared to like this idea). I told him that every military job that I have had would have a specialist flight chief (supervisor). He agreed and imparted the knowledge that even the C-17 flight had a specialist flight chief. I gave him the Donna Pruitt story. Lesson is that you should not let the least technically skilled individuals manage the most technically skilled individuals, even though that is the cheapest way to run things from a short term perspective.

1. I continued to remind of him of what my priorities were and how they had changed in the last six months. I told him that at first I was concerned over security, the environment, and safety (batteries). I mentioned that I had talked with my co-CNAD workers (Dawn Depew & Tammy Romero & Mike Gross), and they had told me that it was useless to tell anyone. They said that they had already tried.

2. Then, I explained that my priorities had changed again. Now they were to find someone who would listen. That was achieved from my knowledge of AFIs dealing with security and with KAMs.I called NSA (National Security Agency), as specified in AFSSI 4001. They told me to call AFCA (Air Force Communications Command), which is run by a two or three star general. I spoke to his vice-commander. He called Altus Base Comm/ Sec for me. He said, "They will be waiting for you to arrive at their office within the hour, Mr. McGrew and they will be more than happy to help you out."

3. I've been trying to fix the battery problem by submitting AFTO 22s, which now have a suspense date that is two weeks old. He told QA to call their HQs and get them on the stick.

4. I told him that we were takin' it big in the rear quarter, because of the way that classify our training records. Crew chief tasks are separated (More of them). Avionics tasks are combined, with as many as three or four tasks combined into one. This shows all Avionics troops as being massively under qualified. I told him that his training system has absolutely no integrity at all. I think that scared him a little or made him mad. I don't care either way, because it's true.

4. Furthermore, he admitted that he had $1.3 million dollars for training over the next six years. He said that it was going to his priority people. Engines, electrics, and crew chiefs. Which means that we high paid avionics troops at Altus AFB will only be able to do one quarter of our jobs for the next six years.

5. He talked about retainability. He said that Altus did not have any. He said that they were working on that, with the step increase package in the works.

Thursday, April 16, 1998

æ½¼ - Mr. Hilley asked me, Kevin Sherill, and a C-5 person to re-do the 2610 JQS's. I sat and talked to Kevin, Don Obriter, Scott, and Mark. They argued against me. They said that the JQS's are useless. They told me that they had been broken down and put back together several times. I explained to them that, it was a management tool. They didn't care. They refused to help me. I did two pages by myself and told the training guy about the problems that I was having. He said that unless I had my boss behind me, I would be sunk. I explained to him that my boss was a crew chief, just like all the other bosses on the flight-line at Altus. My boss does not comprehend, or want to comprehend avionics, or our problems. He certainly is not interested in helping us. He agreed.

Friday, April 17, 1998

263 - Worked on the HF TCTO with Dawn Depew.

æ½¼ - Had to leave and go to a Dr.'s appointment. Took 5.5 hours of sick leave.

Monday, April 20, 1998

263 - Assisted launch.

946 - Refuel (SPR), wind 15G25, lots of rain. No jacket, no raincoat. They are in the back of my El Camino, it is broken and in the shop. Lightening within 5 miles, had to stop fueling a/craft.

263 - Recover, awaiting fuel truck (lightening within 5 miles), fueling called off.

æ½¼ - Don Obriter tried to force everybody off the '10' truck to push back an a/craft. "Boss Hogg" told him that he couldn't tow with lightening within 5 miles. Don insisted, some people got off the truck and some stayed. I stayed on the truck.

Tuesday, April 21, 1998

172 - Moved radar control head to the Navigator's position. Wrote up an ADF control box. Asked '7' truck driver to order a new one. R2 and ops checked ADF control box. Assisted Mike Gross with R2 and ops check of the FSAS control box.

æ½¼ - Mike says to show a little Gusto. He says, I should have gone ahead and ordered one. I told him that the Air Force did not teach me to do things that way. I was trained to check it out and make sure first.

æ½¼ - '7' truck driver George showed me the outdated MOI on the severe weather. Mr. Francis gave us a briefing this morning on that same MOI.

172 - Assisted recovery. Repaired U-94/A connector at the crew entry door. Assisted launch.

610 - Assisted Mr. Hubbs, checking the X-dimension (strut inched=psi). Aired strut to 1480 psi=5¼". Left and right struts.

æ½¼ - Denise (Denis as everybody, but me, calls her) tripped in the cargo area of an a/craft and fell and ripped the skin between the two last digits on her right hand. The ambulance came and picker her up and took her to the base hospital.

Wednesday, April 22, 1998

0219 - Fixed the left troop door interphone cord. Ops checked good. The Flight Engineer did not want to write it up. Like a lot of other CNAD jobs, because then they would need another ER (Exceptional Release).

æ½¼ - We were all sitting around talking about the ambulance that came out to the a/craft yesterday and picked up Denise. Someone noted that the ambulance checked its tires at the ECP (Entry Control Point), but no one else ever did.

263 - Watched Dawn and Tammy try to repair a wire on an 'FSAS' master caution light. 781B's are out-of-wac on the a/craft. There are two copies. The new ones have the wrong serial numbers and the old ones do not have all the correct parts. They were done by Kevin Sherill. I told Mr. Prator that they were not correct. He asked me to fix them when I got a chance. I told him that I had a/craft to tow and refuel. I told him that I didn't know when I would be able to get back to that a/craft. He said that he understood. He said that he would take care of it.

172 - Assisted closing engine cowling doors for the washrack people.

219 - Assisted recovery, checked oil. Refuel (panel). VOR/LOC write up. Rx %. Write up pilot's hand mic will not key.

Thursday, April 23, 1998

7946 - Got to a/craft. Carl came by and picked me up.

50263 - Towed (left wing).

7946 - Assisted Greg Nunnly in changing a #3 hydraulic system, #1 pump. Re-filled the #3 hydraulic reservoir, system ops checked good.

æ½¼ - George '7' truck driver and Carl let me go and check on my form 457 and make another AFTO 22.

æ½¼ - Today was the first time, since I've been here, that I've heard anything negative (derogatory) said about Dawn Depew. This occurred while I was helping Greg and Ron with changing the #1 hydraulic pump. They started talking to the flight engineer about Dawn's award. Dawn's award was presented by a Colonel at roll call yesterday. They said that they were certain that she didn't deserve that award. They said that she wasn't a crew chief. They said that she was just an avionics person, and that she brought the a/craft back all trashed out and broken, because she didn't know what she was doing. They said that she got that award because she was a woman.

Friday, April 24, 1998

272 - Fixed light bulbs in the flight engineer's intercommunication control panel. They were broken out in the socket. I tried to go to the backshop to get the light bulbs, because our flightline CTK did not have them. I did this under much duress as they were trying to replace me, because I wanted to get the thing fixed. Blue shirt '7' truck driver George was behind the thrust to replace me. I got back in time to fix the control panel and keep them from replacing me. Assisted launch.

æ½¼ - Went by base comm/sec office and talked to Msgt. Roror. He was a 2E3 (Crypto-person), like me, before the AF cross-trained him. He says that they got a KIT to de-classify the KG-84s, at his old base. He said that it was about 8 to 10 years ago. I asked him if he and Ssgt. Cody (a 3C - operator) could find me a copy of the message that came with that KIT. He said, "Okay! We'll see what we can do." I went back and looked at the KAM with them both. We looked through the KAM and the modifications. We all agreed that there was nothing in the KAM to indicate that the KY-58 was de-classified.

æ½¼ - I got my AFTO 22 for the KY-75s through QA (Hilley signed this one)

272 - Assisted recovery, checked oil with John Aspinwall. Mike Gross got sick and had to leave the a/craft.

æ½¼ - Flagged Hilley down and got into his truck, as he requested (because he said that we were blocking traffic). He assured me that my last appraisal would disappear, and that my next one did not have any '4's on it. I showed him a page of the KAM 337 that said that the KY-58 are still classified 'Confidential'. He said that he wanted to arrange a meeting with me later about that. I said, "Sure!"

Monday, April 27, 1998

æ½¼ - Today was a NO FLY day (down day).

æ½¼ - I made two more AFTO 22s. One to take care of the KITs and one to take care of a/craft going to the boneyard.

æ½¼ - I had to leave early, so I took my lunch late. I told Don and Carl, they said that it was OK. So, I skipped lunch and left at 1500 hrs.

æ½¼ - I talked to Hilley in the hallway of the hanger. He wanted to do the 797 thing for training. I showed him the AF JQS that Mr. Sam Kennamon gave to me. I told him what Sam told me, that the AF spent millions of dollars making those JQSes, why waste that money. But, he still wanted to break down the 797s, because that's what Mr. Bradley wanted. I told him that no one wanted to help me with the training stuff (breaking down the 797s). I told him that I would do it myself if he wanted me to. He said, "Don't worry about it. I'll have my training guy do it for me." I said, "OK!", "I wish that I could do more." He said, "That's Ok.", "Thanks."

Tuesday, April 28, 1998

263 - Tow (hand brake). George '7' truck driver assisted us. He rode bakes. He didn't talk to me the whole time, from hanger 510 to spot 25 (the wash rack). I noticed that he was wearing the kind of boots that you can buy from Wal-Mart. I had a pair like that, when I was little. However, they are not steel-toed, and are not Air Force issue. He is a work leader, and should be setting an example. Oh well. Refuel. We had a little problem. Leonard did not want to fuel an a/craft. That's because it was sitting on the washrack. It is within 50 ft of a water drain. That is an EPA violation. George just replaced him, and found someone who would do it anyway. That person was Ron (The new hydraulic guy).

æ½¼ - Turned in two AFTO 22s. One on the 34GS and one on the 00 T.O. Series.

223 - On the North ramp with 10 other technicians. Wow. The flight-line is pretty empty. Helped re-install a right main landing gear door.

Wednesday, April 29, 1998

629 - In hanger 514. No VOR/ILS test set available in our CTK. Could not ops check the co-pilot's ADI, ILS bug, yet. Got ramp tester from the KC-135 CTK. G/S bug works fine, but the pitch steering bar, on the ADI, is missing. Tammy had an appointment, so she told me to call Mike to help

me out. Mike went to lunch. Refuel (panel). Swapped VOR/ILS Rx, ops checked good.

æ½¼ - Received a re-call phone call from the 707th Comm Flight, at Tinker AFB. It was just a test.

Thursday, April 30, 1998

272 - Assisted launch. (Air cart - No APU).

æ½¼ - Got a message from Mr. Weaver about my AFTO 22s. He said that for changes to the 00 TO s. I would need to send my AFTO 22 to another address, so we changed the address.

172 - Changed all batteries in Cryptographic equipment. Tried to change the ELT battery, but we couldn't get the land all situated correctly. It was about time to get off work, and George (crew chief) said that we should just wait until tomorrow to fix it. Denise and Kevin showed up to stand ground for us and to check out a TPLC circuit breaker that was popping.

æ½¼ - found a sticker stuck to the back of some of the KY-58s. It references an AMC message #021406Z Aug94 (OTI) One time inspection 1C-141B-003, phase length pattern 105ms. Req's more research.

Friday, May 1, 1998

610 - Spot 21 - assigned to a/craft for wash prep with Mr. Hubbs and Denise. Stood ground during two engine runs. One to check out a sticky starter button, and another one to open the TR s. Denise left at exactly 0800 hours. Buttoned up #2 engine cowling doors. Denise came back at 0900, left a toolbox and took off at 0915. She said that she had an appointment to get her stitches out. John came back and told me that she told him, that she needed Kevin out here, because only a highly skilled -ism (integrated systems mechanic) could operate a DMM. She told John ('10' truck driver, today) that I couldn't operate a DMM. Denise came back at 1015. She asked me if I knew anything about flight symmetry. I said, "No." She said, "Good." She told me that she had nulled out the flap symmetry, and that I needed to do an auto-pilot and stall prevention ops check. I told her that George ('7' driver) said, "Don't worry 'bout it!"

629 - Assisted recovery (debrief). Push-back (right wing), refuel (panel).

Saturday and Sunday, May 2 - 3, 1998

Reserve Weekend

Gave Marilyn a ride back and forth to the chow hall and to the hotel. She doesn't have a car here. She flies in to Oklahoma. STU-III Training. Self-aid and buddy care training. Got Linda's commissary card. Looked for someone to talk to about mom's commissary card. Talked about training AFMSS, whatever that is, but they use it at Cannon AFB. Talked about getting scheduled for 7-level school and the CDC that I will need.

Monday, May 4, 1998

172 - inside of hanger 285. Pilot's AOA (angle of attack) transducer bad. TPLC computer bad. Hooked up 205 test set & ops checked FSAS (fuel savings advisory system), INS (inertial navigation system), & auto-pilot. Checked INS batteries.

272 - Refuel (SPR). Troubleshot interphone. New interphone control box %. Right seat engine run.

Tuesday, May 5, 1998

172 - Re-installed stall computer connector. ELT does not Xmit properly. Pulled off job, at lunch, to help recover 272.

272 - Assisted recovery. Checked oil, refuel (SPR). T-shot VHF radios, had constant transmit (shift change - to Marvin Leveritt).

Wednesday, May 6, 1998

161 - Assisted launch.

æ½¼ - saw the IG, made an appointment to get my reserve physical done (Monday) the 11th.

161 - Assisted recovery, checked oil, refuel (SPR). Msgt. Clem Farley retired. They met him at the a/craft with a fire truck and wet him down. Brian Adrian was pushing a power cart by himself, while we were putting landing gear pins in. George and Scott were watching him from their '7' truck. They never said anything to him about it.

æ½¼ - During refueling, Brian Adrian pulled me off refueling (SPR), because he said that I was sitting on the ground. George called me into the office and fussed at me about it. However, he did admit that he couldn't see whether I was sitting or not. I told him that I was kneeling down. He said that he was sorry. Dawn jumped on him and said that everybody else sits during refueling, even CSS refueling jobs. She said, "Why are you jumping on Dan?", "You better make that rule apply to everybody, George!"

æ½¼ - Brian Adrian is strangely turbulent waters. He appears to get his entertainment value from the misery of others. Much like the 'Green River Killer'. As if he were that way from childhood. He is rude, loud, and often obnoxious. Especially to the older people on our shift. This appears to appeal to a few. He uses an 'Adolf Hitler' emotional appeal, as he twists a dagger into someone else's misery, for the pleasure of the crowd. I think that he might have learned it as a child, probably as protection from some evil in his environment (self-defense), and it has become natural to him.

Thursday May 7 , 1998

610 - Drained the fuel lines. Cleaned up a spill under a halon fire extinguisher on the flight deck. assisted launch.

æ½¼ - a colonel asked for a placard for his a/craft. Brian called back on the radio and told them to get a few dead pigeons from the hanger for the colonel. They gave Brian Adrian a little talking to for that one.

610 - Recovery ('b' man). #2 UHF will not transmit - could not duplicate.

æ½¼ - Don asked me if I wanted to work overtime. I said, "Sure!"

Friday, May 8, 1998

æ½¼ - I asked George and Scott if I could work on Saturday too. They said that they would check into it.

629 - Wiped down engines. Drained fuel lines. Moved radar control head to the Nav's position. Assisted launch. Assisted recovery, refuel (spr).

æ½¼ - Dawn was sleeping in a chair on the flight deck. She told me that she was taking a medicine for depression, called "Paxil". She said that the depression was caused by working at Altus.

æ½¼ - Lawrence Burgeos forget to get his bag off an a/craft before it took off. Big safety thing. The a/craft flew with his bag on it. The flight crew found it and gave it to supervision. Bob Bagg called Lawrence into his office and had a talk with him about it.

Sunday, May 10, 1998

0243 - Wiped bottom of engine doors (all four), wiped MLG (both of them) swivels. Unchained & uncovered aircraft. R2 cable holding clamp by the left aft troop jump door. Assisted launch. The flight engineer waved me on, so I started to push the fire extinguisher away. As I neared the wingtip, a hand-held radio flew by me and crashed to the ground. I looked back and Tammy was in front of the #4 engine. The flight engineer was in front of the a/craft. She had thrown a hand-held radio at my back. I asked her about it and she said that I couldn't very well call in that the a/craft was blocking, unless I had a radio. I really don't see where that allows a person to throw a radio at another person's back. Personally, I think that she lost her temper and threw the radio at me, while I had my back turned. She had wanted me to stop, in front of #3 engine. I did not think that it was wise to sit and talk in front of a running engine. I couldn't really hear what she was screaming anyway. She said later that she telling me to take the radio. But, I didn't hear her, and that made her mad and she threw it at me, when I started to walk away.

æ½¼ - Tammy Romero - Obeys and demands that everyone obey "her favorite" set of rules. She cares nothing for other rules, especially yours. She leaps over tow bars that connect power carts to trucks, stating "That only applies to towing aircraft.", "If they don't like it. They can bite my butt." She forgets a lot of stuff. She borrows my pencils and breaks the lead off them, because she presses too hard on the paper. She tells me that she will not allow me to do oxygen servicing on an a/craft (George was training us), because I had a short sleeve shirt. She had a t-shirt on and was servicing away. To Tammy Romero, rules are for everybody else, but her. She tells us that everyone in her family is a lawyer, except her. If that's true, I think that it is a source of depression for her.

Monday, May 11, 1998

æ½¼ - Did the first half of my physical. It was done by an airman. He did a hearing test and took my blood pressure, pulse, and all that good stuff.

219 - Did CNAD workcard #17. Tammy Romero showed up. I saw her at the shoe and she told me that she was going to the North Ramp. I had also seen Don Obriter at the Shoe and told him about Tammy throwing the radio at my back. He said that he would talk to her, about her temper. Swapped the INS batteries. INS ops checks good.

æ½¼ - Tammy seems to be a different person today. Like HOT & COLD.

946 - Stood ground for engine run.

æ½¼ - The unusual has occurred. Mr. Francis, Mr. Bagg, (Blue shirt) George, and Harold Church, all came out & sat down with us at the picnic tables, after work. They also listened as three or four of the usual mal-contents harassed Lawrence, and accused him of being gay. Of course he's married, has two kids, and his wife is pregnant right now. He and I have had extensive conversations about his life and background, while babysitting a/craft. He never mentioned anything about being gay. Personally, I don't think that he is. I think that Lawrence Burgeous is Still water.

Tuesday, May 12, 1998

610 - Took out pilot's and co-pilot's seats. Removed the floor panels under the seats, for the sheet metal people. Worked with Gary Hubbs and Ed Taylor. Ed took off the a/craft yoke and we cleaned up the yoke bearings.

æ½¼ - Gary tells me that Eddie got out of the military to become a policeman, like his dad. But, he failed the psychological exam. So, he's here at Altus now.

æ½¼ - Went to the clinic to finish up the second half of my physical. I saw Dr. Scott. Dr. Scott suggested that I come in and do the 5 day blood pressure check. She said that since I quit smoking again, am exercising, and trying to eat right, I've eliminated most of the long term risk factors. She said that the short term risk factor that sticks out the most in my life now is violence. So, we talked about my stressful job. I told her that I relieve my stress by writing and organizing a diary.

æ½¼ - Got back to work at 1500 hrs.

Wednesday, May 13, 1998

50263 - Defuel 20000 lbs (SPR). Right rear troop door got stuck open. Ed, Bob, & I muscled it closed. Assisted launch.

æ½¼ - Gary Tignor's wife had a baby boy yesterday. Gary is a real proud father. Their baby's name is Dalton Wayne Tignor.

8087 - (Wash Rack) Closed engine cowling doors.

161 - Helped put some screws into the tail cone.

50263 - Assisted recovery. Checked oil. Refuel (SPR), R2 right jump door interphone cord.

Thursday, May 14, 1998

64000610 - Wiped down engines.

629 - flight engineer's interphone foot switch inop. Roy (hydraulics) had switched it to the nav's position before I got out to the aircraft. Assisted launch. I rebuilt the switch, and will put it in, once the a/craft is on the ground again.

219 - closed #3 & #4 engine cowling doors.

172 - assisted chain & cover.

629 - assisted recovery. R2 flight engineer's interphone foot switch. Assisted raising #1 engine cowling doors. Assisted removing CSD generator.

Friday, May 15, 1998

0700 - 0900 Safety Briefings. USAF Safety Day...

223 - Stood ground for Edward Callefell.

æ½¼ - Ethics class.

Saturday, May 16, 1998

172 - Assisted launch.

æ½¼ - Came in at 0500 hours. Left at 0800 hours.

Sunday, May 17, 1998

272 - LOX'd (Liquid Oxygen) the front of the a/craft to 24 liters.

610 - LOX'd the front to 24 liters. Checked tires.

219 - Assisted recovery and push-back (left wing) to spot 37. refuel (SPR).

172 - Defuel (SPR).

Monday, May 18, 1998

263 - Bob Clark moved the radar control head from the Nav's position to the center console. Bob Clark is a crew chief. He didn't do a quick check to see if the radar still worked.

8087 - Put radar RT in. Someone (Theo, Kevin, or Carl) took it out to swap to another a/craft (because a crew chief swapped a radar control head, and didn't plug the cannon plug up correctly), but they didn't write any of it up.

æ½¼ - Went to lunch at 1100 hrs. to get my blood pressure checked. B/P = 133/63.

161 - Tow (right wing).

263 - Recovery (debrief), push-back (brakes).

Tuesday, May 19, 1998

64-000629 - I asked George ('7' truck driver) why he was assigned to this a/craft with me. He said we were short on people. Drained SPR. Installed two hydraulic pressure switches and ops checked good. Assisted launch.

æ½¼ - B/P checked at lunch, per Dr. Scott's request. B/P=137/63.

172 - Tow (Hand brake).

Wednesday, May 20, 1998

æ½¼ - Comm/Sec class. Mr. Leismister tells us that supply has refused to play, according to the regulations, and account for their equipment. Like they are supposed to.

æ½¼ - B/P=129/72.

219 - Assisted recovery ('B' man), checked oil.

æ½¼ - Tried to tell Hilley about the QA thing. Turned in two more AFTO 22s.

Thursday, May 21, 1998

629 - I was assigned to work a #2 HF coupler fault. George "10" truck driver for today, because we don't have enough people (he's usually the '7' truck driver), George said that Taylor would bring a landall, as soon as his a/craft blocked out. His a/craft blocked out, then aborted, so he had to recover it. Therefore, I didn't get the landall or another person to stand ground for me, so that I could not fix the a/craft.

æ½¼ - B/P=144/76.

629 - Went to do a cure check for a new window. However, they put the RTV over the glass cover. So, I had to re-do the RTV.

æ½¼ - Don called me into the office. He talked to me about turn-over and z-ing out forms. I told him that George came and picked me up to recover and a/craft, so I didn't have a chance to give turn-over. I told him that I did go through the forms and GO-81 classes, but there is nothing in the 00 TO s about how to z out a job. That is a local thing and they didn't teach that in class. He said that he knew and then explained real quick how to do it.

Friday, May 22, 1998

629 - #2 HF coupler bad. Scott ('7' truck driver) told me to go get turn-over on it. He said, "If it's not a quick fix. Then hang it up." Swapped Rts, because mid-shift told me that one of the HF s sounded weak. I went through the whole FI. I started to do the last step (check the feed horn continuity) and we had a weather (wind) warning. Cannot go up on the T-tail and finish.

æ½¼ - I sat down with Bob Baggs at lunch time. He told me that he had two many isms (Integrated Systems Mechanics - 2610s), me that is, on dayshift. He said that he could make do with two, but he had five.

Tuesday, May 26, 1998

629 - Sat on top of T-tail. Helped Dawn take out both HF couplers. Ohms checked the feedhorn. It was shorted. Ordered new feed horn. Dawn and I went up in the landall to look at the lightening arrester. It was not cloudy, as Tammy said that it might be. Tammy kept calling it a fuse. It took me a while to figure out what the heck she was talking about. Finally she said

that it was panel under the stinger, just in front of the black painted circle. That clued me in. The coupler relay appeared shorted to me. But, Dawn did not want to change it, until they had the new coupler feedhorn in.

æ½¼ - Took my lunch at 1300 hrs and two hours leave, so that I could come home and get rid of all the old carpet that we have piled up, while putting down the new carpet.

Wednesday, May 27, 1998

219 - Assisted launch.

8087 - Tow (Right wing).

- Took four hours leave. Moved into our new house, at 600 South Broadway, in Tipton, Oklahoma.

Thursday, May 28, 1998

263 - Assisted Roy & George in fixing a life raft pull cord.

219 - Had to swap with Tammy because 263 had a co-pilot's HSI problem. I don't know much about HSI s. Assisted launch.

263 - Swapped HSI s, New HSI %. R2 HSI, ops checked good. Assisted launch.

- Black Flag - Temp over 900. The MOI says to "Work 15 mins./Rest 45 mins." Bob and George still encourage people to work a lot more in the heat. They say, "You know your bodies. If you start to feel the heat, then sit down and take a break."

Friday, May 29, 1998

263 - Drained SPR. Fuel totalizer is about 8K lbs off. Called the '10' truck, who is Mike Taylor today, and asked for Mike or Theo to come look at it. They told Mike that that was my job, and that I should be able to fix it. I pressed the push to test button on some of the individual tanks and watched the totalizer roll up and down. It finally settled on the correct amount of fuel.

- Mike Zawicki and his (-21) crew tells me that they never take time for their jobs in the computer. They told me that their jobs are never written

up at all. He said that they just fix their stuff and move on to the next job. They fix a/craft cargo rails and stuff like that.

\# - I have a crew of engineers and load masters. But, I have no crew chief to help me out. Bob Clark is supposed to be here. But, he never showed up. He didn't come to work today. They just didn't know that he wasn't here. Finally, they sent out Joe Bates.

\# - I notice that Denise still picks up and moves to whatever a/craft Kevin is on.

0272 - Put in FSAS CDU. Had a bug bite me on the neck. I just itches, but I flicked some spiders off me and I think that it was a spider bite.

' - Went to the restroom to wash my hands. The bug bite looks a little worse. It doesn't itch any worse.

Saturday, May 30, 1998

' - Took our air conditioner condenser apart and cleaned it out. It really needed it, bad. Then, I turned on the air conditioner and the air stopped blowing. I checked it out and the evaporator was frozen solid. So, I gave it a chance to thaw out and cleaned it up too. Then, I cleaned its intake vents and filtered them. When I turned it back on it started blowing like a champ.

& - Linda made me go to the doctor. My Friday bug bite was 3 inches across, red, swollen, and hot. It's 2200 hrs here at the emergency room.

Sunday, May 31, 1998

' - Went to the doctor, at the ER, again. Per the doctor's orders. The spider bite has not gotten better. No phone. Cannot call work.

Monday, June 1, 1998

\# - Told Don Obriter about the spider, and gave him all the paperwork that I had accumulated at the ER. I did this as soon as I got to work. It was 0645 hrs.

8087 - Found a big spider web in the #1 avionics bay. Working with Lawrence today. Assisted pulling out 6 life rafts and 2 survival kits.

; - Kevin Sherill stopped by, went up to the cock-pit, and took two of our KY-58 by-pass panels to a/craft 272, because it didn't have enough of them. He didn't write anything about it in the forms. That appears to be really common here at Altus.

- Got a new initial/annual evaluation. It has all '5's on it. I'm not happy about it, but I'm tired of messin' with it. Don said that I would still get an annual appraisal in September.

4629 - Assisted recovery. Checked oil.

Tuesday, June 2, 1998

946 - Walk around and talked to Ron and Gary. They didn't need any help. I was told, by George '7', to be at the LOX/LIN plant by 0800 hrs.

æ½¼ - Assigned to LOX/LIN plant for 2 hours.

610 - Assisted jacking and installing the #1 engine.

; - Bob Bagg called a lot of people into his office today. It wasn't for appraisals, all the people who he called into his office, had already had their appraisals done two or three days ago.

172 - Held bucket under belly of a/craft for George Liley. He drained some hydraulic fluid.

; - Other flight-line injuries noted.

Dawn Depew - fell down the T-tail ladder and got a hematoma, at least six inches long and three inches wide, under her left arm (interior). I told her to see a doctor, she said, "No!"

Ed Callafell - had three scratches on the inside of his right arm. The scratches are at least 2 - 3 inches long. They look pretty deep, very reddened area, surrounding scratches about 1/8 of an inch. Slightly infected. I told him to see a doctor. He said, "No!" I said, ok then, you should at least put some triple anti-biotic and some kind of a bandage on it. He said, "Ok!"

Wednesday, June 3, 1998

7946 - I was supposed to help with a cargo door actuator, but Gary got pulled to another a/craft. Then, I was supposed to work the Nav's altimeter, #1 & #2 INS inop lights intermittently. I got pulled off to sit right seat on an engine run.

610 - Sat right seat. Opened #3 engine cowling doors, and switched EGT leads. Engine ops checked good.

0144 (Rodeo Plane) - Moved power unit for tow. Assisted launch.

; - Supervisors here at Altus, on the flight -line, namely Bob Bagg, encourage workers to work outside of AETCI 48-101 (Heat stress instruction). Yesterday's temp was 1130 F. We worked on an engine for 3 straight hours. Did anyone tell us it was "Black alert". No. Did Bob or George get out of their air conditioned trucks to tell us to take a break, or to make us take a break. "No!" Hense! The reason that everyone here, at Altus AFB, says that our supervisors have NO BALLS! Moral here is rather low. But, our supervisors keep reminding me, it's been a lot lower. Especially, when they first started. WOW! That makes everything better. NOT.

- I asked Hilly why they stopped announcing the heat range (color) over the radio. He said that they talked about that in a meeting yesterday and decided to stop. Scott told me that they announced yesterday as "Yellow".

946 - Stood ground for engine run.

v - Mike Gross tells me that Mr. Bagg's, big meeting yesterday, was about things that were said on the '10' truck last Thursday and that Dawn Depew was the person who reported them. I asked why Mr. Bagg always had these meetings about Dawn when she was on leave or gone for some other reason. He said that he didn't know.

Thursday, June 4, 1998

- T.O. 1-1-3, pg. 2-3, para. 2-4.7 is a fuel shop T.O. (Climatic conditions).

610 - Assisted launch.

219 - Tow (Rode brakes).

- Truck conversation yesterday was about rugae. Started by Lawrence.

629 - Blocked through spot 21 (twice) to spot 22. Checked oil, refuel (SPR).

Friday, June 5, 1998

629 - #2 BDHI pointers will not point to station.

\# - Truck conversation today, started by Testerman. "What a screw-up George (Big George) is... ", "... and they keep letting him do it."

219 - Looked at the #2 aux fuel gauge, it rotates counter-clockwise continuously. Disconnected & reconnected the push-to-test button. No help. I found the correct FI, but couldn't get a fuel quantity test set from our CTK. They didn't have any. I went over to the KC-135 CTK and got one. Brian stopped by and helped me figure out how to use the GTF-6 test set. There were some bent pins on the fuel probe cannon plug. We straightened them out, reconnected the fuel probe, and the gauge ops checked good.

Sat & Sun, June 6 -7, 1998 (Reserve Duty)

Î - Had address changed at pay and personnel

Ï - Assisted putting up tents, putting up HF antennae. Drove the ton and a half truck. Set up beds & sleeping bags.

Đ - Day two - assisted putting everything up. Talked to Maj. Collins. He gave me a lot of phone numbers to call. These are chief master sergeants who have a few WG-2610-12 jobs, on KC-135s.

Monday, June 8, 1998

8087- Re-assigned and pulled to a/craft 243.

243 - VHF & INS problems. R2 #2 VHF control head, ops checked good. R2 #1 & #2 INS batteries. Someone had shoved them into the rack improperly and damaged them, so the INS system had a battery fail. Pulled to a/craft 610.

610 - Add fuel (panel) to 90,000 lbs, assisted launch.

\# - Mr. Hilley is calling people into office today, except me [Don't know why?]

8087 - Opened #2 engine cowling doors and pushed Denise around on the B4 stand so that she could check the fire loops.

\# - Went to QA and talked to Bill Weaver. One of my AFTO 22s is finally completely approved. Now, I can fill out the AF form 1000 for it.

219 - Stood ground for engine run. #1 engine needs to be trimmed.

\# - Lightening within 5 miles. They actually cleared the flight-line. There is a first time for everything.

Tuesday, June 9, 1998

219 - Assisted launch.

- Went to the inspector general's office about two of my suggestions. I talked to Msgt. Nichols at the IG's office.

- Talked to the OSI about getting something in writing from them, about the KY investigation.

- Talked to the base comm/sec (Information Security) person, Msgt. Bruha about getting something in writing from them.

(- submitted my AF form 1000 for one of my suggestions (improvement # 20J0097AMW8028U) [Idea # ALT 980051, "Dangers of Storing Fill Mercury Batteries in non-used KY/KIT equipment installed on a/craft".

Wednesday, June 10, 1998

219 - Assisted launch.

; - Don tells me that Margaret Malone (Civilian Personnel – Building 52) insists that I make an appointment with her anytime that I want to talk to one of her people. I just walked by their office and they called me in and started talking to me.

629 - Put in EDC for Theo.

219 - Checked oil, pushed back (right wing).

8087 - Refuel (panel).

' - Tammy told me that the secret meetings were about the same thing that the last one was about.

' - There's some kind of standard joke now. It's about being too afraid to come to work. I think that this has something to do with Dawn's EEO complaint.

Thursday, June 11, 1998

610 - Did engine run for the fuel flow indicator problem. It ops checked good. I stood ground.

\# - George & Theo sat in the cockpit for an hour and read the AF Times. Boss Hogg read Dune.

\# - Junior left for camp Monday the 8th. It's a church camp. I hope that he has fun. The preacher assures me that he will. An elderly church woman paid for him to go. Junior comes home Friday.

\# - Linda, the girls, and I played softball Wednesday. Well, I pitched about 20 to 30 balls to each one. They had batting practice. I got hit a lot. They can all hit a softball and they can hit it hard.

610 - Towed from spot 33 to spot 32 for pictures. Helped wipe down a/craft for picture. Did ½ of trascribing forms for Gary Hubbs.

\# - Listened to Gary Hubbs, Theo, Baggs, & Obriter get into how to get Theo off the truck & make him work. He never did get off the '10' truck.

610 - Finished entering all of the MDC data, like Mr. Hubbs, showed me.

Friday, June 12, 1998

\# - Altus is throwing a party for Altus AFB today in hanger 509 (the new washrack) at 1530 hrs.

(- Junior comes home from camp today.

\# - LOX/LIN plant for two hours.

629 - Dropped off life rafts & picked up new ones and dropped them off at the a/craft for T & T. (Team Swank). I'm not sure about the initials or the name.

172 - Chain & cover.

Sunday, June 14, 1998

243 - Installed troop door winch hand switch.

\# - Don is the '7' truck driver.

\# - Tammy is the '10' truck driver.

Monday, June 15, 1998

8087 - Pushed Lawrence around on a B-1 stand to lube the flap screws and tracks.

- Rob Testerman & Don Obriter hang out together a lot. Rob also hangs around Bob Bagg, George Standard, and Scott Johnson (all brown shirts, except Rob) a lot. I'm waiting to see if Rob becomes a brown shirt.

623 - Refuel (SPR).

Tuesday, June 16, 1998

8087 - SKE. Two masters problem. Ordered SKE coder/decoder (By the FI). I helped Denise, Theo, and Kevin with a #1 crossfeed switch problem. It had a broken terminal wire.

- I saw Dawn today. I told her about the suggestions that I put in. She told me that she was working in the HSC/ISO doing T.O.s now. I think it has something to do with her EEO complaint. She told me that all the female trouble-makers wind up there. I would wonder where all the male troublemakers wind up, but since I'm him I guess I know. Greenwood's (swing shift brown shirt) Ex-wife is there. The red-haired Tammy (who slept with here boss, when working on KC-135s) is there. There are some other women who claim to be trouble in there. However, I haven't gotten all of their stories straightened out enough to put into writing yet. Tammy, Dawn, and Greenwood stories have been gotten from them, and then verified by at least two of my friends and one or two of theirs. Sometimes they collaborate each others' stories.

(; - I'm both happy and sad at the same time. Lawrence (my friend) told me that he got a job in Saudi Arabia. I will miss him a lot. He was a good friend. I hope that he makes out great in Saudi.

- Hilley showed us some slides about the civil service rules on workplace violence.

610 - Auto-pilot problem. FI tells me that this a/craft needs an elevator computer.

Wednesday, June 17, 1998

610 - Loaded the #1 UHF presets, drained the SPR, assisted launch.

0172 - Stood ground for engine run.

\# - Roy "10" truck driver is complaining about Kevin & Denise. They go to lunch (for an hour) and come back. Then they go to their a/craft and eat lunch. The '10' truck drivers are wondering what the heck they are doing on their lunch hour. Every time a '10' truck driver tells them to do something, they say that they are eating lunch. Denise is also mean to crew chiefs and a lot of other people. Lawrence was trying to help her out, and she said, leave me alone and do your crew chief thing. She says that to all the crew chiefs who try to help her. They don't want to work with her. They tell the '10' truck drivers that.

Thursday, June 18, 1998

219 - Assisted launch.

\# - Talked to Msgt. Swift. He is going to adopt an 18 year old boy. This boy is about 17½ right now and has had a troubled life. Swift is one of a/crew members on 219. Aspinwall and I talked with him about God for a while. Mr. Swift is a devout Christian.

172 - Helped Tshoot #2 main fuel gauge.

219 - Refuel (Panel).

<u>Friday, June 19, 1998</u>

187 - Chain and cover.

219 - Chain and cover.

\# - 3 people called in sick today.

\# - George (light blue shirt - WL) & Scott (Brown shirt - WS) threw us out of the air conditioning. Francis walked by them once and told them to kick us out. It was temperature condition red (work 30 mins/rest 30 mins - by doctor's orders/AFI). Roy the '10' truck driver let us (Bob Clark, John Aspinwall, Raymond, and I) out at the shoe for a legitimate 15 minute break, at 1000 hours. John and Ray told him twice, while Mr. Francis (White shirt) was present, that we were on our 15 minute break. John asked Scott three more times if he was serious. Scott said, "Go take your break on an airplane, or we'll have you sitting in CTK sorting bench stock and checking tools." We took this as a threat and left. John and Ray were visibly upset, and rather vocal. I can't say as I blame them. Rob Testerman heard about what happened and got us all together and got Roy to take us over to the union rep. Then, we all came back and put it in writing for the union guy. Roy got chewed up by Scott and George for taking us to the Union office.

Sunday, June 21, 1998

'My anniversary. I drove, with Linda and the kids, to Tinker AFB. I have a set of orders to be at the 707th Communications Flight at 1500 hours, to arrange for government travel to Cannon AFB. I drove because the Chevrolet dealer came and picked up our car (El Camino). That's because they said that they fixed it, but they didn't. So, they said that they are going to fix it for free.

Monday, June 22, 1998 (Reserve Annual Tour)

List of jobs in the military leading up to civil service.

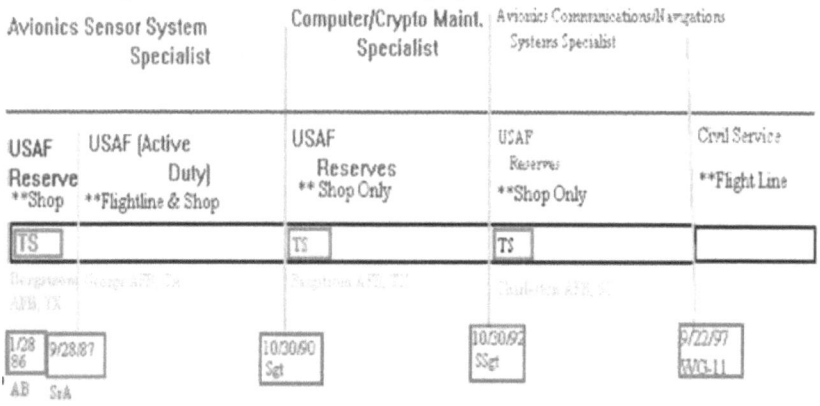

*** TS = Technical School (Formal Training)

0730 - 1100 ± Cannon AFB familiarization. Conducted by Msgt. Greenlee.

1200 - 1600 ± Cannon AFB, unit (27th Communications Squadron) Familiarization.

Tuesday, June 23, 1998

0730 - 0900 ± Discovered user's problem was with a phone jack, not with a network jack (CAT 5 cable). Called (Baker) civilian telephone contractor on base.

0900 - 1100 ± Watched Allesbrooke and Zane install a CD-ROM drive and an HP printer driver.

1200 - 1600 ± Watched Allesbrooke install Win '95 on the wing kings computer. Helped install Win '95 on the 707th CF computer that we borrowed from the 27th CS.

Wednesday, June 24, 1998

0730 - 0900 ± Helped set up E-mail accounts on the 707th desktop computer.

1000 - 1200 ± Learned about the Catalyst 5000 switching system. Instructed by T Sgt. Lovely. Simplified Block Diagram follows.

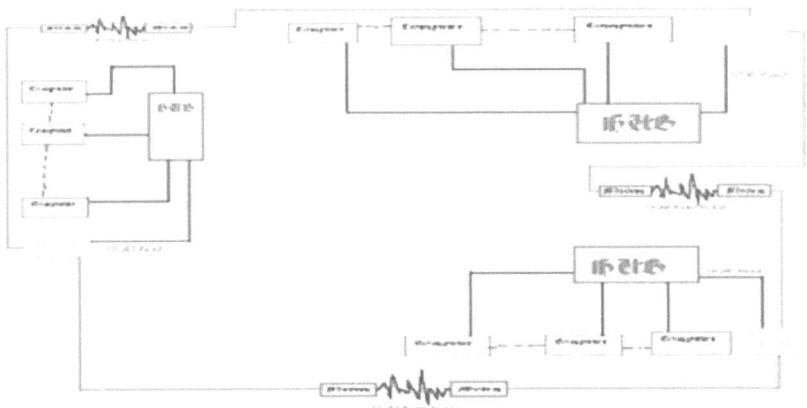

1300 - 1630 ± Troubleshooting Mitch's IBM thinkpad laptop computer. It needs some CD-ROM Drive drivers. Got the CD-ROM Drive drivers and installed them. Ops checked good. Now, it needs some audio drivers. I haven't been able to find them on the IBM website yet.

Thursday, June 25, 1998

0730 - 1200 ± Studied different memory configurations, for TSgt Lovely's computer.

1300 - 1630 ± Changed two over-drive processors on two computers, to no effect. One of the computers has a bad BIOS chip.

Friday, June 26, 1998

0730 - 1630 ± Warrior Day. Erected a medium tent. Put up camo netting around tent and pick-nick area. Attended a retirement ceremony for a MSgt.

Saturday, June 27, 1998

Rode back from Cannon AFB to Tinker AFB. I Drove from Amerillo.

Monday, June 29, 1998

0187 - IFF mode IV check. Ops checked good.

0263 - IFF mode IV check. Ops checked good.

- I signed a paper today, to let the union represent me. John Aspinwall is now our new shop steward. Still no word on the grievance that we all filed two weeks ago.

172 - Checked tires. #1 main tire is at 185 psi, all the others are 200 psi. Got nitrogen cart, and assisted Gary Hubbs in filling the tire back up to 200 psi.

Tuesday, June 30, 1998

0610 - Assited launch.

- Talked to Tracy Britt about military leave. She gave me an AF form 3598 to fill out, and take over to the civilian pay office.

\# - Talked to Yvonne at civilian pay about my missing 15 days of military leave. I gave her the AF form 3598. She said that she would see what she could do with it.

\# - I also filled out a form to start an allotment for our house payment. I gave that to Yvonne also.

0172 - Talked to MSgt. Hall about the KAM 334B. She said that thought it was on the base. She said that she remembered seeing it. I told her that I had been told by the base comm/sec office that it was not. I told her that I did not know how the C-5 comm/nav guys had modified the KY-75s to KYV-5s without a tech-manual. But, hey that is her job (Safety NCO).

' - Condition black announced, at 1310 hours.

0263 - Dropped off to put 781D in the aircraft forms.

0629 - Recovered. Checked oil. Fixed brake pressure gauge (co-pilots). Refuel (Panel). George told us to clean all the wheel wells on the aircraft. Mike Gross and I cleaned for two and half hours with George Standard, the crew chief, and the QA guy watching us from their air conditioned truck. The QA guy told us to use JP-8 instead of the 'general purpose' cleaner that I had gotten from CTK. I think that you could safely call Altus AFB, Oklahoma an out-door sweat shop, sponsored by the United States Government.

Wednesday, July 1, 1998

\# - Talked to Bill Weaver. 7 of my suggestions are still awaiting approval from depot. They have all been approved by their respective HQ s.

0263 - Assisted launch. Swapped radar control head.

\# - MSgt. Hall told me that Col. Ayers left the base. He retired, and is no longer the IG for Altus AFB. She said that our base does not have an IG at the present time.

0610 - Mode IV check. Ops checks good, R2 IFF mode IV computer batteries.

Thursday, July 2, 1998

8087 - Babysat spare. Drained SPR and cleaned windows.

\# - Bab Bagg & Don Obrieter still contend that SCD (Service Comp Dates) mean absolutely nothing here at Altus. The union maintains the same thing. However, all the workers think that the opposite is the case. We, the employees, feel that SCD should be incorporated into our system.

263 - Chain and cover.

161 - Assisted recovery, checked oil. Nav's interphone, #1 UHF inop. CND.

Friday, July 3, 1998

********Independence (Fourth of July) Holiday

Monday, July 6, 1998

243 - Drained SPRs. A/craft is going to Germany; the crew chief asked me to (please) do an IFF mode IV check. I said sure. I started to get all of the equipment together and Mr. Obrieter and Mr. George Standard asked what I was doing and why. I told them, that there is an AFI that says that anytime an a/craft goes over water or a border, we must do an IFF mode IV check. They said that they didn't know of an AFI like that, but that I could do it. Mike Praetor, Mark Fletcher, Tammy Romero, and Mike Gross all told me that they remembered that AFI, but couldn't remember exactly what number it was. I told them that was ok, and did the checks anyway. The KY batteries were over two years old, so I replaced them also. R2 standby ADI.

\# - Turned in radar RT for Tammy.

\# - Arranged for another house payment ($382.00) through the bank to Mr. White's bank account, on the 10th of July, a Friday.

Tuesday, July 7, 1998

0610 - Moved radar control head to the Nav.'s position. Drained SPR. Engine trouble. Something hard went through the #3 engine during a mid-air refuel, yesterday. The engine had plenty of dings on the turbine blades. The engine shop borescoped it and had to call Tinker AFB to talk to some of the engineers there, to see if they could blend the blades that much. The engineers said that it was ok, barely. They faxed a letter here telling us that. That was last night. Now, the crew chief (Gary Hubbs) and some members of the flight crew wanted to make sure that the engine would hold together during take-off. So, they asked Don if he could arrange to have a ground engine run done. Don said, "No!" So the air crew said that they would take another a/craft.

- Personally, I just wish that these managers here would take some lessons in humanity. That is, people before a/craft. They don't seem to be able to distinguish between what is actually mission essential and what is not. They certainly do not appear to realize that we can replace a/craft. We can never replace a person. To top it off, this is a training base.

#- John Aspinwall recanted his scary tale. He tells us that Mr. Francis (who loves middle men) sent George Standard over to tell him to drop the grievance that we all signed against him, or we might get hurt. That sounds a lot scary out here on this dangerous flight-line to me. Already, they don't obey any of rules, especially safety rules. They just keep re-canting, "We are not in the Air Force", "You are not in the Air Force."

0263 - Crew moved from a/craft 0610. #4 engine oil low light came on. We put 7 quarts in it. I used 15 spill pads to mop up a spill that was approx. 50 ft. in diameter. It had been leaking for a couple of days. Joe Bates (engine troop) says that the gear box is bad and has been leaking for weeks. Don Obrieter has been notified. He kept telling the crew that there was nothing wrong with the plane. But the flight engineer wanted an oil consumption run done on it. He told Don that he saw the oil low light come on two hours into flight last time he flew that plane. He said that they had to put 11 quarts in it. Don finally said, "Ok". I asked him (Don) if we should notify the spill response team. He said, "No!" ADC (Air Drop Cargo) training mission aborted.

187 - Engine run (stood ground).

- George Standard is the '10' truck driver today. He told me that he hates driving the '10' truck. John, the rest of the crew, and I believe that it is his job. He only drives the '10' truck when everyone else refuses to do it. The '10' truck involves making a lot of management decisions, and if you volunteer to do it, you don't get paid a penny more. But, you do get all of the blame, and all of the flack. So, it's not worth it.

' - Lunch 1230. Condition BLACK.

263 - Stood ground for engine run, for 30 mins straight.

8087 - Refuel (panel).

\# - I talked to Ray Leismeister about my suggestion for the C-5s. He told me that he was made the #3 evaluator for my suggestion. He told me that he thought I was just trying to get more money. He likes to pick at me about money, because I have five kids. He didn't tell me what he was going to suggest. He did tell me that it was a different perspective for him, because he was usually sitting where I was (the suggestor). He said that he had to do all the calculating for the idea and that was the part that was killing him. Re-evaluation letter from one of my sillier moments follows:::,

To: 97 AMW/MO
        212 S. 7th Street
        Altus AFB, OK 73532-5307
From: Daniel Leroy McGrew
        600 S. Broadway
        Tipton, OK 73570-0766
        Re: Request for Re-evaluation of Suggestion ALT 98-0051
        Date: DATE \@"DDDD', 'MMMM\ D', 'YYYY" Saturday, December 29, 2007

1.   Request reconsideration of the intangible award benefits of approved AFTO form 22, improvement report number 20J0097AMW8028U.

2.   AFTO form 22, improvement report number 20J0097AMW8028U was approved on 03 June 1997 with intangible benefits valued at minor and broad. However, this appears to be an inappropriate value of benefits for the annual potential (<u>Estimated</u> - AFI 38-401, page. 10, chapter 4, section 4.2.1.1.1) amount of savings generated.

3.   The cost of a KY-58 (NSN: 5810-01-050-8116, P/N: ON241800-4) is   <u>$2,600.00</u> . The cost of a KYV-5 (NSN: 5810-01-236-5246, P/N: ON347805) is <u>$6,740.00</u> . The cost of a KIT-1C (NSN: 5810-01-273-7820, P/N: ON389698-1) is   <u>$1,253.51</u>   . These units did not have inspection requirements in the C-5, -6 Technical Order in the past. The BA-5372/U, BA-1372/U, and the BA-5567/U vented batteries have potential corrosive effects upon equipment, when left in de-energized equipment for extended periods of time. Checking fill batteries is a three-fold benefit.

    Î   Prevents sending useful batteries to the base pharmacy.
                Price of new batteries:
                        a.   BA-5372/U --- $ 70.84 (NSN: 6135-01-214-6441)
                        b.   BA-1372/U --- $ 70.84 (NSN: 6135-01-801-3493)
                        c.   BA-5567/U --- $ 4.68 (NSN: 6135-01-090-5365)

Price of battery disposal:

a. Lithium batteries: 1.43/.454Kgrams

172.0 grams of lithium batteries per aircraft

860 grams total for C-5 aircraft at Altus AFB, OK.

Ï   Increases reliability of Identification friend or foe information, in war-time environments.

Đ   Knowledge is power. If your/our enemies know where we are going and what we are doing. Then, they will have power over us. (Example: one army helicopter shot down by two Air Force F-16 fighters, over the Iraq - No Fly Zone) In either case Î or Ï, the United States of America just lost one C-5 aircraft, its invaluable crew members, and all of its important cargo. (No one should ever have to die, because of a $70.00 battery)

Price of one C-5 aircraft:

a.   C-5B (Galaxy) --- $ 184.2 Million dollars per aircraft

b.   C-5 aircraft built to carry expensive Army equipment.

4.   This technical order affects all of the C-5 aircraft at every Air Force Base in the world. If the value of this idea at Altus Air Force Base is $200.00. Then, that value should be multiplied by the number of Air Force Bases maintaining possession of C-5 aircraft. This would include 8 Air Force Bases. They are: Charleston AFB, SC; Altus AFB, OK; Dover AFB, DE; Travis AFB, CA; Kelly AFB, TX. C-5 aircraft are also maintained in 2 Air Reserve Units (Kelly AFB, TX and Westover AFB, MA) and 1 Air National Guard Unit (Stewart ANG, NY). This suggestion is actually of greater value, when the environmental impact is properly extrapolated.

5.   In my personal opinion, I would place the value of benefits, for this suggestion, at substantial and broad. Signatures of other technicians who agree with me are included on the reverse side of this memo.

6.   My suggestion appears to have a greater value of benefits than Mr. Moya and Mr. Gonzalez have attributed. I am fairly certain that they were not thinking of the modern, potential, military benefits of information protection. Therefore, I respectfully requested an objective re-evaluation of my suggestion award.

Daniel L. McGrew, WG-2610-11

2nd ½ of reserve annual tour

Saturday, July 11, 1998

Went to DP (Disaster Preparedness) / CW (Chemical Warfare) Briefing.

Sunday, July 12, 1998

Assisted setting up the AFMSS Ï system.

Monday, July 13, 1998

Tsgt. Moorehead gave me the 7-level upgrade training, student workbook (E6AZS2EX7X-000).

Tuesday, July 14, 1998

Studied workbook, took safeware test and got password.

Wednesday, July 15, 1998

Studied workbook. Went to the computer expo at the O-club.

Thursday, July 16, 1998

Studied workbook. Went to the computer expo at the O-club. **PQA 529, Plymouth Voyager. Little girl in the front seat was rocking back-and-forth unusually hard and fast. Normally I don't notice much of what is going on in other people's automobiles, but that was strange. She appeared to be in the 10 -12 year range. Her dad (I think) was sitting next to her, she looked like she was talking & rocking forward and backward in her car seat. I remembered a little girl who used to ride the school bus with us. She would do that when people bothered her.

Friday, July 24, 1998

The union asked me to fill out a paper telling what Bob Bagg told us all, sign it, and give it the president. I did that with the information below in the letter. YES! I, Daniel L. McGrew, heard Bob Bagg say that we were not going to be conducting union business during working hours, anymore. He said that Mr. Obriter would be getting out to the flight-line more often now. He also said that he was going to start getting tougher on people who say, "I can't do that. That's not my job. I don't know how to do that."

Saturday and Sunday, July 25 - 26, 1998

Rescheduled August UTA because of Keesler Tech School. While at the LaQuinta hotel across from Tinker AFB, our van window was smashed & all of my bags were taken. My training records & shot records were in my blue bag.

Monday, July 27, 1998

- Told my supervisors about the theft of my stuff at Tinker AFB. They are arranging to get me some boots, Davis-Clark head-sets, a line badge, and some other things that I need for work.

243 - Pilot's N1 RPM indicator reads 8% less than co-pilot's. I've been put on this job alone. I've never worked on engine instruments before. I read the FI, and told Scott '7' truck driver, to order another gauge.

- Filled out paperwork to get new line badge. Got new head-sets.

243 - Assisted installing #8 MLG tire. Jack handle fell down & smashed 3 of the fingers on my right hand. Talked to Scott & we filled out some paperwork on it.

Tuesday, July 28, 1998

243 - Changed #1 engine N1 RPM gauge.

- Got new line badge.

- Scott gave me the paperwork to go to the hospital to get my fingers looked at. Now, I just need transportation.

0187 - Helped Brian Shettler change 5 fuel probes.

- Boss Hogg is driving the '10' truck today.

172 - Picked up HSI & coupler.

8087 - Recovered, checked oil, push back (left wing). Refuel (SPR).

- Went to ER after work to get fingers X-rayed.

Wednesday, July 29, 1998

- Tammy Romero tells me that she dropped her grievance against Kevin & Denise.

629 - R2 right troop door interphone cord. Assisted launch. Recovery. Removed broken latrine door handle. Assisted launch.

610 - Pulled off panel on top right wing, back by spoilers, so that we could send it to sheet metal. It was beginning to delaminate.

Thursday, July 30, 1998

610 - Found fuel leak #3 engine pylon mounting bolts. Removed 2 panels FOM (facilitate other maintenance).

8087 - Checked oil, a/craft has an FSAS problem. Kevin & Denise pulled up in a mule and took out the FSAS computer, then drove the mule to the back shop to check out the computer. A call came out over the radio that told Boss Hogg to bring Kevin, from the back shop, into Mr. Bagg's office pronto.

8087 - Refueled (panel).

- Overheard Bob Bagg on the phone saying that Tammy had dropped her grievance, and Denise had dropped hers, but Kevin did not/would not drop his. This was verified later by Tammy, and then by John Aspinwall.

@ - 0219 - Volunteered to do 2 hours overtime to help swing shift jack this a/craft in hanger 435.

Friday, July 31, 1998

8087 - Called in 5 write ups. 3 Hydraulic and 2 fuel problems. Assisted launch.

- Had to go get a new line badge. They put some incorrect information on my last one.

- George (blue shirt) is driving Kevin and Denise around in the back of his truck, out to the parking lot to their cars. I've never seen him give anyone else a lift to the parking lot. Not in the little truck, just when he drives the big truck.

8087 - Assisted recovery.

263 - Assisted recovery, checked oil, refuel (panel). Ramond Carrion (Hydraulics) told me he couldn't stand Denise, because she told him that she hopes that we all lose our jobs. R2 & ops checked an EPR gauge at the pilot's position. Turned in the old EPR gauge.

I - Scott (Brown shirt) told me to report to Mr. Curiel (C-5s) Monday, and that Mr. Tully would be my trainer.

Monday, August 3, 1998

First night on C-5s with Mr. Tulley.

466 - Initial Orientation.

9018 - Moved to watch engine run. It was not that involved, because it was a single engine run.

466 - Helped deliver B2 stand, B2 stand has excessive hydraulic fluid leaking at the RAM. Have to get new B2 stand. Got new stand, put it in place, beneath the anti-terrorist entry point, under the tail.

Tuesday, August 4, 1998

018 - Tow (Brake accumulator observer).

- Talked to Larry Collins. He was limping. He said that he had a bone spur in his right leg. He's the person with the masters' degree in abnormal psychology (the religion of pagans). He told me that there was too much violence and not enough sex on TV (in American). I think he's a Freudian philosopher.

- Neil Tulley, my new trainer has two children by his first marriage and one child from what he calls a local girl, whom he never married.

Wednesday, August 5, 1998

\# - Went to SATO, got plane tickets.

\# - Went over training record with Tulley. Tulley was bought out. He got out of the military early, because he couldn't hack it anymore. He said that he was getting too close to being overweight and they probably weren't going to let him retire anyway. So, he took something like $30,000.00 dollars to get out of the Air Force. He told me that that gives him something like 15 years of service comp. time in civil service (or so he keeps telling me). I'm with Mike Gross. I don't think that people who couldn't hack it in the military and were kicked out or got money to get out early should have more service comp. time than retired people (like Mike, who has no service comp. time to start with) or people like me (who never got $30 or more thousand dollars or a big fat retirement check every month).

0466 - Tow (Rode in the tow vehicle).

001 - Assisted launch.

9018 - Training. That is Tulley sits down and talks to me about how things work on a C-5. Just AFIN stuff, that is. He is an AFIN person. He is all systems qualified, and thinks that that makes him an expert on all systems. Well, maybe he is. He certainly knows more about everything on a C-5 than I do. For now. I will learn. But, I'm not going to learn to be a crew chief. I don't care how much they want me to be one. It's not in my job description; they didn't hire me for that. If they want me to be one, they can add it to my job description. I'm starting to mirror the feelings of my co-workers. I wonder if I'm doing that in order to try and fit in.

Friday, August 6, 1998

\# -Got a ride with Grandpa, Mom, Dave and family to Keesler. We are going to stop by Dannette's house first. Then, I get to go on to Keesler to AFMSS training.

Saturday, August 7, 1998

\# - Dave and grandpa worked on Mom's car air-conditioner. The compressor burnt up. They replaced it and took it to the dealer, with same results as always (for us poor people). $400.00 later and it still doesn't work.

Something about a stuck orifice. You know, I've gone through the better business bureau (BBB) about these kinds of things before, it never works. Then, the BBB starts hounding you too. Got up at 0630 with everybody, at Dannette's house, ready to go to Keesler. We stopped and had supper at the Edgewater Mall, Bilouxi. Arrived at Keesler at 1030 hours.

Sunday, August 8, 1998

- Went to the BX and got all the stuff that I thought I was going to need. Laundry detergent, stamps, envelopes, ect...

Monday, August 9, 1998

- Went to the wrong orderly room twice. First, I went to the triangle orderly room. That's the orderly room for NPS (non-prior service students). Finally, I went to the right one and got checked in.

Thursday, August 12, 1998

(- AFMSS training is going fine.

; - I have 3 African-American classmates. They are all SrA. However, while we were all talking, one of them informed us that he was HIV positive. He told us that he didn't do drugs and he has never had sex with a man. We were all rather stunned about his having HIV. We hadn't asked. I've helped take care of AIDS patients in the hospital before. This brought back some unpleasant memories. Through-out the rest of the day, with no probing from any of us, he spoke of having sex with lots of women while in England. He said that he didn't have any steady girl-friends. He talked about his local girlfriends (dates) in the civilian area around Keesler, AFB, having to put out, because he had bought them a drink or bought them something else. He never said that he told them of his disease or whether he used a rubber or not. He did keep telling us that all women were evil. He told us that he got his disease from a girl in Europe. I think that he will/is trying to infect as many women as he possibly can, out of hate or for some kind of revenge. As a matter-of-fact that is what he told us. My infected classmate's name is SrA. Griffin.

- One of the airmen in my class, keeps talking about becoming a doctor. His name is SrA. Love. He is a 2E2 (Computer repair), like my other two

classmates. He told me that he met a girl on his plane trip. He knows that I am up on my security stuff, so he asked me, if it was OK for him to talk to her. This is because she is a foreign national (Canadian). I told him that I thought it was OK, just as long as he doesn't talk about his job. He also asked our instructor (Mr. Van), who told him the same thing. He also told our instructor that this girl is over 50 years old. All the airmen in my class, SrA Love included, are in the 20 year old range. The oldest one just turned 21.

Monday, August 17, 1998

; - I was awakened by my telephone ringing, incessantly at 2230 hours. I kept answering it, but no one was there. I called the front desk, they told me that lightening had struck their answering machine and that it was going crazy. It kept ringing from 2230 hours to 2330 hours.

(- I went to the pay phone downstairs, so that I could call my wife and make sure that she wasn't trying to call me. She wasn't but, she was glad to hear from me. She had lots of stuff to tell me about the kids. They just started school. This was their first day. Anyway, she told me that the children's new birth certificates had finally arrived. We have all been waiting for almost a year. The children were so happy. It's too bad that I had to hear all this over the phone. It reminded me of the song, "I watched my baby grow up in pictures." I can't let that happen. I won't let that happen.

;(- We had home-schooled them all in the South Carolina for a while, because the crappy teachers kept trying to kill them, by denying them medical treatment for injuries received at school. As a matter of fact, they appeared to be bound and determined never to call us at all, when any of our children were injured at school. I wrote letters to my congressmen and to the governor of South Carolina. All to no avail. This happened five times, so we just said the heck with it.

; - Biloxi, Mississippi - When I got back to the room, I found a note on my door. The note said, "Big Guy, if interested. Let's meet in the 3RD floor dayroom. Will give you the best blow job ever. Willing to pay you. Name price." I found the note positively revolting. I immediately called the security police. The security policeman on the phone asked me three times if I was certain that I wanted to make a statement. He kept telling that I didn't have to make a statement. Like he had better things to do, or something. I kept telling him that I was certain. He sent over SSgt Masters to take a statement. SSgt Masters told me the same thing that I didn't have to make a statement. SSgt Masters told me, after he gave me a pad, and

I wrote down my statement, that this kind of thing had been happening a lot in the dorms. He said it just started to happen a lot, in the last two months.

Tuesday, August 18, 1998

- The 332ND TRS first sergeant called me into his office the next day. He said that they found my name on the police blotter, but it didn't say what my name was on there for. So, he said, would you mind filling in the blanks, SSgt McGrew. I said certainly, pulled out my diary, he took notes from it and said thanks. The first Sergeant's name is MSgt. Thomas. I did tell him that the security police were strongly discouraging people from making complaints about homosexual harassment, in the dorms. I told him that I am not a homosexual. I told him that I have a wife and five children. I told him that I do like to keep to my room when I am TDY. Again, he just said thanks.

- I didn't get to tell them that I thought that the security police are covering up the fact that heterosexuals, like me are being discriminated against and harassed by homosexuals in the dorms.

Monday, 23August1998

I missed the airport shuttle that was supposed to take me from Altus to the Oklahoma City airport. So, Linda and the kids took me to the airport. The SATO/TMO people hadn't told me where to catch the shuttle at. I was supposed to catch it at billeting, but I thought that I was supposed to catch it in front of the SATO/TMO office. They also didn't tell me that I was supposed to get a rental car at the Philadelphia International Airport. So, I didn't get one.

Wednesday, 26August1998

I thought that the other techs from Altus were going to have a cow, because I didn't have a rent-a-car. They insisted that I call SATO/TMO and get one. So, I did even though I was fine walking back and forth to class and the chow hall. My instructor told me that one of the Master Sergeants here didn't want me hanging around the admin. office, where Mrs. Patricia works. Mrs. Patricia hasn't even been here, because she has been on jury duty. My instructor told me not to be offended. He said that it was nothing personal. I told him that all I did was go in the office and call SATO/TMO. He said, "Don't worry about it...","...He's leaving soon anyway, and no-one here will miss him any." The SMSgt's name is SMSgt. Moorow. My instructor's name is MSgt. Daugherty. I found another woman, by accident, as always, who left her baby in her hot car alone, with the windows rolled up. White Honda, Delaware plates, 480803. The baby was secured in a baby-seat, in the back seat of the car. Baby's age, approx. 8 to 10 months old. Temperature outside was about 91 degrees F, and sunny. Maybe she had left the AC on. Oh, well, I was just there to get some cheese for my sandwiches. The place, Dover AFB, shopette. MSgt. Daugherty told me that the office thing absolutely had nothing to do with the secretary. That would be Mrs. Patricia. That's interesting, because I hadn't asked him anything about it. I did tell him that I didn't know how it could have anything to do with her, because she had been gone for jury duty. Oh, well, this kind of confusion is way above my pay grade.

Tuesday, 1September1998

Stock market fell 512 points. That's what the news said, last night. So What??? I think that Dover, Delaware is more of a police state/city, than even Los Angeles, CA. There are two (2) civilian police channels here (that is channels that show crimes and criminals) and one (1) military. They are on all the time. I heard about police using active IR in what they called a FLIR (Forward Looking InfraRed) system. I worked on those systems over a decade ago for the military. AFP1 talks about a coordinated effort to put military technology in the hands of the civilian police force. I saw the thing about the police using the FLIR systems on the Police Technology channel here in Delaware. I thought that using the military, or even apart of the military against the civilian population was unconstitutional. We are talking about an enormous amount of power. The government is already rather abusive with its civilian tools. I can see/feel where this is going. It's just the opposite of what Jefferson, Madison, Adams, and all the other founding fathers talked about. I can see this kind of power being abused, and abused a lot. Thomas Jefferson obsessively believed that our founding fathers should create a government so weak that no citizen would have to be afraid of it. He also believed that they should create a people so strong that they didn't have to be afraid of their/our government. I got that from Thomas Jefferson's notes on the state of Virginia. It was an incredibly interesting book. There are already a lot of reports about civilian police abuse of power and authority. Imagine what they are going to do, when no citizen(s) can touch them. Ouch....

Wednesday, 9September1998

Northwest Airline is striking. So, I called SATO/TMO and asked them if I needed to make some other arrangements, since my tickets are with Northwest. They said, sure! Come On down here and we'll take care of you. They gave me new tickets and told me to give my old tickets to the SATO/TMO office at Altus. They also told me that there would be a drop-off charge for the Enterprise rent-a-car that I had. They said that it would be about $75.00. So, they gave me a list of shuttles that drive to Philadelphia airport. I called them and they will drive a person to the airport for $40.00. I can save the government some money. Some of the guys here told me that Civil Service is supposed to pay you for traveling. That is, I should get about 12 hours over-time for traveling home on a Saturday. They also told me to look out, because they keep putting people down for 8 hours, even though they travel more than that. They said that they did that to Gina Pyle, and she filed a grievance against them. They told me that I might have to do the same.

Monday, September 14, 1998

002 - Tully showed me how to ops check the ALDCS system. Howey showed me how to hook up the DFDR test set. Then, Tully & Howey showed me a little about how to use MADAR. Stood ground for engine run.

- Talked to Rickter about travel to Dover and back. He said that all you could get was 8 hours travel for a travel day, no matter what. I told him that it took me 12 hours get there & 12 hours to get back. He said that 8 hours is all that you can get for a travel day. It's good to know someone who knows the rules

- I'm starting to believe that the WSs get better appraisals for cheating workers and workers get bad appraisals when they complain about it. That is, I agree with Dawn's assessment.

Tuesday, September 15, 1998

\# - Watched maint. Courses (sleepy slides we call them).

\# - There are 29 techs, total, on C-5 swing shift.

\# - Rick (Brown shirt) sent me to watch the C-5 egress training film. Larry Woody (Training Super) says that there is no C-5 or C-141 egress films. Here are only KC-135 films. Watched 5 more films.

Wednesday, September 16, 1998

002 - Checked out a MADAR printer with Tully. We were going to do an IFF mode IV check, but got switched in transit to help with an engine change.

018 - Helped to 3 point (mount) an engine.

014 - Helped down jack.

002 - Helped put nitro in tires.

002 - Did IFF mode IV check, changed batteries (they were below 6 VDC, and over 2 years old) ops checked good.

\# - Neil's motorcycle is in, he drove it to work and showed us all. It is a Honda Shadow 1100.

Thursday, September 17, 1998

018 - Towed from hanger to north ramp II. Helped R2 two main fuel tank probe seals. Sat in right seat during engine run.

\# - Talked to Richter & Rick Curiel about switching with Don. Don works grave shift and wants to switch to swings. I volunteered because it would let me see my kids a little more. I could watch my son's football games and help my kids with their homework.

\# - Neil has been asking me a lot of questions. Personal ones, like were was I from, where did I live. He wanted to know all the places that I lived. He said, "Why did you move so much?" I said that circumstances moved me. He said, "That must put a lot of stress on your family." I said, "Probably not. I moved a lot more when I was a kid, it didn't bother me any." I was thinking to myself, about his past, having two wives and sleeping around (having kids by mistresses) must be pretty stressful on a family too. Anyway, his questions went on all night. My objective, as always. To learn, not to talk, even a little, get lots of information.

- I talked to Richter about getting Friday off. I told him that I had to make up a UTA, and pick up some of my stuff from the Del City Police Department. He said ok and got out the leave book. I signed the book.

- Claude stopped me by the water fountain and told me that Neil Tully was NOT my friend. I gave him a perplexed (questioning) look. He said, "Just between you, me, and that book you write in.", "I heard Tom Richter and Neil Tully talking.", " Neil said that he didn't want to be your trainer.", "Tom said - you will teach him." Then I said, "Thanks Claude!" We both went to the parking lot and got into our respective cars and left.

Friday, September 18, 1998

- Went to the Del City Police Dept. I asked them to please mail my stuff to me COD. I wrote them a note saying so, and giving them permission to do that. I showed them my ID cards and stuff.

- I went by base claims and spoke to Ms. Rhonda L. Westerman. I gave her copies of all the stuff that Linda gave to the insurance company. She said that she would take care of all that.

- I went to billeting. They gave me the same hotel, to stay in, that I stayed in last time. When my van window got busted into. The LaQuinta manager told me that they had beefed up their police patrols since then.

Saturday - Sunday, September 19 - 20, 1998

v - Reserve Make-Up Weekend

- Took two CBT courses.

- WOW! I sure do miss my wife and kids when I have to sit in these hotels all alone. Every time I go away from home it's this way. I just can't wait to get back. It's just killing me not to have my little Laura and Teresa jumping on me. I miss Junior trying to get on my nerves. He's gotten it down to such a science that I really miss it. Of course, once I get home that will sure be different (ha!). He'll start using his highly individualized and super specialized 'get on dad's nerves' techniques. I miss Bertha. She is getting to that age, when she looks at me, almost like she understands what I'm talking about. That is, I don't have to go back over every other word and explain what I meant. I miss Eva a lot too. I feel so bad that she

needs my help, with her homework, and I'm not there to help her. I wish that I were.

Monday, September 21, 1998

\# - Tammy Romero told me last Wednesday that she filed an EEO complaint against Bob Bagg. She said, "Let's see how he likes that." She also asked me if I had gone around showing the grievance that we filed, to everybody. I said, "No!" Because, she had never given me a copy of it. Plus, I mentioned. I have been TDY for a month and a half. I wasn't even here.

466 - Neil is replacing the rudder limiter linear actuator. He said that he wasn't going to bother teaching me about that, because it wasn't rightfully ours (a comm/nav AFIN job).

Tuesday, September 22, 1998

0466 - Went in T-tail to help Bill adjust the linear rudder limiter actuator. T-shot TACAN ID tone to interphone system.

\# - Kevin & Denise are now working together on C-5s.

018 - Recovered, checked the oil, & launched. Arnie (graveshift brown shirt) told me that it was OK to swap with Don.

Wednesday, September 23, 1998

The union asked me to write a list of items that I wanted to have accomplished. This is what I gave to them.

To whom it may concern,

I have submitted, on five occasions, the Sheppard AFB form 127. This is the form that I was told to fill out by the admin. people at bldg. 52. This form 127, is to update personnel records. I have submitted the form and attached supporting evidence, generally stapled to this form, when submitted to the proper offices. I have also paid $12.00, twice, to have official transcripts sent to the civilian personnel office, at Altus, and once to the office at Randolph AFB. My records have not been properly updated. It is advertised in a civil service pamphlet at the civilian personnel office, on Altus AFB, that personnel records will be updated within 90 days. This has not happened to my records and I have submitted changes over a year ago.

- I want my two college degrees listed on my Employee Career Brief.
- I want my supervisory experiences listed on my Employee Career Brief.
- I want my nursing job listed in my experience history on my Employee Career Brief.

I want to have my Network Administrator job at Tinker AFB, added to my Employee Career Brief.

Thursday, September 24, 1998

69001 – Helped ops check a FF transmitter on #1 engine, t-shot VHF KY-58s. Ordered #2 VHF KY-58. Requested issue of #2 UHF KY-58 RCU. Î - - I sat down and talked to my bosses (Mr. Francis, Mr. Hilley, and Mr. Greenwood) and the union (Union President [Ron} and Chief Stewart [Harold Church]) people. We talked about training, the CCIs, Dennis, and over-time.

Hilly said to submit an AFTO 22 and an AF form 1000 for the batteries in the CCIs. He said that I wouldn't have any trouble doing that on duty time. I have had nothing but trouble doing that on duty time. I had already been trying to do that.

I told them that Dennis did not want to train me. I told them what he said. That everyone he trained, went off and left him. Mr. Greenwood told me that Dennis told him, that I did not want him to train me. He said, that I told Dennis that I already knew everything about the a/craft. I told them that Dennis lied to him. I never said anything like that.

Hilley, Greenwood, and Mr. Francis suggested that I go to day shift, get my formal training, and some OJT, and help Mr. Prater. Mr. Hilley also said that I could go to any shift that I wanted to, after I had finished my training. I said, OK. Mr. Hilley said that we could do that 2 week thing to keep the union happy, if I wanted to. I was so anxious to get some training, I told him not to worry about it.

Ï - I went to day shift on, Monday, 23February1998.

Ð - - Don Obriter came to me with a letter sending me back to swingshift C-141s. I told him that I wasn't trained like Hilley said I would be. He said, we have too many eisms (2610s) on day shift. You have to go to swingshift. So, I was going to talk to Hilley and I saw Jerry. Jerry the 97th airlift training manager told me that no one had asked him about formal training courses for me, since I had been there. We walked outside and talked some more. Jerry left. Then, Hilley walked up. I told him that I wasn't trained yet, like he said I would be. I also told him what Jerry said. He said, I'll fix that, wait here. He walked inside and came back out in a few minutes. He said, you will have a set of orders to go to school in about week or two. I said OK.(I didn't realize it at the time, but he had arranged for me to go to a CNAD school - this was helpful but not needed and not requested. I have always asked for an AFIN school, which I still have not receive, as of the date of this grievance) I also said, they want me to go back to C-141 swingshif. That is were I was in the beginning, when Greenwood waited five months to tell me that the only person on the flightline, namely Dennis Scott (who got bonuses, 7s and 8s on his appraisals) who could train me (in AFIN work) did not want to train me (while he gave me 4s and 5s). Mr. Hilley said, I'll fix that. He went inside again, and came back out and said, you're going to be on swingshift C-5s, with Mr. Neil Tully, as your trainer, now. I said, thanks.

Ñ   - Now, I have wasted five months on day shift. I was never given any formal training as mentioned in my meeting with my bosses and the union. Therefore, I request restitution for the ills that have been done me. That would be approx. $1205.64, as of September 24, 1998. My calculations are that I lost $0.98 an hour for 1232 (154 days or 22 weeks) hours. These calculations are at WG11 Step 1. I did not figure in the fact that I am a step 2. Furthermore, I still request formal AFIN training.

É   - To begin with, in our meeting, Mr. Hilley spoke of loyalty and trust and dedication to you employer. When we spoke about training, he said that he didn't play games with his people. I told him about the trick that Glenda played on me. She said that she signed me up for all those AFIN courses, but she never sent me to any of them. Mr. Hilley said that he was sorry about that, but they probably ran out of money, or stopped offering those courses or something. I agreed with him then, about the loyalty and dedication part. I agree with him now about loyalty and dedication. However, I also believe that an employer should show some loyalty and dedication to its workers. I'm getting tired of my employer always erring on the side of the worker (me). Always.

What I want...

- I want to go to Grave-shift. I want the 1205.64 that was taken from me.
- I want AFIN training as mentioned at our meeting.

I want to see submission of AFTO 22s, safety/improvement reports encouraged more on all Shifts and at every level.

Friday, September 25, 1998

69001 – KY-58 stuck in 'c' mode. Ordered new KY-58, ops checked good.

466 – Right wing tow from North ramp to wash hanger.

Sunday, September 27, 1998

First day of grave shift.

001 – Talked to Rich Roy. Ron (AFGE President's right hand man). I talked to Rich about AFIN stuff.

Monday, September 28, 1998

466 – Changed #2 INS battery.

Tuesday, September 29, 1998

014 – Assisted Vance in a pre-flight check. Found bad comm. Cord at left fwd crew entry door position. Watched Vance show me how to LOX a C-5.

- He told me more about Greg Nunley. His mother works at the Tipton Elementary school & teaches my 6 year old daughter (Teresa). His brother works here on the KC-135 side.

Wednesday, September 30, 1998

457 – in hanger 435, it's a cann bird. Missing HF RT. Found RT in A/C 467, swapped #1 RT back to 457. T-shot an INS problem, found #1 &

#2 INS system cabling swapped @ the control console under the CDUs. We hooked up the cables properly. Could not ops check the INS system because the DC power was removed for work on other systems. So we wrote it up as req's ops check.

Thursday, October 1, 1998

0466 – R2 pilot's AMI, ops checked good.

Friday & Saturday, October 3 & 4, 1998

Reserve Weekend. Grave shift worked out great because I was off on Friday nights and could drive 3 hours up to Tinker on Friday and get a room for my reserve tours on Saturday and Sunday. Another bonus was that I could work as a reservist on Sunday and drive 3 hours back to Altus and work grave shift starting Sunday night at 12 MN.

Sunday, October 4, 1998

\# - Talked to Doug & Rockman, C-141 engine mech & electrician , respectively. They said that Kim Kough & Terry quit, & Claud & Marvin put in for xfer to KC-135s.

024 – Worked the corrosion out of the magnetic compass lighting wires. R2 airspeed indicator.

\# - Doug & Rockman also told me that Randy Greenwood went to dayshift C-141s.

Monday, 5 October, 1998

001 – R2 a/craft 28 VDC backup normal batter. Assisted tire change, cleaned up cargo bay as ordered by Steve (Brown Shirt)

Unity of Command Grievance

I. Unity of command, which is a right of all employees, as directed by AFI 39-1.

A. Justification

1. To prevent confusion at all levels.

2. Allows WG employees to do the job described in their job description, instead of driving a truck, which a WS should be doing.

3. Demands that WS employees, as front line managers (not GS or GM employees, desk watchers) get off their butts and do their jobs (drive the flight-line truck and make all necessary decisions concerning work-load, employee responsibilities/duties, lunch times, employee safety, aircraft parking, and training.)

4. At least one brown shirt, permanently assigned, to the flight-line trucks (C-5, C-141, and KC-135 aircraft), on each shift.

5. To promote effectiveness and efficiency of all civil service employees at Altus AFB.

II. A list of exactly what... management, does and does not, consider mission essential.

III. A sticker on the dashboard of every supervisory, flight-line, vehicle that states: "Nothing! Nothing! At Altus AFB, is important enough to jeopardize safety." - Col. Lewondowsky

1. This rule is not obeyed by the C-141 or C-5 side.

A. As a matter of fact, I have been directed by my supervisors to refuel three C-141 aircraft, during a lightening within 5 miles warning.

B. I have also been directed to assist in towing aircraft during lightening within 5 miles warnings.

2. These important safety rules (AFIs) established by the long, and hard won experience of the Air Force, have been purposely reduced to save money. That is, MOIs (Maintenance Operating Instructions) have been introduced to severely limit the effectiveness of these safety instructions. The MOIs now put the direction to obey these safety instructions, to the discretion of the flight-line supervisors.

A. As anyone with a brain can certainly see. My Supervisors have no discretion for their workers. Only the almighty dollar of Civil Service. YES. I have brought several issues such as this one up to our almost union (AFGE) They are often unable (for some reason) and/or unwilling to press ahead with the wishes/safety of the worker.

C. I would like to work in a safe environment. I want supervisors who shut down the flight-line during dangerous weather extremes. Instead of people who say, if you feel dizzy sit down. I've five-pointed engines, when the pavement was 121 degrees F. The AFI, written by a doctor says, 15mins. work, and 45mins. Break, in a cool area. It takes hours to five-point a C-141 engine. My supervisors didn't even tell me that it was condition BLACK. They just watched me from their air-conditioned trucks.

D. Workers have died, in the past, because supervision did not have guidelines to help protect their workers. Now, they have the guidelines and have thrown them away. It appears that we (the workers) are doomed to repeat the past, because our supervisors have forgotten it (for the sake of money).

E. Here is my name, Daniel Leroy McGrew, WG-2610-11. But, please keep me anonymous, because my supervisors have already given me fours and fives on my annual appraisal for telling them that they were violating Air Force security and safety instructions.

F. I keep a rather complete work diary. It is available upon request, from Congress and/or the military. However, all warnings and exclusions listed in it apply.

G. I would like to formally request a Congressional Investigation into safety and security at Altus AFB.

Tuesday, October 6, 1998

\# - Went to QA (Bill Weaver) he has re-submitted four of my C-141 AFTO 22s.

466 – Worked weak TACAN ID audio

Wednesday, October 7, 1998

466 – Traced TACAN audio signals through the interphone system.

Thursday, October 8, 1998

001 – Assisted Gary in fixing an auto-pilot problem. Helped swap pitch & yaw aug computers.

450 – Jack team member

Sunday, October 11, 1998

018 – Swapped IP interphone control panel cannon plug.

Monday, October 12, 1998

Holiday

Tuesday, October 13, 1998

- Sick – sore throat, no temperature.

001 – Worked auto-pilot AFCS problem.

014 – Attached octopus to help t/shot auto-pilot problem on 001.

Wednesday, October 14, 1998

466 – Research ANDVT

452 – Assisted moving T.O.s & tool box. Tow right seat.

Thursday, October 15, 1998

014 – Helped Aaron Wright remove six screws, holding the brackets for an air conditioning duct.

450 – Tow (Accumulator motor).

- Talked to Arnie about AFIN classes. He said that he would talk to Manny & get him to talk to Jerry. Jerry is the Air Lift training manager.

- Two airman showed me around a C-17. It looked just like the ones at Charleston AFB, SC. All the radios are identical to the C-5 & C-141 radios plus I've already worked on this GPS system.

014 – Refuel (SPR)

- Jerry told me stories about Bob Bagg & Julian Vargas.

- 'D' told me stories about her Dr. friend.

Sunday, October 18, 1998

452 – Helped Wanda take the screws out of a rudder pack. This a/craft has no 781Bs. It does have a full compliment of crypto equipment.

Monday, October 19, 1998

\# - Manny talked to me about a battery change on 001.

024 – Helped change a tire on the RMLG. Refuel (SPR – 1st truck). Vance showed me how to do the flight engineer's panel on the 2nd & 3rd trucks.

Tuesday, October 20, 1998

452 – Helped Rich Roy change a MADAR power supply & a POU.

\# - Hearing appointment

\# - Talked to Rich about my grievances. He's dropping them all, except the one about my overtime to Dover AFB, Delaware.

Wednesday, October 21, 1998

466 – Put in new MADAR tape.

\# - Researched C-17 stuff for AFTO 22s.

Thursday, October 22, 1998

452 – R2 co-pilot's ADI.

\# - Went to QA to put C-17 info into AFTO 22 format.

Sunday, October 25, 1998

024 – Helped pull sticks & take off pitot covers. This is part of general servicing. I've done this on other C-5s.

Monday, October 26, 1998

452 – Helped Jerry R2 SAR #1 & fix an engine vib problem. Swing shift turned over a radar ant. Stab problem, however winds exceeded 25 mph, we couldn't finish the job.

Tuesday, October 27, 1998

452 – Swing shift R2 radar ant., we ops checked it good.

Wednesday, October 28, 1998

- Sick leave

Thursday, October 29, 1998

- Sick leave – went to Maria's in Texas.

Sunday, November 1, 1998

018 – Roll Yaw pac's comp. bad, since 22Oct98. Ordered roll comp.

450 – Assisted tow, changed a/craft batteries.

Monday, November 2, 1998

014 - #1 main fuel gauge fluctuations intermittently. CND.

Tuesday, November 3, 1998

014 - #1 main fuel gauge intermittent, pulled 8 fuel probes. Hooked up PDS 60 to fuel gauge. Everything looks good. Told dayshift that the problem was most likely in the wiring harness.

Wednesday, November 4, 1998

014 – Tow to fuel hanger (watched accumulator pressure)

Thursday, November 5, 1998

450 – Sitting on the spare.

Friday & Saturday, November 7 & 8, 1998

Reserve Weekend.

Sunday, November 9, 1998

450 – Changed INS battery. Helped change 2 tires on #4 MLG.

Monday, November 10, 1998

018 – Worked #1 UHF with 'D'

- Actually 'D' did crew chief work & refused to work on the UHF problem me & Jerry. Then she told us it was because she was on her period. We told her that we didn't want to know that. Everything got quite and 'D' left.

Tuesday, November 11, 1998

018 – Worked #1 UHF with Jerry.

Wednesday, November 12, 1998

018 – Fixed #1 UHF with Looney.

Thursday, November 13, 1998

018 – Baby sat a/craft. It was a spare. Filled Hyd. Sys. #3 & 4.

Sunday, November 16, 1998

014 – Sat on spare.

Monday, November 17, 1998

024 – Helped Jerry service oil * check out a leak on #4 MLG. Helped Anthony work on #1 & 4 engine fire lights.

- Saw some meteors.

- A POL (fuel truck/cart) caught on fire in the KC-135 section of the flight line.

- Rich Roy announced that is individual appeal for WG-12 was approved, and it should affect all WG-2610-12s.

Tuesday, November 18, 1998

018 – Refuel (Left SPR). Helped Jerry work on a SAR #14 & #25 problem. SAR #25 is backordered BQ and is entered in the 781Ks. Serviced #1 & 2 hydraulic systems. R2 MUX processor. System ops checked good.

Wednesday, November 19, 1998

- Rich came in and told us that we would all be getting the wage increase to WG-12 next payday.

455 –Ordered, R2, & ops checked FE's interphone control panel. Refuel (Left SPR).

Thursday, November 20, 1998

024 – Stood ground for Jerry to put in fan sticks & check oil. SPR (Left side)

- Rich Roy was born in Boston and grew up in California.

- At some point in the night, 'D' told me that she had an operation for severe endometriosis, and had to have her uterus removed. That led to talk

about adoption. She told me about her doctor friend in California who had some female trouble and was thinking about adoption.

- At some point in the night Evalon talked to me about her female problems. She confided that she had gone through menopause. She described some of her feelings, including suicide, during her doctor's attempt to normalize her hormones.

- At some point in the night Dave Turner started telling Jerry and I about three union cases. That is, three people two of whom we worked with and knew, who had been fired for drug use. We didn't know the other person because they worked on the KC-135 side.

- The three things that we see written on the bathroom walls are slanderous comments about the women we work with, our bosses, and anyone who works for the union.

Sunday, November 23, 1998

455 – Retracted all the walkways from around the right side of the a/craft, so that it could be towed. Right wing for tow.

450 – Towed from north ramp 1 to hanger 485, right wing.

Monday, November 24, 1998

455 – Auto-pilot roll problem. Helped Jerry R2 the auto pilot roll servo. Ops checked good.

- Jerry, Carrion, & Vance have continuously told me that there is a lesbian on our shift. Looney & Tully told me that 'D' was the lesbian. I asked them why they thought that. They told me that she told them she was a lesbian.

Tuesday, November 25, 1998

024 – SPR (Right side). Helped the sheet metal shop put up their equipment after fixing the #2 engine.

Wednesday, November 26, 1998

024 – SPR during defuel (Left wing).

Thursday, November 27, 1998

Off for Thanksgiving Holiday

Sunday, November 29, 1998

455 – Tow (waited for broken condor to get pulled out of the way).

Monday, November 30, 1998

024 – Helped Jerry work on the auto-pilot

Tuesday, December 1, 1998

- Took sick leave. Went to hospital Wednesday morning for an endoscopy. Went to ER to get splinter from fan stop 2X4 taken from my hand. The fan stop 2X4s were all weathered and old and splintering.

Wednesday, December 2, 1998

455 – Attempted to help 'D' install & check out the pilot's HSI. She didn't want to help me. Did fwd & aft crew compartments of pre-flight & helped Vance service the #6 access door, emergency ladder bottle.

Thursday, December 3, 1998

018 – Did fwd & aft crew compartments for pre-flight.

Friday, December 4, 1998

018 - #3 CDU bad. Helped jack a/craft.

Tuesday, December 8, 1998

455 – Helped t/shoot a CARA & FSAS problem.

018 – Helped down jack as nose jack team member.

Sunday, December 13, 1998

455 – Pitch autopilot w/u. CND.

- The guys picked this night to talk about how much Evelyn & 'D' are like men, only uglier & fatter – especially in the rear. I stay out of these conversations and for some strange reason they never ask me what I think.

Monday, December 14, 1998

452 – Refuel, left SPR

455 – Down jacked, right fwd nose jack team member, refuel left SPR.

Tuesday, December 15, 1998

455 – Assisted Jerry with finding a SAR 4 problem, w/u is FE & co-pilot's N1 & TIT indicator do not agree with MADAR.

Wednesday, December 16, 1998

455 – Checked out a VHF w/u. CND. Assisted Jerry with an N2 w/u. Found bad connector at circuit breaker.

Thursday, December 17, 1998

452 – (North Ramp) – Turned in generators to supply.

- Hurt Left knee while helping Rich Roy carry the generators.

A/C	70% Avionics	20% Aircraft Electrician	10% General Serv.
0200 10/17/97			1
8087 10/17/97			1
Daily Totals			2
0146 10/20/97	1		1
0263 10/20/97			1
Daily Total	1		2
0146 10/21/97	1		
Daily Totals	1		
0146 10/22/97	1		1
0161 10/22/97		1	1
Daily Totals	1	1	2
0200 10/23/97			1
Daily Totals			1
087 10/24/97		1	1
*X1 & X2 10/24/97			*2
Daily Totals		1	3
0610 10/27/97			1
0829 10/27/97	1		1
0161 10/27/97			1
Daily Totals	1		3
0293 10/28/97	1	1	1
0141 10/28/97	1		
Daily Totals	2	1	1
0243 10/29/97	1		1
0161 10/29/97			1
Daily Totals	1		2
0629 10/30/97			1
8087 10/30/97		1	
Daily Totals		1	1
8087 11/3/97	1		
Daily Totals	1		
0610 11/4/97	1		1
Daily Totals	1		1
0223 11/5/97			1
Daily Totals			1
11/6/97 Slides #94			
*X1 & X2 11/6/97			*2
Daily Totals			2
*X1 & X2 11/7/97			*3
Daily Totals			3
*X1 & X2 11/10/97			*5
Daily Totals			5

Veteran's Day Holiday 11/11/97			
0203 11/12/97			1
0223 11/12/97	1		1
Daily Totals	1		2
0223 11/13/97	1		
0161 11/13/97	1		
Daily Totals	2		
0146 11/14/97			1
8087 11/14/97			1
Daily Totals			2
0204 11/17/97			1
*X1 11/17/97	1		
Daily Totals	1		1
*X1 11/18/97			1
0203 11/18/97			1
0161 11/18/97			1
Daily Totals			3
0204 11/19/97			*2
0146 11/19/97			1
0263 11/19/97	1		
Daily Totals	1		3
11/20/97	Class - Pollution prevention	Class - Pollution prevention	Class - Pollution prevention
8087 11/20/97			1
0161 11/20/97			1
0223 11/20/97			1
Daily Totals			3
0263 11/21/97	1		1
0243 11/21/97			1
Daily Totals	1		2
*X1&X2 11/23/97			2
Daily Totals			2
*X1 & 0161 11/24/97	1		2
Daily Totals	1		2
0219 11/25/97			1
0243 11/25/97			1
Daily Totals			2
0203 11/26/97			1
0219 11/26/97			1
0161 11/26/97			1
0146 11/26/97			1
Daily Totals			4
8087 12/01/97			*2
Daily Totals			2
12/02/97	781 Forms class	781 Forms class	781 Forms class

8087 12/03/97			1
0269 12/03/97			1
Daily Totals			2
0161 12/04/97			1
0200 12/04/97		1	
0243 12/04/97		1	
Daily Totals	2		1
0161 12/05/97			1
0146 12/05/97			1
0243 12/05/97			1
8087 12/05/97			1
Daily Totals			4
0219 12/08/97			1
Daily Totals			1
0219 12/09/97			1
8087 12/09/97			1
7946 12/09/97			1
Daily Totals			3
0219 12/10/97			1
0610 12/10/97			1
0223 12/10/97			1
0203 12/10/97			1
Daily Totals			4
8087 12/11/97			1
0223 12/11/97			1
Daily Totals			2
8087 12/12/97	1		
0243 12/12/97			1
Daily Totals	1		1
8087 12/15/97			1
7946 12/15/97	1		1
60203 12/15/07			1
Daily Totals	1		3
0223 12/16/97			1
Daily Totals			1
0243 12/17/97	1		
60161 12/17/97			1
0243 12/17/97	1		

Daily Totals	2		1
50243 12/18/97			1
40629 12/18/97	1		1
0610 12/18/97			1
Daily Totals	1		3
0810 12/19/97			1
60144 12/19/97			1
0263 12/19/97			1
670946 12/19/97			1
Daily Totals			4
0144 12/22/97			1
0283 12/22/97			1
66172 12/22/97	1		
Daily Totals	1		2
0144 12/23/97	1		
Daily Totals	1		
172 12/24/97			1
Daily Totals			1
0263 12/29/97			1
0161 12/29/97			1
Daily Totals			2
0610 12/30/97	1		
629 12/30/97	1		
60144 12/30/97			1
Daily Totals	2		1
223 12/31/97			1
Daily Totals			1
223 01/02/98			1
144 01/02/98			1

Daily Totals			2
7946 01/06/98	1		
8087 01/05/98	1		
Daily Totals	2		
7946 01/06/98	1		
8087 01/06/98			1
Daily Totals	1		1
144 01/07/98			1
8087 01/07/98	1		
Daily Totals	1		1
8087 01/08/98			1
70022 01/08/98			1
57946 01/08/98			1
50161 01/08/98			1
243 01/08/98			1
146 01/08/98	1		
7946 01/08/98	1		
263 01/08/98	1		1
Daily Totals	3		6
7948 01/09/98			1
263 01/09/98			1
243 01/09/98			1
Daily Totals			3
0219 01/12/98	1		
50263 01/12/98			1
146 01/12/98			1
948 01/12/98			1
0141 01/12/98			1
0172 01/12/98			1
948 01/12/98			1
Daily Totals	1		6
219 01/13/98			1

610 01/13/98			1
Daily Totals			2
610 01/14/98			1
946 01/14/98			1
223 01/14/98			1
610 01/14/98			1
Daily Totals			4
610 01/15/98		1	
8087 01/15/98	1		1
0223 01/15/98			1
Daily Totals	1	1	2
946 01/16/98			1
0172 01/16/98	1		
0223 01/16/98	1		1
610 01/16/98	1		1
0144 01/16/98	2		1
Daily Totals	5		4
946 01/20/98	1		1
219 01/20/98	1		1
8087 01/20/98			1
0629 01/20/98			1
Daily Totals	2		4
263 01/21/98			1
Daily Totals			1
0144 01/22/98	1		
0161 01/22/98			1
Daily Totals	1		1
8087 01/23/98			1
7946 01/23/98			1
50219 01/23/98			1
8087 01/23/98			1

Daily Totals			4
8087 01/26/98			1
263 01/26/98			1
Daily Totals			2
8087 01/27/98			1
529 01/27/98			1
222 01/27/98			1
Daily Totals			3
8087 01/29/98			1
Daily Totals			1
243 01/30/98			1
161 01/30/98			1
Daily Totals			2
263 2/2/98			1
161 2/2/98			1
Daily Totals			2
0172 2/3/98			1
40645 2/3/98	1		1
263 2/3/98			1
Daily Totals	1		3
223 2/4/98			1
Daily Totals			1
223 2/5/98			1
Daily Totals			1
948 2/6/98			1
610 2/6/98			1
172 2/6/98			1
Daily Totals			3
219 2/17/98	1		

	First	Day Of	Day	Shift
629 2/17/98	1			
Daily Totals	2			
946 2/18/98				1
8087 2/18/98				1
Daily Totals				2
946 2/19/98			1	1
Daily Totals			1	1
946 2/20/98			1	1
Daily Totals			1	1
	First	Day Of	Day	Shift
0629 2/23/98	1			
Daily Totals	1			
172 2/24/98	1			1
610 2/24/98	1			
Daily Totals	2			1
2/25/98	L-band Sat Comm Class	L-band Sat Comm Class	L-band Sat Comm Class	
219 2/26/98	1			
610 2/26/98	1			
Daily Totals	2			
223 2/27/98	1			
Daily Totals	1			
223 3/1/98				1
610 3/1/98	1			
Daily Totals	1			1
172 3/2/98	1			
Daily Totals	1			
172 3/3/98				1
0151 3/3/98	1			1
141 3/3/98	1			

Daily Totals	2		2
629 3/4/98	1		
7946 3/4/98	1		
629 3/4/98	1		
141 3/4/98	1		1
Daily Totals	4		1
937 3/5/98			1
Daily Totals			1
223 3/6/98	1		
8082 3/6/98			1
629 3/6/98			1
5144 3/6/98			1
Daily Totals	1		3
263 3/9/98	1		
Daily Totals	1		
223 3/10/98			1
172 3/10/98			1
Daily Totals			2
7946 3/11/98			2
629 3/11/98			2
Daily Totals			4
My Birthday 263 3/12/98	1		
161 3/12/98			1
610 3/12/98			1
Daily Totals	1		2
263 3/13/98	2		
8087 3/13/98			1
Daily Totals	2		1
946 3/16/98			3

Daily Totals			3
8087 3/17/98	1		2
946 3/17/98			1
Daily Totals	1		3
629 3/18/98	1		1
8087 3/18/98			1
Daily Totals	1		2
946 3/19/98	1		1
144 3/19/98	1		
8087 3/19/96	1		1
Daily Totals	3		2
144 3/20/98	1		1
Daily Totals	1		1
243 3/23/98	1		1
219 3/23/98	1		
Daily Totals	2		1
172 3/24/98			1
Daily Totals			1
0200 3/25/98	1		
629 3/25/98	1		2
Daily Totals	2		2
283 3/26/98	2		
8087 3/26/98	1		
Daily Totals	3		
283 3/27/98	2		1
144 3/27/98			1
283 3/27/98			1
Daily Totals	2		3
629 3/30/98			1

	Reserve	Weekend	Tinker AFB
255 3/25/98	1		
219 3/30/98			1
272 3/30/98			1
Daily Totals	1		3
263 3/31/98	1		1
Daily Totals	1		1
263 4/5/98	1		1
629 4/1/98			1
Daily Totals	1		2
261 4/2/98	1		
Daily Totals	1		
272 4/3/98	1		
263 4/3/98			1
Daily Totals	1		1
4/4/98 & 4/5/98	Reserve	Weekend	Tinker AFB
144 4/6/98	2		1
219 4/6/98			1
Daily Totals	2		2
610 4/7/98			1
629 4/7/98			1
8087 4/7/98	#1		
Daily Totals	1		2
8087 4/8/98	#1		
Daily Totals	1		
8087 4/9/98	#1		
Daily Totals	1		
272 4/10/98	1		3
7948 4/10/98			1
144 4/10/98			1

Daily Totals	1		5
219 4/13/98			1
0243 4/13/98			2
50272 4/13/98	1		2
Daily Totals	1		5
60172 4/14/98	1		
629 4/14/98			1
172 4/14/98			1
Daily Totals	1		2
200 4/15/98	1		
40629 4/15/98			1
Daily Totals	1		1
4/16/98 Worked	on JQS	for Mr. Hilly	******************
263 4/17/98	1		
Daily Totals	1		
283 4/20/98			2
946 4/20/98			1
Daily Totals			3
172 4/21/98	3		2
610 4/21/98			1
Daily Totals	3		3
0219 4/22/98	1		
263 4/22/98	1		
172 4/22/98			1
219 4/22/98	2		2
Daily Totals	4		3
7946 4/23/98			1
50263 4/23/98			1
7946 4/23/98			1
Daily Totals			3
272 4/24/98	1		1
Daily Totals	1		1
4/27/98	No	Fly	Day
263 4/28/98			2
223 4/28/98			1
Daily Totals			3
Totals:	103	9	243

RE Diary 2			
679 4/30/98	1		1
Daily Totals	1		1
272 5/1/98			1
172 5/1/98	1		
Daily Totals	1		1
172 5/4/98	2		
272 5/4/98	1		1
Daily Totals	3		1
172 5/5/98	1		
272 5/5/98	1		1
Daily Totals	2		1
161 5/6/98			2
Daily Totals			2
610 5/7/98	1		3
Daily Totals	1		3
629 5/8/98	1		2
Daily Totals	1		2
0243 5/10/98			2
Daily Totals			2
219 5/11/98	2		
946 5/11/98			1
Daily Totals	2		1
610 5/12/98			2
Daily Totals			2
50263 5/13/98	1		3
8087 5/13/98			1
161 5/13/98			1
Daily Totals	1		5

6400610 5/14/98			1
629 5/14/98	1		2
219 5/14/98			1
172 5/14/98			1
Daily Totals	1		5
0700 to 0900 5/15/98	USAF	Safety	Day
223 5/15/98			1
1300 to 1500 5/15/98	USAF	Ethics	Training
Daily Totals			1
172 5/16/98			1
Daily Totals			1
272 5/17/98			1
610 5/17/98			1
219 5/17/98			1
172 5/17/98			1
Daily Totals			4
263 5/18/98			1
8087 5/18/98	1		
161 5/18/98			1
263 5/18/98			1
Daily Totals	1		3
629 5/19/98			2
172 5/19/98			1
Daily Totals			3
219 5/20/98			1
Daily Totals			1
629 5/21/98	1		1
Daily Totals	1		1
629 5/22/98	1		

Daily Totals	1		
628 5/26/98	1		
Daily Totals	1		
219 5/27/98			1
8087 5/27/98			1
Daily Totals			2
262 5/28/98			1
219 5/28/98			1
263 5/28/98	1		1
Daily Totals	1		3
263 5/29/98	1		1
272 5/29/98	1		
Daily Totals	2		1
8087 6/1/98			1
4629 6/1/98			1
Daily Totals			2
946 6/2/98			1
610 6/2/98			1
172 6/2/98			1
Daily Totals			3
7946 6/3/98			
610 6/3/98	1		1
0144 6/3/98			1
948 6/3/98			1
Daily Totals	1		3
610 6/4/98			1
219 6/4/98			1
829 6/4/98			1
Daily Totals			3

629 6/5/98	1		
219 6/5/98	1		
Daily Totals	2		
8087 6/8/98			1
243 6/8/98	1		
610 6/8/98			1
8087 6/8/98			1
219 6/8/98			1
Daily Totals	1		4
219 6/9/98			1
Daily Totals			1
219 6/10/98			1
629 6/10/98	1		
219 6/10/98			1
8087 6/10/98			1
Daily Totals	1		3
610 6/11/98	1		
610 6/11/98	1		1
610 6/11/98			1
Daily Totals	2		2
629 6/12/98			1
172 6/12/98			1
Daily Totals			2
243 6/14/98		1	1
Daily Totals		1	1
Jobs	70% Avionics	20% A/C Electrician	10% General Service
AC1 Totals:	103	9	243
AC2 Totals:	43	1	73
Complete Totals:	146	10	316

—   all asterisks indicate multiple jobs. Such multiple jobs without a/ craft numbers indicate multiple general servicing jobs. Such as, launching, recovering, fueling, checking oil, assisting with pre-flights, assisting with thru-flights, post-flights, changing light bulbs, ect.....

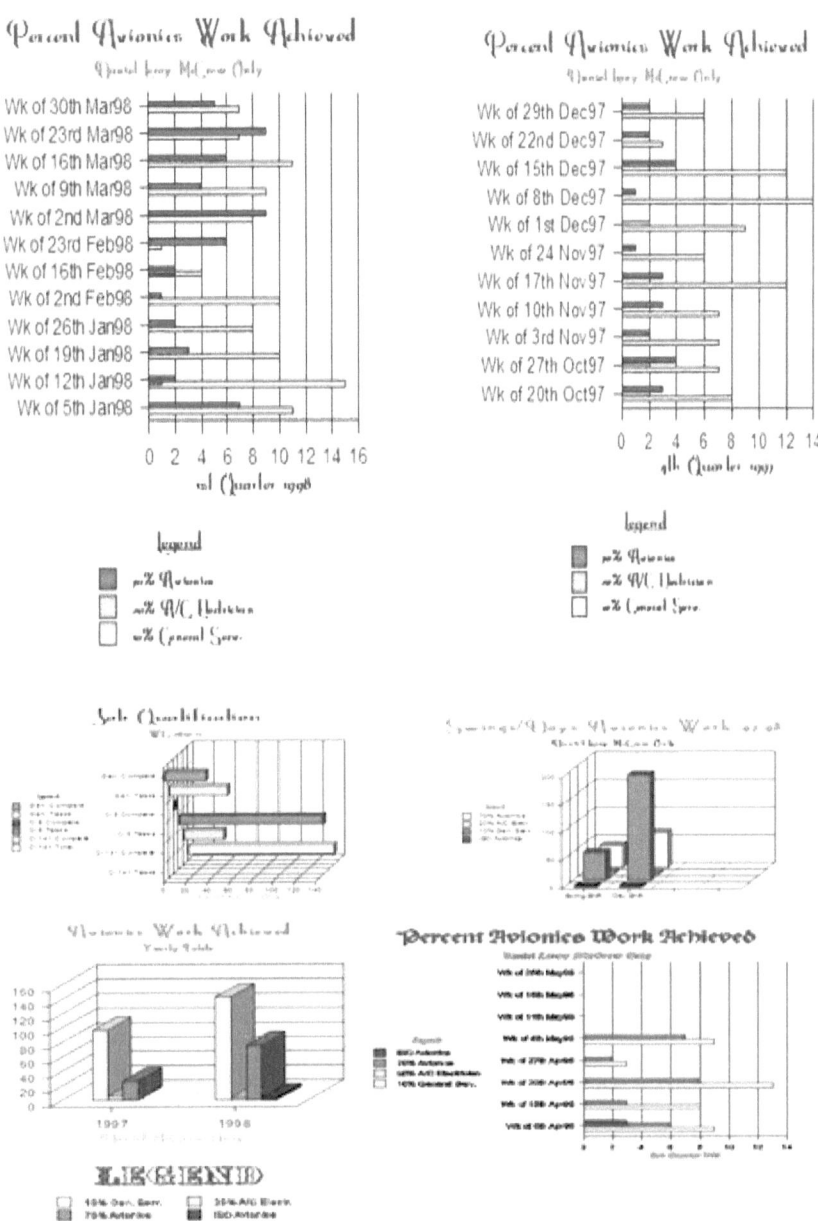

After my first knee injury in December 1998

Friday, February 19, 1999

\# - Jerry, Arnie, & the 97th ALW passed a school list around, while I was doing military duty at Tinker AFB. I have been telling them that I needed those AFIN classes for over a year now. Now they are sending everyone but me. I told them that they missed me. They (Arnie & Jerry) said they would look for some more classes for me. I told Rich Roy about it. He told me to have patience.

\# - Talked to Steve & Arnie about my appraisal.

Tuesday, June 1, 1999

452 – R2 3 INS batteries.

Wednesday, June 2, 1999

054 – R2 PTU hydraulic monitor. Towed (Right wing), refueled.

Thursday, June 3, 1999

001 – Helped kneel.

\# - Steve & Arnie gave me my appraisal. It was all 5s & one six. I told them that I didn't like it. I told them that I did better than that. Claude told me that he got 6s & 7s. Devin told me that he got 6s & 7s. Arnie told me that they were going to change it.

Monday, June 7, 1999

8306 – Fixed an interphone problem.

Tuesday, June 8, 1999

8306 - Refueled, right SPR.

Wednesday, June 9, 1999

8306 – A/craft is a reserve a/craft. I am TDY to Kelly AFB, Texas to help maintain it during it's FMS-800 modification. Working on a GPWS problems, fixed, ops checked good.

- I am taking Vance Roger's place. I was told that it was because his wife wouldn't let him go. Delia (aka: 'D') left her multimeter on the a/craft for about a week. A bird flew up into the cockpit and scared Neil Tully. James caught it and put it outside.

- The hotel room that Scott put us up in is great. It is right on the San Antonio River Walk. I called my wife and told her to get the kids ready, put them in the van, and come down here.

Thursday, June 10, 1999

8306 - It flew and came back with another FMS problem.

Friday, June 11, 1999

8306 – This is our only a/craft anyway, for now.

- Scott & the other fellows have been having fun, in this lagtime, by dogging other employees, who are not here. They spent two days dogging JJ, on day dogging Delia, who didn't even show up for work her first day here. Harold Church, my Indian buddy, didn't make it his first day either. Neil & James like to dog out a swing shifter who is called, "SKE".

Monday, June 14, 1999

- Within a week, while we've been gone, more people quit.

Andrew – ISO docks – 8852

Marvin Leveritt – C-141 – 2610

Kevin Sherill – C-141 – 2610

Denise Hamerick – C-141 – Electrics

8306 - #2 VHF no side tone at the co-pilot's station. Ordered VHF RT via Scott.

\# - James tells me that he hurt his back at Altus and has been having trouble getting the medical bills paid for. He says that Workers' Compensation is supposed to for it. He's going to CPO to get it fixed when he gets back.

\# - The a/craft is back over with the 433rd. This means that it passed the acceptance inspection.

\# - We were told that another a/craft would not arrive until Monday, the 21st.

Wednesday, June 16, 1999

I mentioned that my son and I went to the Alamo last weekend.

Friday, June 18, 1999

\# - Still no new aircraft. We're having a BB-Q just like last Friday. We all contribute $5.00 & the reservists cook the food.

Saturday, June 19, 1999

\# - Drove back to Oklahoma.

Sunday, June 20, 1999

014 – R2 MLG RND CCA#16 & repaired #1 touchdown c/b (pops after 30 secs) with Rich Roy.

Monday, June 21, 1999

90001 – Assisted launch & recovery, refuel (Left SPR). Worked HF#1 problem.

Tuesday, June 22, 1999

052 – R2 seal on #3 main tank comp probe with Looney.

\# - Got scheduled for 2 more AFIN classes.

Wednesday, June 23, 1999

052 – This a/craft is the spare for flying, so we're just babysitting it, with Evelyn.

Thursday, June 24, 1999

052 – Assisted towing from the active taxiway. The flight crew left it there because of the lightening.

\# - Evelyn battery started the APU, without a fire truck or anyone on the ground.

\# - Arnie showed me the appraisal that was re-accomplished for me, because I had told him & Steve (The black belt Karate instructor at the Karate school downtown) that I didn't like the first one that they did. The re-accomplished one is all 5's and three 7's.

\# - Steve had chewed by behind during the last interview. He said that "…other people were doing my work for me, while I sat on my a - - and filled out AFTO 22s." I told him that I never used duty time for my ideas.

\# - I told Rich Roy, our new Union President, about the whole thing. He said that, "Steve should've said that", but didn't offer to do anything about it. Rich also said that, "I hope that you are aware that they send their favorites on the avionics jobs, so that they get the experience and good appraisals."

052 – Stood ground for engine run.

\# - This is the second day that I've seen Rich & Jerry walk off a plane toward the shoe at 0700 hrs, without giving turnover

Sunday, June 27, 1999

\# - I have an appointment with Dr. Gunderson tomorrow at 0900, about the knee injury I received at work.

455 – In hanger 518 reseated & B and a ½ed the #1 main fuel probes. Cont checked fuel probes at the boundary disconnects.

Tuesday, June 29, 1999

001 – Worked FMS/FSAS data invalid problem with Rich Roy.

- I had another talk with Steve & Arnie about my appraisal, on the 28th.

Wednesday, June 30, 1999

Rebuttal to my annual appraisal and it's accompanying feedback session!!

Employee:	Daniel L. McGrew
Department:	97th Air Lift
Reviewer:	Steve Brown & Arnie Garner
1st Review Date:	3Jun99	2nd Review Date: 24Jun99
Date of Last Review:	28Jun99	Reporting Period: 98 04 01 to 99 03 31

	Rating
1. WORK EFFORT:	8
2. ADAPTABILITY TO WORK:	9
3. PROBLEM SOLVING:	8
4. WORKING RELATIONSHIPS:	9
5. COMMUNICATIONS:	8
6. WORK PRODUCTIVITY:	9
7. SELF-SUFFICIENCY:	9
8. SKILL IN WORK:	9
9. WORK MANAGEMENT:	9

Comments:

1. I disagree with my immediate supervisor's(Steve Brown) opinion that, "how do you think your co-workers feel, when you sit on your butt filling out AFTO 22s, and they have to pull your weight." I have always started, carried out, and completed (to the best of my ability/training) every job assigned to me, in an effective and timely manner, on any shift, and any airframe(C-141s or C-5s) at Altus AFB.

2. I can pick up new ideas and procedures. I have also assisted depot level engineers with inventing new ideas and procedures for C-141s, C-5s, and C-17s. I responded to an oral request from T.O. Hilley, and my immediate supervisors (Tom Richter and Randy Greenwood) at the time, to go to day shift for formal training in the guidance and control portion of my job position. I waived the formal two weeks notice, to show my ability and willingness to follow verbal and written instructions. In my eagerness to prove this, I lost over $1,000.00, changing shifts, for promised training that I would never receive.

3. I have devised and assisted in the creation of solutions to problems. I have identified problematic objectives and have devised effective methods and procedures for accomplishing these objectives. Through co-ordination with NSA and AFCA, I provided the impetus that started our current comm/sec program, and followed it up with solutions to several safety

concerns on the C-5, C-141, C-17, and other aircraft Air Force wide. This program is currently ran by Ray Lesmeister and Mike Prator. I supplied them both with all of the information that I had collected, at their requests. I feel that this information was of great assistance to them and to the 97th airlift. I feel fairly confident in stating that they have both received better appraisals than I have for this contributing to this project.

4. I have friends whom I have assisted and who have assisted me on all three shifts and both airframes (C-141s & C-5s), our personnel office, our quality assurance office, training, safety, security, depot, other Air Force bases (Travis, Dover, Charleston, ect...). I maintain effective working relationships with the most knowledgeable avionics people in the world. I have traded assignments with two other employees, for their benefit, and for the 97th Air Lift. My working relationships would probably have been better if my immediate supervisor (Steve Brown) have not raised his voice when he made the statement listed in item number 1. It is my belief that the C-141 employees, who normally dominate his office, easily over-heard this statement.

5. I have demonstrated my ability to communicate orally to my supervisors, my co-workers, inspector general, and our union. I have explained to my supervisors and co-workers, on three different shifts and two airframes, that my resume was/is accurate. I have been taught and understand radio communication/navigation. However, I have never stated verbally or in writing that I can perform any guidance and control work. I requested, but have never been taught or instructed in the methods and/or procedures to maintain these types of systems. My ability to communicate, both orally and in writing, can be evidenced by our organizations current willingness to send me to formal training. Furthermore, by my ability to co-ordinate with our quality assurance personnel to submit over 30 AFTO 22s, FORM 1000s, and zero overpricing challenges, 8 of which have been approved. I have also assisted three co-workers with submission of the same. These three employees, and my wife, can vouch that I performed these extraneous tasks during lunch and after work, to the contrary of my immediate supervisor's statement in item number 1. I also have two college degrees, one of which is from the Community College of the Air Force in Aircraft Electronics.

6. I quite smoking during this reporting period. This means that I no longer take smoke breaks. This allows me to concentrate, more time, on my work. Therefore, I can complete assigned projects, duties, and tasks much quicker. I have been asked by supervisors on two different shifts and both airframes to train/assist employees, who were new to our shift. This is

evidence that I can complete my work in a timely manner. If that were not the case, my supervisors would not laden me with further complications.

7. I can perform all of the tasks that I have been trained and taught to do. I can complete all of the tasks to complete my jobs, on my own. I have been asked on many occasions to show others. I had no supervision or help at all, in these instances.

8. I perform all of the job-associated tasks that I have been taught and trained to perform, well. I have been asked, and have been successful at accomplishing the same. I have shared my knowledge and training with others, at the request of supervision.

9. I have/can effectively plan and organize work. I have/can properly follow(ed) and/or implement(ed) management procedures, directives, regulations, and/or technical orders. I have demonstrated an ability to direct/evaluate/substitute for an absent supervisor. This statement is evidenced by the fact that I have been a civilian supervisor for years, as a nurse. It is also evidenced by the fact that I have been a military (active duty) supervisor, in operation Desert Storm, and a current reserve supervisor.

* These are features of my employment that have been accomplished during this reporting period. Since my supervisor continually asks me to do things, without properly documenting them in my 971, I have been attempting and partially successful at adding some of these accomplishments myself.

** I also do not agree with my immediate supervisor's comment that he cannot be held responsible or knowledgeable for what happens on other shifts. During this appraisal session, in his comments, he uses statements like this as a license to forget to communicate with other shift supervisors, workers, and his own supervisors.

*** I have been loyal and supported my immediate supervisor, during this reporting period. This can be evidenced by that fact that I continually attempt to remind him that he does not properly communicate his verbal instructions at roll call/turn over. He is consistent in his efforts to confuse people by calling the aircraft number first, instead of people's names. This is a common communication process that is taught at every level in the military and civil service. Steve has also asked for my opinion of other employees.

018 – Changed 3 tires with Shorty.

Thursday, June 31, 1999

455 – T/shot FSAS & BDHI with Vance.

Tuesday, August 3, 1999

- I went to an INS/FSAS school in July, and made up 3 reserve UTAs.

- I had another talk with Arnie & Steve about my appraisal. They had given me all 5's. Then, they changed their minds and gave me all 5's and three 7's. I told them that I deserved better than that. They told me that they weren't going to change it anymore.

001 – Baby sitting a/craft.

- Mike Morshing went and told Manny & Arnie, who told us, that James and I were lazy. Mike also signed off a "2610" write-up, "fluctuating fuel totalizer", as within limits. He's a crew chief. He's not supposed to sign off "2610" jobs. Oh well! This kinda' thing happens a lot at Altus AFB.

Wednesday, August 4, 1999

451 – Assisted jack job, R2 one master caution annunciator cluster for stall limiter audio 2 w/n reset.

018 – Monitor panel edge lighting bad. Pin 'F' recessed, ordered new cannon plug.

Friday, August 6, 1999

- Annual Tour – Did 2 wks at Cannon AFB, NM, playing help desk and fixing computers.

Monday, August 23, 1999

451 – No 781 Ls or Bs for the Crypto stuff.

Tuesday, August 24, 1999

455 – Performed MOC of YAW/LAT aug computer.

464 – Refuel (Right SPR), ops checked vertical accelerometer.

Wednesday, August 25, 1999

014 – T/shot & R2 AVVI (Pilots), t/shot #2 CDU, ordered new CDU. Refuel (Left SPR).

Thursday, August 26, 1999

052 – Babysat a/craft.

- Talked to Rich about becoming a union steward. Dave (Engines) Turner says that he doesn't want to be a steward anymore.

- Took annual appraisal worksheet to John. He said that he would find a union rep to help me.

Sunday, August 29, 1999

464 – W/u nav's CDU & ordered standby ADI – ADU.

Monday, August 30, 1999

014 – All the parts that I have ordered on Wednesday are supposedly in, but Cecilio tells me that they are lost. He says that Vance and Looney were looking for the parts last week. I will have to keep my eyes open.

- Steve is away and Manny is doing the supervisor thing.

- Harold Church jumped into the back of the truck and started talking to Willie Simms about getting the NAACP out here to Altus, because there are NO black supervisors in the airlift. I know that there haven't been any since I got here.

Tuesday, August 31, 1999

001 – Refuel (Right SPR). Assisted Mike with a bad aux 2 outboard boost pump inop, found bad relay.

Wednesday, September 1, 1999

464 – T/shot nav's VVI, ordered new VVI. Started to check out the GAAS MADAR w/u & twisted my left knee. Told Arnie, filled out the paperwork, & went to the ER.

Monday, September 6, 1999

- For the last few days Arnie & Manny have sent me to CTK to work, because I'm on light duty again. I built a tool box, put touch-up paint on another, & inventoried about five other boxes.

- Today, I leave work at 0500 hours to have my first knee surgery at 0700 hours. I tore the ligaments in my left knee in December 1998, Dr. Gunderson put me in a knee brace and sent me back to full duty status. I went to the ER on Wednesday, and I had a follow-up appointment with him and he was mad. Looking at his notes he said that someone on his staff was supposed to contact me after our last appointment in January 1999 and schedule me for an MRI on my knee. It never happened, so I kept trying to work because he had sent me back to work full duty status.

Sunday, October 3, 1999

- I'm back for the first time since my knee operation at Jackson Country Memorial hospital. Of course, I'm back in CTK with not a lot to do. I had to leave at lunch time because I have a cold.

Monday, October 4, 1999

- Workers' Compensation specialist (Kim Bailey) said that I should get paid this Friday. The last time they paid me was the 11th of September

\# - I've been fitted for a new knee brace, now I'm waiting for them to finish building it.

Sunday, October 11, 1999

\# - Got paid by workers' comp., $2,000.00. Paid lots of bills

\# - Started physical therapy. Manny told me to go to CTK again tonight. I just keep inventorying test equipment & fixing comm. Cords.

\# - Fred Weller (Union Steward) looked at my appraisal grievance and told me that I only had 5 days to grieve the appraisal, so he couldn't help me. I told him that I talked to John (Union Steward) immediately after I got the appraisal, but he gave me paper to fill out, which took me a while to fill out and get back to him, because I work grave shift.

Thursday, October 15, 1999

\# - Went to a 2 day FMS/GPS class here at Altus.

\# - Back in CTK today.

\# - Talked to another union steward at the union office. He showed me the spot that Fred was talking about, in the union agreement. It does say 5 days, but it does not say whether it has to be in writing or not. I talked with Rich the day after my appraisal & Dave the day after that. They told me to talk to John Aspinwall, which I did the next day. So I am going to tell them to keep at it.

Monday, October 18, 1999

014 – Assisted cargo bay pre-flight, refilled #2 hyd. Res., filled out tags for AMI. Tried to ops check ALDCS by the book, but 'D' wouldn't let me.

Tuesday, October 19, 1999

059 – ALDCS moc checked good.

018 – Switched by Steve to help ISO, went home because of knee pain.

Wednesday, October 20, 1999

018 – Refurbishing the CANN bird, with Jerry & 'D'.

Thursday, October 21, 1999

014 – Assisted recovery, checked oil, did thru-flight on cargo bay, assisted tire change..

- Last night 'Demo' told 'D' that she was a comm./nav wanna' be, because she didn't know where of what a radar roll compensator was.

Friday, October 22, 1999

464 – R2 two monitor panels & 2 relays for a pitch a/p problem (overtime)

Sunday, October 24, 1999

464 – Baby sat a/craft.

Monday, October 25, 1999

454 – Changed AFCS light bulbs & R2 #2 INU for excessive drift.

Wednesday, October 27, 1999

- Arnie told me and Jerry to work on the C-141, because they don't have any eisms (Electronic Integrated Systems Mechanics).

187 – R2 nav select panel & flare computer. Ops checked good.

- Jerry went home at lunch.

612 – t/shot auto-throttle problem.

Friday, October 29, 1999

Did two weeks at Tinker AFB (Annual Tour)

Monday, November 16, 1999

451 – T/shot & signed off a #1 VHF & G/A comp problem.

- Gary was made a temporary WS tonight, according to Arnie at roll call

Tuesday, November 17, 1999

451 – Baby sat a/craft. Refueled (Panel)

014 – R2 & ops checked CVR control panel

Wednesday, November 18, 1999

454 – Assisted Jerry & Lonney with t/shooting a leaky #4 pitot-static system.

001 – Cann'd NSP to a/craft 451

451 – Installed NSP & ops checked NSP & HIS good. Refueled (Panel).

Thursday, November 19, 1999

Sick leave (Knee pain)

Sunday, November 21, 1999

452 – Lube job

Monday, November 22, 1999

452 – HSI CDI problem

- Talked to union about closure notice for appraisal grievance. They said that Fred not turned it in yet.

Tuesday, November 23, 1999

451 – Refuel (Panel). Signed off KY battery checks.

- Talked to Steve about my semi-annual appraisal feedback. He said that I would get a copy.

Wednesday, November 24, 1999

451 – Worked autopilot problem with 'D'. She rode in on the a/craft from Travis and talked to the pilots, so she signed off the problem as CND.

Thursday, November 25, 1999

Thanksgiving

Sunday, November 29, 1999

001 – R2 MADAR filter, Morshing told me that he was moving the write up to the k's, just to piss Neil Tully off. I watched him do just that.

018 – Tow (Right wing)

Military TDY

Tuesday, December 14, 1999

025 – Helped Andy install and ops check a #3 BTC.

- Talked to John and Fred Weller about my grievance. Fred's quitting the union, like Dave did, which leaves me out in the cold again, with no real union representation. I guess I should be getting used to that by now.

Sunday, December 19, 1999

454 – Spare, changed tire

Thursday - Sunday, January 6 - 9, 2000

- Annual wing planning meeting at Tinker & reserve UTA.

Sunday, January 9, 2000

025 – GAAS comp. problem with Rich Roy. Ordered new GAAS comp.

Monday, January 10, 2000

- Linda's Birthday

Monday, February 21, 2000

I have submitted an AF form 1000, through the suggestion program for the following idea. The following is a chain of events, produced by this idea.

1. I suggested that all Aircraft 781 forms, be printed on both sides of the paper.

2. My idea was returned as not economically feasible at the present time, with the suggestion that the below mentioned printers would be phased out, through attrition.

3. A fact, the printers that print the aircraft forms are connected to the base LAN system.

4. I sent a copy of my idea to Senator Inhoe and the Altus AFB, Inspector General. They returned my letter, with some comments from an AF Colonel. She stated that, it was AF policy (also, included in an AFI) to utilize both sides of the paper, when possible.

5. Money was suddenly given to the 97th to purchase high-speed duplexing printers. The tractor fed models are still connected however, the senator and his acolytes (AF Colonel) apparently do not realize that they are simply using the high-speed duplexing printer to print hundreds

and thousands of sheets of paper on a single side now. Basically, they are now able to waste paper at a much faster rate.

Today (**Monday, February 21, 2000**), I would like to ask a question. If these computers are connected to the base LAN, and I know that they are. There are network printers connected to the LAN. As a matter of fact a network printer (A Lexmark Optra Se 3455) is physically positioned in the same room with these computers, and is connected via CAT 5 to the network, as a network printer. It has a duplexer box connected, specifically for printing forms on both sides of the paper. This printer has been in the room for almost two years now. My question is, AWhy are the Output Technology 4140" printers still connected to the LPT1 printer ports of these computers, when there is a $1000.00 network printer (Lexmark Optra Se 3455) sitting across the room from them, and logically connected to them? I don=t understand the terrible waste of money and resources, in the light of such environmentally friendly AF directives/policies.

I ask the 97ᵗʰ Airlift. Why was my idea rejected? I ask my Senator, Mr. Inhoe. Can you help me, with this idea?

Therefore, I would like to submit this request for re-evaluation.

Cost analysis of single sided printing and cost savings of double sided printing. It would be to the credit of the Air Force to be more environmentally aware in this respect. That is, to encourage companies, such as NetSoft and FutureSoft, Inc to make their computer programs able to use double sided printing. Double sided printing has been around for over two decades. My Commodore 64 had the ability to print double sided. That is, it would print the odd numbered pages first and then ask the operator to insert the paper again, so that it could print the odd numbered pages.

At present Altus AFB uses McGregor Printing Corps paper (1210 Avenue S. Grand Prairie, Texas 75050). It is called teletypewriter paper. NSN:7530-00-823-8040. 4,000 sheets per box. There are 8 C-5 aircraft at Altus. The crew chiefs print new forms (781As) every night. There are approximately 20 - 50 pages of 781As in each set of forms. The number depends upon whether an HSC or ISO inspection is being done. I have used the lower number for these calculations. The actual number is probably much higher. Now for the calculations.

One box of Teletypewriter paper costs $33.32 per box, according to the DO43A printout.

C-5 Cost analysis

8 C-5s X 20 pages per day X 365 days = 58,400 pages (used) per year X $0.00833=

$484.72   2(for double sided printing)=$242.36(Savings for the year).

C-141 Cost analysis

14 C-141s (assigned) X 20 pages per day X 365 days=102,200 pages per year X $0.00833=

$851.33   2(for double sided printing)=$425.663(Savings for the year).

Altus AFB - TOTAL Cost analysis (Year 2000)
22 Total aircraft (assigned) X 20 pages per day X 365 days = 160,600 pages per year X $0.00833=$1,337.798(cost per year)   2 = $668.899 (yearly savings)

Altus AFB - TOTAL Cost analysis (Year 2007)
22 Total aircraft (assigned) X 20 pages per day X 365 days = 160,600 pages per year X $0.012906=$2,072.8106(cost per year)   2 = $1036.4053 (yearly savings)

* These calculations do not include the environmental impact of saving trees.

** The active duty AF, C-17s at Altus, AFB print on both sides of their aircraft forms.

However, when civil service takes over a C-17 aircraft they switch to using a single side of the paper for the aircraft forms. I was told (by Arnie) to stop trying to print forms on both sides of the paper because two sided forms would confuse the crew chiefs.

Sunday, August 27, 2000

024 - Arnie Garner (My supervisor) assigned me to this aircraft at roll call. After roll call, I went into the office and reminded him that I was on "light duty", and I asked him if he was certain about assigning me to the aircraft. He repeated the instructions for me to go out to aircraft 024 (C-5) and stated that I should not "…over-do it out there." I assisted Vance & Anthony with checking tires. I climbed the ladder and got to the flight deck. Every other step up the ladder was like having a knife stuck into my left knee. Every step down the ladder was like having knives stuck into both knees, and my left shoulder.

On The Job Injuries (Disabilities) – The road to nowhere in Civil Service.

C-5 Galaxy Crew Boarding Ladder (50ft. high)Very wobbly and shaky especially with my 6'6"

Personal Experience – The diary of Dan McGrew

The height of a C-5 is 65.1 feet making the ladder to the flight deck approximately 50 feet high. Arnie had told me that my light duty excuse from Dr. Hullender didn't say anything about climbing. Actually, it had a check mark in a block with the words 'Light Duty' behind it, signed by Dr. Hullender. I told Arnie that I couldn't climb that ladder again. He said, "OK!" and told me to do "9 alpha". "9 alpha" is a desk job, ordering parts for everyone on the shift (C-141s & C-5s). The job also includes transcribing everyone's forms into the GO-81 computer system. I remember as an airman, on active duty. There was an AFR that instructed everyone to input time their own time into the CAMS computer system. It stated that no one person was to input time for everyone. Each person was responsible for their own time. That was 10 years ago. I wonder if there's a similar AFI for GO-81. I did the "9 alpha" job the best I could, propped up my legs, and put an ice bag on my knees. Next morning, 0810 Hrs.

I let Jan Spence know about this problem. She said, "Light duty employees are not to be assigned to aircraft!" She said that they had had this problem with Arnie before, and that she would remind him. She also gave me a gentleman's name & number to call if he persisted.

I couldn't do all of the tasks that I was required to do in physical therapy (PT), because my knee was hurt & swollen.

Tuesday, August 29, 2000

I was assigned to do the "9 alpha" job. I was keeping ice on my knee due the increased swelling caused by Sunday night's ladder climbing.

Vargas told me to go do a FOD walk & ground AGE line inspection on the North Ramp. I reminded him that I was on light duty. I reminded Arnie that I was still on light duty because of my knee. I explained that a lot of walking and/or standing would not help my knees. He told me that I could do it because I didn't have to climb. I did some of it, and came in at lunchtime and told him that I couldn't finish it. My knees were hurting, from all that walking.

Next morning, 0805 Hrs.

Gina Fuller (union W/C rep) told me that my work hours could be arranged so that I wouldn't have to pull an 8 hour shift and then tack 2 hours of PT onto it, 3X's a week, for months. I told her that I had already asked Arnie, Steve, and Harvey. They told me to forget it. I told her that I would ask them again anyway. I asked if she knew a reference for that rule. She told me that she would look for it.

Wednesday, August 30, 2000

024 - I asked Steve about the adjusted work hours. He laughed and said, "No way!"

I told him that both my knees hurt now. I told him that walking & standing hurt my knees, and would make them worse. I told Harvey about all this. I told Steve and Harvey that I just wanted to sit down and put a bag of ice on my knees. Harvey laughed and said, "Without a note from you doctor telling you to do that. You don't have a leg to stand on."

Steve assigned me to a jack job on 024. They hadn't finished putting the gear on the aircraft, so I went in to see if Steve would let me take over the "9 alpha" job, sit down, & put some ice on my knees. I told Steve, and he said, "OK! Be 9 alpha!"

Thursday, August 31, 2000

I had my Dr.'s appointment today. The Dr. gave me another light duty excuse. Dr. Hullender had hand written the words, "No Climbing!" I gave a copy of it to Steve along with the *green form that Arnie had forgotten to give me for my, Aug 9th appointment. I had given it to Kim & she had FAX'd it to Dr. Hullender's office, they had FAX'd it back to us.

Arnie was on my back for two weeks about that *form. He kept telling me that the last *green form I had given him had expired. He said that I needed to get another one from the doctor. During the following week, Steve & Vargas began telling me the same thing. It was like working with a bunch of parrots. I kept calling the Dr. about it, as Arnie had insisted.

Finally, this morning, it was FAX'd back to our civilian personnel office (CPO).

Friday, September 1, 2000

I have an appointment with Dr. Hullender today. The CPO gave me a copy. It said that I could climb, lift, bend, twist, ect…. At my appointment (1400 hrs), I asked Dr. Hullender why he had given me a light duty excuse that emphasized, "No Climbing", then turned around and told them (via the *green form) that I could do almost anything. He told me that it was because he didn't understand the *green forms. He advised me to see a specialist who does ACL's.

I got a bill from Dr. Gunderson for some blood work. I took it to Gina. She said that she wanted a copy of it. I gave it to her. I took it over to Annetta and gave her a copy. She looked up my W/C stuff on her computer and said that she understood what had happened. Dr. Gunderson's office had billed W/C for the money and W/C only paid a certain amount of money. So, they me billed me for the rest. She said that this was illegal and assured me that she would take care of it. I thanked her.

Friday, September 8, 2000

I've been doing the "9 alpha" job for about a week now. Tonight, Arnie told me to be "9 alpha" for the first half of the night & then do a FOD walk on the 40 row for the second half (after lunch). I FOD walked for about an hour and went back in to tell Arnie that I couldn't finish it all. He started giving me a bunch of crap about the definition of climbing and how it doesn't even have the word bend in it. He even pulled out a dictionary and read me the definition. I told him that I wasn't interested in what Webster had to say. The common sense that GOD gave me, tells me that you have to bend your knees to climb. I told him that I just wanted to sit down somewhere and put ice on my knees, because they hurt. He said, he thought I wanted to argue technicalities with him. I said, "No! I just want to get well!" He said, "OK! Be '9 alpha'". Arnie told me that he wasn't allowed to have …"too many injured people on my shift." He said that he may have to send me to some other shift, probably dayshift to do Technical Orders. I told him that it sounded like a threat to me. He said, "No! Don't take it that way." So, I returned to the '9 alpha' job for the rest of the night.

Monday, September 18, 2000

Steve called me at home (0030 hrs.) and asked me what was going on. I told him that I had talked to Kim & Annetta at the CPO. I told him that they were trying to get a second opinion from a Col. McPherson at the base hospital. They told me that the Colonel was going to have a chat with Dr. Hullender and together they were going to decide what to do with me. That is, what kind of light duty work I could actually do. He told me that he was calling because the people at CPO were not telling him and Arnie anything (…"they are leaving us out of the loop."). He told me to call work every now and then and let them know what was happening. I told him that as soon as they told me anything, I would call him and let him know. Kim & Annetta told me that they would call me this morning.

Tuesday, September 19, 2000

OK. It's tomorrow. I called Annetta twice and left messages. Finally, I called and talked to Kim. I informed her of Steve's concerns. I also expressed some of my own, like the fact that I'm out of sick leave. They have told me all along that I could use my leave for this, and that I could buy it back at a later date. Kim told me that they would get right on the leave buy back thing, under a different work injury number. Gina keeps telling me that I can't buy this leave back. I get a little confused sometimes when CPO tells me one thing and Gina tells me something totally different. Gina, Steve, Arnie, & Vargas are telling me to go back to work, even though I'm injured. The doctor, Annetta, Kim, & Jan are telling me not to go back to work. It's very confusing. Finally, Gina tells me that it's up to me. Kim said that she would e-mail Arnie & Steve. She said that she would let them know what was going on with me, at the present time. I should have asked her to e-mail that to me too. ha…. Anyway, she also said that she would call me first thing in the morning and let me know what the Colonel had said. I called work and left a message on the answering machine, as to current events, at 1045 hrs.

Wednesday, September 20, 2000

I called Annetta twice today. Once at 0900 hrs & again at 1000 hrs, she was not there either time. I left a message for her to return my call, as it was urgent, because I have run out of sick leave. Dr. Hullender's secretary called me at 1300 hrs, and cancelled my appointment. He had told her that since I was making an appointment to see Dr. Coupens, there would be no point in him seeing me also. I asked her about the referral to Dr. Coupens. I explained to her that I couldn't see Dr. Coupens without it. She said that she had mailed it out to me, but stated she would check my file just to be certain. She came back to the phone and said that she was sorry, but she had forgotten to mail it out to me. I asked her if she would just FAX it to Annetta, at our civilian personnel office, instead. She said that she would do that.

I called Annetta Wetts and asked her what Col. McPherson had said. She told me that she had just finished getting all of my records together and sent them over to him. I asked her how long she thought that it might take to get an answer back from him. She told me that she expected to hear something from him by the end of today.

I re-asserted my concerns, about my sick leave running out. She said that she would talk to Kim, in the morning, about putting me on leave without pay, and getting me paid through my workers' compensation claim. I told her that that would be fine.

I informed her of Dr. Hullender's decision to cancel my appointment for today, and related the explanation that I was given. She said that she had gotten the FAX and that she was already working on getting me an appointment with Dr. Coupens.

I called Annetta again at 1525 hrs to find out what Col. McPherson had said. Her phone rang around, as it usually does to the gentleman in the office out front. He told me, as he always does, that he would put a message on her desk. I guess handling the W/C cases for an entire base must keep a person rather busy. She has never returned any of my calls.

1600 hrs

I called Annetta again and asked what Col. McPherson had said. She told me that she hadn't heard from him and that she didn't expect to hear from him until tomorrow, or possibly Friday at the latest. I asked her for some more information about going on 'leave without pay' until I could get an appointment with Dr. Coupens, unless Col. McPherson advised me to go back to work. She said that I should talk to Kim about that. I asked her if Kim had filled her in about what Steve had told me. She told me that she had made contact with Arnie and Steve several times over this matter. She said that she had not talked to Kim, today. She asked me to wait, and she put me through to Kim's phone.

Kim's phone rang. I spoke with Kim about the leave thing. I told her that I wanted to use leave until we heard something from Col. McPherson. Then, if he advised me 'not to go back to work', I would use workers' compensation until my appointment with Dr. Coupens. I broached the subject of Steve Brown and she told me that she had e-mailed him and Arnie and explained everything to them. She said that he e-mailed her back and said that if we didn't get more information to them, he would start coding my timecard as AWOL. She said, that she wrote back and told him that he been given the 'duty status report', signed by Dr. Hullender. It said that I was not to return to work. She e-mailed him about Col. McPherson (base hospital) intervening. She stated that he was told (via e-mail), "…it is being handled." She said that it was silly for him to expect me to call in every night. I told her that I would call Steve tonight and talk to him. She said that she felt relieved by that.

2300 hrs

I called work and talked to Steve. I told him everything I knew about this whole situation. He said, "OK! I'll write it down." He didn't mention the AWOL thing. He didn't say anything about my *green form being expired either.

Wednesday, September 20, 2000

0705 hrs

I called Annetta Wetts. I asked her if she had heard from Col. McPherson. She said, "I don't know. Hold on, let me check my e-mail." I said, "Ok!" I heard the music start (0715 hrs.) as she put me on 'hold'. At 0803 hrs I hung up the phone. I figured what the heck. I'll give her some time to check her e-mail, then I'll call her back or she'll call me.

0900 hrs

I called the Union office and spoke with Tammy. She told me that Gina would be gone for the next three (3) days. I gave her this information.

1000 hrs

I called Annetta Wetts. I asked her if she had heard from Col. McPherson. She told me that she had not gotten any e-mail from him. She said that since I was getting low on leave, she would talk to Kim about paying me through my workers' compensation claim. Annetta re-emphasized the fact that they had communicated to Mr. Brown that I was not to return to work, per Dr. Hullender's order. I told her that I would call Steve and let him know about the decision to file with workers' compensation and select leave without pay. First, I need to talk to kim again, and find out how to do it.

1015 hrs

I called work. Arnie answered the phone, asked me to hold, and brought Steve to the phone. I gave Steve all the information that I had. He told me that someone needed to get that girl (Annetta) on the stick. He said that it was her job to co-ordinate all this stuff. I told him that I was going to call her in the morning anyway. I let him know that I had spoken with Kim and that I might start taking leave without pay. He said ok.

1030 Hrs

I called and spoke with Annetta. She told me that Col. McPherson (Base clinic) had spoken with Dr. Hullender. Dr. Hullender was sticking with his opinion that I should not return to work. I told her ok. She told me again that I was approved for an appointment with Dr. Coupens. I asked her if she had made an appointment for me. She stated that she couldn't make the appointment. She told me that Dr. Hullender or I would have to make the actual appointment. I asked her to please talk to Kim, because I wanted to start leave without pay and let workers' compensation pay me. She told me that Kim would be gone for a while. She informed me that Jan Spence was there and that they would confer. Ok, I told her.

1115 Hrs

I called and spoke with Veronica, at Dr. Coupens office. She made an appointment for me on October 2nd, at 1430 hrs, at his southern OK city office. Maybe I can get my knee fixed, finally. It stinks to have your knee swollen & painful for two years. I had asked Dr. Gunderson about it. He said that it would be that way for a while. He told me that it was normal. I asked the techs at 'Rebound' about it. They told me that it was normal.

1200 hrs

I called our civilian personnel office and left this appointment information in a message for Annetta.

Friday, September 29, 2000

I called and left a message with Tony. I told him, to let Annetta know, that I wanted to take leave without pay and get paid by workers' compensation. He said that he would put the message on her desk.

Bobby from Dr. Coupens office called me. She said that someone had lost all of my workers' comp. Information. She asked me for someone's name & number at Altus who would be able to give them all of the information again. I gave her Annetta Wetz name & number.

Monday, October 2, 2000

I went to my appointment with Dr. Coupens at 1430 hrs. He X-rayed my knee. He brought the X-rays to the room and we talked about them. He showed me what Dr. Gunderson had done. He explained to me that Dr. Gunderson had broken the pin in my knee, when he installed it. He also told me that Dr. Gunderson had made (drilled) the holes for the screws to large. Furthermore, he told me that the screws were in the wrong places.

I said, "OK!" All that being as it may, how do we fix it? Dr. Coupens said, "I hate to be the one to drop the bomb, but we need to re-do the ACL." "When I get in there. I may not be able to repair this." "Dr. Gunderson messed your knee up pretty bad." I gave them the *green form that Arnie gave me. He wrote down, no bending, stooping, climbing, ect…. Also, no walking for over 2 hours. I told him that both my knees hurt if I walked for

166

more than 30 mins. He told me that 2 hours was cumulative for the day. I told him that 1 hour would work better for me. He told me that he would add it in an addendum to workers' comp and FAX it in to them. He said that I could get it tomorrow. I don't know anything about getting stuff from the workers' comp people, but I'll try to get that paperwork from Annetta Wetz, at Altus. I had sent the *green form back to him, via his nurse, Paula three times. She brought it back to me and left it with the comment that, "… these forms are horrible!" I nodded my head in agreement. I told her that I had had problems with my employers over this form in the past. I said that there were stairs to the bathroom where I worked. She told me that I could return to work, if my employers could meet the conditions on the form.

Tuesday, October 3, 2000

I took the CA-17 (*Green form) to Annetta & Kim today. They told me that they had e-mailed Arnie and asked him to see if he could accommodate my injury. Annetta & I called Paula at Dr. Coupens office and left a message on her machine. Annetta asked her if she could get Dr. Coupens to clarify some things on the form for her. Also, Dr. Coupens filled out the CA-17 and added his own form (Form 5) to the pile. The two forms did not match, as far as my limitations go. So, we asked Paula to get that fixed too. Paula called me at home and told me that she had gotten those things fixed. Arnie called at 1500 hrs. evidently he can accommodate my injury because he called and left a message on my answering machine. He stated that Kim Bailey had told him that I was OK and could return to work. I will go to work tonight and speak with him.

Thursday, October 5, 2000

Took sick leave. Going up & down the bathroom stairs just got to be too much for my knees.

Wednesday thru Thursday, October 10 thru 12, 2000

Did '9 Alpha'.

Monday, October 16, 2000

Did '9 Alpha'.

This Afternoon

I called Annetta Wetz and was put thru to Kim Bailey. I asked her if my surgery had been authorized. She told me that she had not heard from Larry Tate (My case worker). She said that it was strange because, they hadn't asked for anymore information. They hadn't told her that anything was wrong. They hadn't said they needed to review anything. She told me that she didn't know why it was taking so long, but that she hadn't seen any indication that they would refuse Dr. Coupens request for surgery. I told her OK, and said that I would try to get in touch with WC and see what the trouble was.

I called Paula at Dr. Coupens office and left a message for her to call me back. In my message I stated that the doctor had told me he may not be able to repair the work that Dr. Gunderson had done. So, I asked Paula if she could get him to elaborate on some of the possibilities, if that were to become the case. I asked her to please return my call.

I called Theressa at Dr. Coupens office and left a message. In my message, I asked if she had heard anything from WC concerning authorization for my surgery. I asked her to please return my call.

I called WC at (###) ###-#### and left a message. In my message I asked them for a way to contact my case worker(s), due to the fact that I had an upcoming surgery and needed their approval for it. I expressed my concern over the matter as I have been waiting over two weeks.

I e-mailed Mr. Tate and asked him to please give an update on the status of my case and Dr. Coupens request for surgery.

The WC administrator at Dr. Coupens office called me. She told me that the surgery authorization request had not been granted by WC yet. She said that she had spoken to Kim at CPO and told her that if there was a problem with the authorization, she needed to know today. She told me that Kim said she was going to call Mr. Tate and call her back, today. She also said that she would call me back as soon as she heard from Kim. I told her about the message that I had left for Paula. I told her about my last meeting with Dr. Coupens. I told her what he said about Dr. Gundeson's surgery on my left knee. Dr. Coupens had stated that the screws were in the wrong place, the holes drilled too big, and a broken wire. I asked her if he had written that in his reports anywhere. She told me that he might have. She stated that their office was about a week behind in getting their dictation done. She said that she would check for me and would call me back about it. I also asked her about my left knee injury causing damage to my right knee and shoulders. I told her that I had been talking to Kim, to get WC to allow Dr. Coupens to examine my right knee and shoulders. She said that Kim hadn't told her anything about that.

Paula from Dr. Coupens office called me. She asked me what I needed. I asked what alternatives the doctor had in mind, if he couldn't repair my knee. She said that he would have to look and see what was going on in my knee first. Then, he could come up with some ideas. She said that in any case, he would do his best.

I explained to her that I needed some pain medication because my left knee was popping out of joint every time I turned around a corner, and hurt when I walked. I told her that I thought it was getting worse. I asked her if she thought that I might be damaging it by walking around on it. She told me that I wasn't going to hurt it anymore than it already was. She said, that unless I took a hit in the knee, fell, or some other similar catastrophe it would be OK. She told me that she would call in a prescription for 'Loritabs' to the clinic pharmacy in Altus. I told her that I appreciated that.

Wednesday, October 18, 2000

I got a call from Kim at CPO. She told me that the surgery was approved. Shortly after that the secretary from Dr. Coupens' office called me and told when I was supposed to show up at the hospital. She also told me that I still needed to call the hospital. I called the hospital and let them know that I had been notified. I am supposed to show up Friday at 0530 in the morning. I called in and let Vargas know that my knees were hurting. I asked him to start putting me down for 'leave without pay' (LWP). He said, "OK". This has become a little easier for me to do now that Kim has told me that I will still get paid. No one ever told me that I could that. I used up all my leave because I couldn't work due to my injury but still had to have money to pay my bills and feed my wife and five children. I was a nervous wreck over the whole thing and no one ever stepped up to tell me that I would still get paid even if I had to take a day off because my knee was swollen or hurt too bad to walk on. The whole affair is a little upsetting.

Friday, October 20, 2000

Drove down to the Oklahoma surgery clinic to have my knee operated on. Woke up and stayed overnight at the 'Comfort Inn'. Went in to see Dr. Coupens at his North Office, at 0900 hours. He looked at my knee, told me not to wear the knee immobilizer anymore. I told him that my knee was hurting real bad. He made sure that I had enough pain medication. He pulled the drain tube out my knee. My wife and kids had accompanied me to OK city. We left town that afternoon. I forgot to give the doctor the green 'Duty status report'. Probably had something to do with those drugs. When we got home, I told my wife and she e-mailed him a copy of it. I called his office and one of his secretaries told me that they would get it filled out and back to me. I also told Annetta at our CP office. She told me that she would put some pressure on them and get a copy of it FAX'd to her.

I called Paula and asked her about it. I told her that I needed that form. She said that she would take care of it. I told her what Annetta had told me. She had said that without that form I would have to return to work, or not get paid. Paula said that no one should be expected to return to work, one week post-op. She told that that was illegal to pressure someone like that. I told her that I would not worry 'bout in anymore. That could be all of the pain medication talking though. I made certain that the doctor understood that I lived 25+ miles from work. I also told him that Arnie and Pat told me that civil service did not require anyone to drive to get to work. I told him that I had no way to work, unless I drove myself there and on-base under the influence of mind numbing medication. Therefore, I asked him not to advise me to return to work, if he was going to advise me to take medication that would induce drowsiness. I wrote him a letter about it in case I were to forget, and handed it to him when I got to his office. I told him that this would be an accident in the making. He replied that he had read and understood the letter.

Monday, November 27, 2000

I had to re-schedule my appointment with Dr. Coupens, because my son (Rafael McGrew) had broken his leg and it required surgery. Dr. Coupens secretary re-scheduled my appointment for Monday, December 04, 2000. I called Annetta Wetz, Kim, & Arnie and let them all know.

Monday, December 04, 2000

I got back home after civilian personnel had closed. I called Arnie at 2230 hours and let him know what was happening. I told him that I would come to work tomorrow because I had been driving all day (3½ hours to OK city, and an hour waiting to see the doctor, & 3½ hours back to Tipton). He told me that Kim had faxed my form 5 to him. He said that it was ok, because he had too many people on limited duty right now anyway. He told me that LeFonte was still on limited duty and now Harold Church was on limited duty also. He told me that he would contact Kim in the morning and tell her that he didn't have a place for me on his shift. I let him know that my next appointment with Dr. Coupens would be in eight weeks (February 2001)

Tuesday, December 05, 2000

My wife & I went to the civilian personnel office today. We spoke with Kim. She told us that she was really sorry that workers' comp had not paid me since my surgery. 27 October, was the last time that I was paid, and that was only for a ½ week. That payment was made by civil service. She told us that she had sent e-mails to my case worker. Furthermore, she told us that she had sent e-mails to the workers' comp liaison. She said that she had not heard anything back from WC, about having my right knee, & shoulders looked at. She told me not to get too awful excited if WC sent me letters or started talking about re-training me. She that this would be because Arnie had told them that he didn't have any work for me to do. She said that they have to ask Eulis Mobeley next. She told us that Arnie would decide if he could find work for me in my job area, and that Eulis Mobeley would decide if he could find work for me on the base. She explained that once Mr. Mobeley told them that he could not find anything for me to do, then WC would try to re-train me into something that I could do.

Thursday, May 31, 2001

Kim called me at home and told me that Arnie has a job for me. She told me that he had shifted the walking wounded around until he had a place for me. WC was going to pay for my A+ & MCSE certifications in three weeks, but now that's void. She told me that Arnie said to come to work this coming Sunday night. I said okay.

Sunday, June 5, 2001

I talked to Stave & Arnie. They told me to go to the GO-81 computer room and work on ordering parts & inputing aircraft forms.

Thursday, June 7, 2001

Steve called me to his office and gave me my appraisal. It was 7's & 8's. I signed it.

Friday, June 8, 2001

Steve told me to work in CTK making comm. Cords (U-94s). I said OK. By 0100 hours, I had already fixed two broken comm. Cords. I asked Steve to let me off work 2 hours early, he said okay, I signed the book for 2 hours of annual leave.

Sunday, July 8, 2001

Went to ER because my knee had swollen up and was popping. ER doctor said to rest, elevate my knee, and put ice on it. I had called Dr. Coupens first, but another doctor was doing standby for him.

Tuesday, July 9, 2001

I went to see Dr. Carter (My primary doctor), he told me that had bilateral carpal tunnel syndrome. He made an appointment for me to see Dr. Villazon (a neurologist). I went to block training with Arnie. I told Arnie what Dr. Carter had told me. I asked if I should fill out a CA-2. He told me to talk to Manny. I asked Manny about filling out a CA-2. He said that we could do it later.

Wednesday, July 11, 2001

I went to see Dr. Villazon. He scheduled me for an EMG (Electromyologram) on Wednesday the 18th.

Xscribed forms for the following a/craft into the GO-81 computer system:

A/craft	Transcription Date	Sets of forms
65000218	18Jun01	
65000220	21Jun01	
65000217	27Jun01	
65000206	2Jul01	
70000462	9Jul01	3 sets
65000217	9Jul01	2 sets
65000014	12Jun01	
65000219	13Jul01	
70000462	13Jul01	
65000217	23Jul01	
65000213	23Jul01	

15 MDC forms.

Wednesday, July 12, 2001

I asked Steve to help me fill out a CA-2 for my carpel tunnel syndrome.

Thursday, July 13, 2001

I asked Steve, again, to help me fill out a CA-2 for my carpel tunnel syndrome.

Monday, July 16, 2001

I did my UTA this weekend, the 14th & 15th. I went to see Dr. Coupens; he pulled my knee some, and gave me a new WC form 5. Dr. Coupens made all of my restrictions permanent. He asked me what I thought that civil service was going to do with me. I told him that I didn't know, because they hadn't told me anything. I got to work tonight and told Steve what Dr. Coupens had said. I asked him if he had heard anything from Kim. He said, "No." Arnie came by the computer room later and told me that he had spoken with Kim yesterday. He said that she didn't know I was wearing hand braces for CTS (Carpel Tunnel Syndrome), I told him that I was going to let her know after Dr. Villazon (Neurologist) got through with me on Wednesday. I asked Manny if he could fill out a CA-2. He said that he was busy, and asked me to hit him up tonight.

Sunday, July 22, 2001

I filled out my own CA-2 and handed it to Steve to sign. He gave it back to me and said that I needed to hand it back in with more medical documentation.

Monday, July 30, 2001

I wrote a letter to the commander's hotline about having to do everyone's electronic a/craft forms (C-5 & C141) for them.

Tuesday, July 31, 2001

My limited duty job has changed radically. I used to input 3 – 5 sets of a/craft forms into the GO-81 computer system every week. I also ordered parts. Last week Arnie started handing out the little MDC sheets to crew chiefs. They are 8½ X 11, and have spots to write in an action taken code, how mal code, ect... he did this at roll call and told everyone to hand these sheets into me at the end of the day. He told me that I had to input them before we left to go home. I him that some of the codes were wrong and that I had some trouble with peoples' handwriting. He told me to call them on the radio. I told him that that would be difficult since it would be at shift change and people would be trying to get away to go home. I told him again that in my opinion everyone should do their own. He gave me some malarkey about how we only have four computer in the comp room for all of our a/craft. I told him that while I was on active duty we had over 250 a/craft (3 crew chiefs each) and four computers. We each got our own computer work done. I told Fred Weller (our union steward) about the whole thing. Tonight Arnie told me to just do MDC. He said that Norm in the DIFM office would order parts. First Arnie told me to go the DIFM office and do MDC there. However, Norm told me to go back to the GO-81 room to do MDC. I told Arnie and he said to go back to the GO-81 room. Anyway the change in the MDC job is obvious. That is, a change in Arnie's attitude. Arnie said that if I didn't have enough to do, he could send me to CTK to build comm. Cords. He started asking me how I felt about vacuuming the floor. He said, "Do you have anything against pushing a vacuum cleaner." Arnie has added building 350 and condition tags, to the job he built for me, for each bad part delivered.

Xscribed forms for the following a/craft into the GO-81 computer system:

A/craft	Transcription Date	Sets of forms
7050462	31Jul01	2 sets
65000219	31Jul01	
70000454	31Jul01	
2 MDC Sheets	31Jul01	
4 MDC Sheets	1Aug01	
Filled out over 50 serviceable tags & tied them to their respective parts		
68000215	2Aug01	2 sets
3 MDC Sheets	2Aug01	
70000454	6Aug01	2 sets
69000026	6Aug01	2 sets
68000217	6Aug01	2 sets
Filled out 20 more serviceable tags & tied them to their respective parts		
2 MDC Sheets	6Aug01	
65000217	27Aug01	
69000018	27Aug01	
68000217	30Aug01	
70000462	30Aug01	2 sets

Wednesday, August 1, 2001

Arnie found a new job for me to do today. He found a roll around mobility bin filled with C-5 junk from the last 2 years. He told me to separate it into, bench stock & found on base (FOB) items. He told me to take the bench stock items to CTK & the FOB items to Norm in the DIFM office, after I tagged them all. I asked him how he wanted me to prioritize the MDC job with this new job. He said, "They both have the same priority."

Thursday, August 2, 2001

Arnie told me that a CTK person was coming over to help me sort through the giant bin. They never came. Arnie came in while I was making serviceable tags for about a hundred parts that I had separated out of the bin. Now, I have to tie a little wax string to each one of the parts. I told Arnie that doing all this writing, typing, and tying little knots in little pieces of string hundreds of times was probably not helping my CTS. He said, "Hell Dan! Looks like you've got a pretty rough life then." Sarcasm. Then he said, "Well, we could have you build up comm. Cords or put you back on workers' comp. That sounded like he was getting annoyed with me because this sounded like a threat, so I just decided to shut up before he tried to find something worse for me to do.

Sunday, August 5, 2001

Tonight, I'm just doing GO-81. After lunch, Arnie came by & started looking for the red, mobility bin full of hundreds of a/craft parts that need to be tagged. He found it & rolled it back into the GO-81 room. He said, "Look like this may be a permanent job for you, Dan!" A month ago I only saw Arnie once a night, now he comes in and bugs me 3 or 4 times a night. I finished tagging all the parts in the med. Mobility bin (3rd bin). I went and told Arnie. Scott Johnson, Paul, & Tammy were there, in the dayshift office. I asked Arnie if he could ask someone to help me push that giant bin over the DIFM office. He began belittling me, insinuating how weak I was, by laughing while repeating that I needed help pushing that little, tiny bin. Finally, he said, "Come on! I could push that little thing myself, but I'll help you!" We met Carlson in the hallway & he belittled me some more. Then, we went to the GO-81 room & moved the bin.

Monday, August 6, 2001

Arnie came into the GO-81 office & was making fun of me, because I wasn't doing forms fast enough. I told him that he was welcome to help if he thought that he could do 'em faster. He just laughed & told me that I would be over helping Norm in the DIFM office. More specifically, he said that I would go help Norm & then come back over to do MDC after lunch.

Tuesday, August 7, 2001

I spoke with Kim today. I asked her if they had a real job for me, instead of this made-up one. She said that she heard something about some supply jobs coming down. I talked to her about my phone interview with Shepard AFB contracting. We talked about my reserve job. We talked about the way that Arnie kept changing my job around from night to night. I asked her again, to please have him put something in writing about my job so that he couldn't change on a whim. She said that she would work on it. Tonight I'm filling out 2005s for Norm Smith & his co-worker. This gives them more time to read books, take long smoke breaks, & play computer games (SAME, tai pai). I went back to the GO-81 room after lunch. Arnie came in & told me that Norm wanted to see me because I had put some wrong parts in the wrong can. I told him that I would fix it. He told me to just go over there (DIFM) & stay. I told him that I didn't want to interrupt the woman over there teaching her kids how to play tai pai on the computers. He told me to go anyway. I said, "Okay! Let me get this straight. You want me to go back to DIFM & tag hundreds of parts by myself, so that Norm and this woman can be free to teach her kids how to pay tai pai on government computers." Arnie said, "She doesn't work for me." I said, "Yea, but I do & you shouldn't let them treat me that way." I slammed the door & walked out. I'm back over at DIFM tagging parts. I was Arnie & Norm walking back from the smoking area, thick as thieves.

Wednesday, August 8, 2001

I wrote a letter (e-mail) to the AFGE union, requesting help with the situation mentioned above. I also told Ed Tautenhaun (Union steward) at roll call. He said that he would mention it to Arnie. I went over to DIFM to do 2005s like Manny told me to do. I asked Norm where the 2005s were at, he gave a slip of paper to me & told me to take time for a job. I tried but GO-81 had a problem with the serial number. Manny walked in & gave me 3 MDC sheets. Time was already taken for all the jobs on them. I asked Norm 2 more times for a stack of 2005s. Manny told me that I had to get that bin emptied. He also said, try to stay busy & keep away from Hitler (referring to Arnie)

Sunday, August 26, 2001

Started back to work in the computer room at Altus, after doing my annual tour (2 wks) at Tinker AFB. Arnie told me to check out that red mobility bin because it still had some stuff in it. I checked it out. It was empty, except for an empty, old, red toolbox. Then, I went & started inputting forms again.

Monday, August 27, 2001

I talked to Norm at the DIFM office. Arnie had me vacuum the floor in the GO-81 room. I talked to Kim & she said that the supply super (Jerry Caldwell) was thinking about retracting the job offer.

Tuesday, August 28, 2001

I did some more forms & MDC sheets. Arnie told me to vacuum the floor again. I did. I talked to Norm he said that the job offer had been retracted, according to his e-mail from his boss. I told him that no one had said anything to me about it.

Thursday, August 30, 2001

Arnie told me last night that he would see what he could do to get me detailed over to DIFM. He hasn't said anything about it yet tonight. I did 3 sets of forms.

Sunday, September 2, 2001

Took 8 hours sick leave for hands and knee pain.

Monday, September 3, 2001

Labor day – Not allowed to work, because I'm disabled.

Tuesday, September 4, 2001

The ceiling collapsed in the GO-81 room (the ceiling tiles fell in because of a leak in the hanger roof), so Arnie sent me over to the DIFM office. He told me that I could start learning stuff from the people there. The MSL people who work in the DIFM office told me that Norm was on leave for 2 wks. They gave me a computer to do MDC on, Arnie came back in the DIFM office & told me to just do MDC because the MSL people don't have enough people to train me.

Monday, September 10, 2001

Did weekend warrior at Tinker. Still being sent to DIFM (MSL) office.

Tuesday, September 11, 2001

Arnie made me sweep the floor in the ready room, then I went over to MSL. They still aren't teaching me anything. They are too busy solving crossword puzzles in the Altus Times. They solve about 2 per night. Kim requested a more detailed explanation of my restrictions from Dr. Coupens. Jerry Caldwell is the man who told me that Hilley told his boss to rescind the Civilian Personnel Office's job offer. He says that all this occurred via email. Got off work this morning & went home. As I walked in the door my wife, Linda, handed me the telephone. I said, "Who is it?" She said, "It's your mother." I said, "Hello! Mom, how are you doing?" She said, "Son! The world is coming to an end." I asked her why she was saying that. She told me to turn the news on, and I did. She said, "An airplane just knocked down the twin trade towers." I told her not to worry about it, they won't fall down. I reminded her that an airplane hit the Empire State building and it didn't fall. She said, "Listen son, it's already fallen." I looked at the news and saw that the building was smoking, but hadn't fallen. I told her that I was watching the news and it hadn't fallen. She told me that what I was watching was a few hours old. As I watched and listened to what she was telling me the news switched to a newer, more recent clip and sure it showed the first tower that was hit falling down. I told mom not to worry about it, and I was sleepy and tired because I hadn't been sleeping well. I told her that I LOVED her and that I was going to bed. I said, goodnight to her and hung up the phone. I told Linda and the kids not to worry about it either. I told them that everything would be find. I said goodnight and went to bed.

Wednesday, September 12, 2001

Tonight Arnie told me to be a door guard all night. So, I checked IDs all night long. 8 hours is a long time to guard a door. It didn't matter anyway; people were still coming in through the wide-open front of the hanger. I was guarding the side facing the flight line.

Thursday, September 13, 2001

Another night guarding the CTK entrance to our hanger. This time the CTK people didn't want to take my place as door guard so that I could go to lunch. Steve had let everybody go to lunch from 0200 to 0400 hours.

At 0200 hours he told me that he would get a C-17 (military) person to take over for me. It's 0330 hours now; I'm still waiting to go to lunch. Its 0430 hours & I asked someone from CTK to relieve me so that I can go talk to Arnie. I asked Arnie if I could go to lunch now. He said sure; don't worry 'bout going over there, we can get those military guys to do their part. I talked to Kim about this scheduled award thing. She said that WC was going to pay me around 49 hundred dollars. She said that I was on the periodic roles. She also said that this was a bigger payment because I was being back-paid to the date when I reached MMI. She said that I would get paid some more money but she didn't know how much or when. She also said that the WC payment said pending in her computer. She said that she didn't understand that since they had been paying me electronically.

Friday, September 14, 2001

I called the bank & discovered that I had 55 hundred dollars in there. Linda, the kids, & I went and paid lots of bills.

Sunday, September 16, 2001

I'm back to guarding the ECP. I handed Arnie the statement about the Carpel Tunnel in my hands, that I had gotten from my doctor. I told him that I had brought it so that he could fill out a CA-2 or something about it.

Sunday, September 23, 2001

I guarded the ECP all last week, until Thursday. I built comm. Cords on Thursday. I took Friday off. Actually, Steve drove up in his truck & asked me if I wanted to take Friday off. This is really strange because he's never asked me anything like that before. Anyway, tonight Arnie told me that I was fired guarding the door. He said that the military didn't like the way that I was doing it. He told me to sweep the floor & see if there was any MDC to do. I swept the floor & didn't find any MDC to do. Now, I'm stuck back in the GO-81 room all night with the bird and rat fecal matter all over the place. Now, there are lots of flies in there too. Arnie came to print out some papers. He clarified the doorguard (ECP) thing for me. He said that a MSgt. came over to his house this weekend and told him that GIs would be taking over the ECP job. Arnie noted the flies & animal feces, and said, "Well, I guess they just don't like the way that we are checking

IDs." Of course, I entered the ECP, by showing my linebadge to a civilian employee today. This morning, I was walking down the hallway with Arnie & we stopped to talk to Jerry before we got the bathroom. Arnie told him that I would be going to his section soon. Jerry had filled out a CA-7, given it to Kim who faxed it to Dr. Coupens, who sent her back a note instead of filling out the CA-7. So, Jerry asked us why I was going over to his section. He said that Dr. Coupens said I could climb, bend, stoop, and all that physical stuff. I interjected that I had read Dr. Coupens note & it said limited climbing, bending, stooping, ect… Arnie & I spent about 30 mins explaining to him just how strenuous my normal job was. Jerry said that I should still be able to do my old job.

Tuesday, September 25, 2001

Bob started telling me that I would be going to swing shift on October 7th. I told him that I didn't want to go to swing shift. I told him that I was under the impression that moving people when by service comp date (SCD). He said that he and Perry had talked about it and they said that I was going to swing shift. He said that I could start working swing shift early if I wanted to. I told him that I would think about it. I asked Arnie if I could go to swings for training. He talked to Steve & told me that he would go over to MSL with me to talk to Roger. I said, "OK". We went over in the morning. Arnie told Roger that he would detail me over to MSL on swings. I interjected that it was for training & then I wanted to go back to graveshift. Roger said that I could go to swing shift for training and permenantly. I said well forget it then. He said well your going to swings on Oct. 7th. I said, "Well let's do this by the contract. Let's use SCD." I started to explain the trouble that I would have, because I had enjoyed the move to graveshift to see my kids and help my wife, when Jerry interrupted. He said, "Look! He's not even over here yet and he's telling us how to run our shop!" I tried to explain that I was only trying to make a suggestion when he shouted, "We don't need you in here! Get out! Get on out the door!" Arnie said, "He's workers' comp." Jerry said, "Get out the door!" I said, "Well then put me out the door big man." He just huffed off & pushed by me & out the door. I might add that I had my lunch box, a 52 oz. water cup, & a reading book in my hand when he pushed by me. When Jerry left, we all left. Outside I apologized to Arnie for bringing him into all this. A treat this morning, they have closed the hanger doors making everyone come in the back (flightline) door so that someone can check their ID. I saw Norm (not a door guard) letting Francis into the hanger through back supply gate. RHIP, rank has its privileges.

Ideas

AFTO 22 Number	Orig. Date *2nd Date	DD Form 1000 Number/ Alt Number	TO Affected	HQ Approved Date
20J0097AMW8134R	7Oct98		1C-5A-2-4CL-1	
20J0097AMW8077R	19May98		1C-5A-2-8-1	21Oct98 (Advisement)
20J0097AMW8078R	20May98		1C-5A-2-8-1	21Oct98 (Advisement)
20J0097AMW8027U Changed to 8128R	4Mar98		1C-141B-6	10Aug98 (Down-graded)
20J0097AMW8028U	4Mar98	ALT980051(A)	1C-5A-6	10Jun98 (Approved)
20J0097AMW8055U Changed to 8129R	23Apr98		1C-141B-2-23GS-00-1	13Aug98 (Down-graded)
20J0097AMW8058U Changed to 8130R	27Apr98		1C-141B-2-23GS-00-1	13Aug98 (Down-graded)
20J0097AMW8059U Changed to 8131	27Apr98		1C-141B-2-34GS-00-1	13Aug98 (Down-graded)
20J0097AMW8061U	28Apr98	ALT980075	00-20-5	17Sep98 (Approved)
20J0097AMW8077U	19May98		1C-5A-2-8-1	21Oct98 (Approved)
20J0097AMW8078U	20May98		1C-5A-2-8-1	21Oct98 (Approved)
20J0097AMW8142R	23Oct98		1C-17A-2-23JG-50-2	
20J0097AMW8143R	23Oct98		1C-17A-2-23JG-50-2	
20J0097AMW8144R	23Oct98		1C-17A-2-23JG-50-2	
20J0097AMW8145R	23Oct98		1C-17A-2-23JG-50-2	
20J0097AMW8146R	23Oct98		1C-17A-6	
20J0097AMW8157R	10Nov98		1C-141B-2-12JG-10-1	
20J0097AMW8158R	10Nov98		1C-5A-2-4CL-2	
20J0097AMW8162R	19Nov98		1C-5A-2-4CL-2	
		1999-12476	C-5 Fuel Quantity Circuit Breaker Position 1C-5A-2-5	14Sep99 (Approved)
		2000-2403	Caster Power-Back System Control & LVDTs	14Jan00 (Approved)
		2000-6769	C-17A Antenna Switch Picture Correction	26Jun00 (Approved)
		2000-6770	C-17A APS-133 color Wx radar radiation hazard area	26Jun00 (Approved)
		2000-6771	C-17A Color Wx radar R/T warm-up time	26Jun00 (Approved)
		2000-6772	C-17A Radar Antenna Removal	26Jun00 (Approved)
		2000-6773		26Jun00 (Approved)
		2000-6772	C-17A Deletion of frequent repetitive steps	26Jun00 (Approved)
		2000-7267	C-17A Improper line selection in ANDVT checkout	24Jul00 (Approved)
		2001-2898	Tire Alignment Markings	20Feb01 (Approved)
		2002-559	SCALX Power on Precaution	5Nov01 (Approved)
		2002-2330	Save paper by re-routing management notices	28Jan02 (Disapproved)
		2003-4168	Insulate Bldg 225 ventilation system	24Apr03 (Disapproved)
		2003-5443	Aircraft INUs	10Oct03 (Disapproved)
		2004-4298	Waste assembly container	5May04

Re-Evaluations

Orig. Idea Number *2ⁿᵈ Number	Re-Eval Submit Date	Re-Eval Finished at Altus AFB	Re-Eval Finished at HQ	Re-Eval Final Answer Date
20J0097AMW8028U - ALT980051A	17Jun98	14Jul98		
20J0097AMW806U1 - ALT980075	16Sep98	28Sep98		
Zero Overpricing forms				
Fill Batteries (No number yet)	5Nov98			
Latrine Latches (No number yet)	5Nov98	Prices adjusted, no award	Prices adjusted, no award	Prices awarded, no award
Solitary Form 1000s				
Double-sided printing (2003-5083)	(2003-5083R) 10Nov98	Disapproved	Disapproved	Disapproved

* 2nd Date on AFTO 22s, are due to the fact that Mr. Rameriz accidentally disapproved these ideas and they were re-submitted at his request.

** Co-ordinated efforts with SMSgt. Ernesto Lads and SMSgt. Moya at Head Quarters (DSN#: ###-####) and SMSgt. Danos at Depot (DSN#: ###-####).

Friday, September 28, 2001

In emails, phone conversations, and office visits, I was told (Can a person take LWOP to work at another civil service position? Rich and Dave had told me that I could be a LAN administrator in a temp position here at Altus and take LWOP from my 2610 job on the flight-line. Is that possible? If so, how much LWOP can a person take? Kim had told me that you can get paid for working at two CS positions at once. However, can you work for both since your only getting paid by one?)

I don't believe it is possible to take LWOP from one Civil Service job to work at another one, even as a temp. But I will check into it.

(Also, they want to put me on swing shift here in supply. Straight from Grave shift WG12 to swing shift GS5. Do GS's have to use the SCD rule also? Can I demand that Bob (supervisor) do this by SCD? I'm not certain that that would help me out anyway, but since I've been on grave shift for decades (even before I joined CS) I like to stay on it. I don't want to go to swings. I've told Bob this and he doesn't seem to very concerned about my needs. What can I do about this?)

Tammy told me, if they told you that you were subject to shift work at the time they offered you the job, or it is reflected on your PD, they can assign you to whatever shift they need you on. When we get the new shift change policy in place, you can use open season to request a shift change. Until then, the only way to change shifts is if you can swap with someone.

This, of course, assumes that there is no vacancy on any other shift. If you have a hardship, you need to tell Mr. Kirouac immediately. His concern is getting Mr. Golden to train you before he leaves in one month. Once that is done, you may want to ask again about changing shifts.

I'll need to mull this over a bit.

Wednesday, October 3, 2001

Email from me to Kim Bailey at Civilian Personnel, building 52.

I'm being discriminated against pretty badly here. Last night Arnie told me to go over to MSL anyway (regardless of what Jerry had said to us) and learn some more. I did what I was told, as I've always done. I've been going over to MSL for over two months, learning how to do things. They've been refreshing me. Anyway, tonight Arnie tells me that they told him to tell me not to go over there tonight for any more training, since I didn't want to volunteer to go to swings for the training (a loss of 3% shift differential). Furthermore, they told him that they didn't want me over there at all until the 7th. I've never had any problems with Norm, Bob, or Kim. I don't get it. They were willing to have me help them out. I always take do all the supply work while they go outside together (all three of them) to smoke cigarettes. They just leave me in there to answer phones, radios, and order parts, while they go out to smoke.

Norm was detailed over there for training, on grave shift. So, was Keith. Now, all of a sudden they don't want any more disabled people over there. This is not fair at all. I've learned that they are putting a new woman in my spot on graves, probably because she is not disabled. I feel very offended and terribly concerned by their behavior as of late. If they are so short, why don't they want my help? Why don't they move this new woman to swings? I have been ordering things, just like they've been doing, for years as nine alpha. I have been tagging parts, for them while they smoked and played video games on their government computers, for months. Now, all of a sudden they don't want me over there anymore. What's the problem here?

Is Jerry's intention to make me quit? What am I to do? The 7th brings up another point. Bob tells me that I'll be going to Monday thru Friday, swing shift. You told me to show up on the 7th which is a Sunday. So, I need to get this straightened out soon. When do I show up for work? I'm supposed to have something in writing, right? I don't want to be a big pain or anything, but I don't want to have my pay messed up anymore than it already is either. Speaking of pay, if I go to swing shift like they want, my business will suffer greatly. As a matter of fact, I'll have to give it up.

Even utilizing working hours like 9 to 2 with a one-hour lunch is only four hours to do business. I'm sorry but that just doesn't work. I'm certain that you can see that. How do I explain to WC that accepting this job offer puts my daytime business (fixing computers), out of business? Is there any kind of relief for this? Can I apply for any kind of hardship? What can I do?

Thanks for helping me to get a new doctor.

Dan

PS

Am I communicating my acute distress effectively enough?

Kim's reply told me that she was still awaiting a reply from AFPC about my doctor's bills. She told me that she was going to check on it again.

Monday, October 15, 2001 (Supply Job)

----- Original Message -----

From: "McGrew Daniel L WG-12 97 LGM/LGMCA" <Daniel. McGrew@altus.af.mil>

To: "'LOCAL2586'" <union2586@intellisys.net>

Sent: Monday, October 15, 2001 3:25 PM

Subject: Thanks

I never would have thought of you as a conformist... ha...

Thanks,

Dan

More correspondence with my local union president, Tammy Ramiro on 15Oct01.

I asked Tammy for help and she told me that she too busy to help me. She said that she had stewards to do things like helping union members. She told me to take advantage of that. I told her that I had had problems with the one that she assigned to me. She said that if I had complaints about a steward then find another to help me. She said that she was just too busy to attend to every grievance of every member. She told me that she so busy all she had time for was to give advice of answer a few questions. She said that she was forwarding all of our email correspondence to Mr. Tautenhahn and that he would handle all of my concerns.

----- Original Message -----
From: "McGrew Daniel L WG-12 97 LGM/LGMCA"
<Daniel.McGrew@altus.af.mil
To: "'LOCAL2586'" <union2586@intellisys.net
Sent: Thursday, October 11, 2001 5:50 PM
Subject: Attn: Tammy - Discrimination

Hello Tammy,

You know Bob Duitt thought that he was going to get this GS7 job, over here in MSL. They've also put him on dayshift. Since he didn't get the job, his integrity may be enhanced a little. If you ask him about it, he may tell you what Norm told me my first night over here. According to Norm the next night, he had e-mailed Jerry about it. That is, that they didn't need or want anymore untrained disabled people over here on grave shift.

Of course, that's when they started telling me that I would be put on dayshift and out of their misery.

Just a thought to assist you in doing a little justice for a member of the bargaining unit. No pressure.

Sincerely,

Dan

Monday, October 15, 2001, 2:06AM

Tammy told me that, from what she had gathered from my email, that it looked like a good EEO complaint, because of a handicapping condition. She told me where to find the definition of handicapping condition was at, 29CFR 1614. I looked it up and it said that it was something that severely limits a major life activity. She told me that she didn't believe that I was being discriminated against. She told me once again to speak with Mr. Tautenhahn.

More emails to the Union (Supply Job 2002)

----- Original Message -----
From: "McGrew Daniel L WG-12 97 LGM/LGMCA"
<Daniel.McGrew@altus.af.mil
To: "'LOCAL2586'" <union2586@intellisys.net
Sent: Tuesday, March 05, 2002 9:08 PM
Subject: Info

Hello,
Does our Union have a person to help us workers' comp people yet?
Dan

On Monday, March 11, 2002

The union finally told me that was had a WC person. His name was
Albert Galvan. They gave me his phone number.

----- Original Message -----
From: "McGrew Daniel L WG-12 97 LGM/LGMCA" <Daniel.
McGrew@altus.af.mil
To: "'LOCAL2586'" <union2586@intellisys.net
Sent: Monday, March 11, 2002 4:46 PM
Subject: RE: Info

That's good to know. Does he have an e-mail address? Like albert.
galvan@altus.af.mil ?
Dan

The union told me that Mr. Galvan had an email address but that he
was detailed away from his section and didn't have access to his email over
there. They told me that I could find him at the base Community Activities
Center.

> -----Original Message-----
> From: "McGrew Daniel L WG-12 97 LGM/LGMCA"
> <Daniel.McGrew@altus.af.mil>
> To: "'LOCAL2586'" <union2586@intellisys.net>
> Sent: Tuesday, March 05, 2002 8:43 PM
> Subject: RE: Thanks
>
> > Dear Tammy & Fred,
> > Thanks for the birthday card. It was nice.

Monday, July 29, 2002 (My hardest battle with civil service)

Dear Union,

I'm having problems with civil service. I have applied for two jobs here at Altus AFB. Their numbers is 02MAY267220 & 02MAY267232. I am qualified for these jobs and have been considered eligible at other Air Force Bases. However, Randolph has told me that I am ineligible for this job because I am, "Ineligible for consideration because you do not meet the federal time in grade requirements."

What's the problem here? Attached you will find reports of correspondence with Jan Spence. She assures me that even though I may be qualified, there is NO way that I can get this job because WG service time cannot be crossed over to GS. She assured me that I need to be a GS for five years before I could ever be promoted anywhere else. Please, read the reports of our correspondence and give me a course of action.

Dan

-----Original Message-----
From: McGrew Daniel L WG-12 97 LG/LGMCA
Sent: Thursday, July 18, 2002 3:43 PM
To: Spence Janice C GS-11 97 MSS/DPCS
Subject: RE: Question about 02MAY267220 & 02MAY267232

So, even if you're qualified for the job. You can't get it because you've been stuck in a GS-05 spot. There must be a way to move through this phase of the hiring process.

I can't believe that Civil Service is just throwing away qualified people like this. Doesn't my civilian computer business qualify me for this job? I do own and operate it. From what I was told it qualifies me as a GS-09. If that's the case then I should be qualified. I have been running this business for well over a year.

[McGrew Daniel L WG-12 97 LGM/LGMCA]
-----Original Message-----
From: McGrew Daniel L WG-12 97 LG/LGMCA
[mailto:Daniel.McGrew@altus.af.mil]
Sent: Friday, July 26, 2002 10:31 PM
To: 'LOCAL2586'
Subject: Daniel L. McGrew - Jobs (Help)

This is the last round between Jan and myself. This isn't making sense to me. Did I forget to put a check in a box somewhere? I'm new at this pushed into a new job thing. I do pay union dues.

I need some help here. Can one of you Union people help me to get this job, or not?

I'm qualified. I'm injured enough. I've been a WG-11/12 here for over five years. Why do I not have the time-in-grade for this job all of a sudden? I've held a WG-12 slot. I've been told that WG's do not have to meet the TIG requirements when crossing over, as long as they are qualified. Can you help me find out where this is stated in the rules? I could really use your help.

I can't believe that civil service is simply throwing qualified information technology people away.

Dan

Jan wrote me back and said that she had never told me that I wasn't qualified. She had simply stated that qualifications and time-in-grade were two different things and that I didn't have the time-in-grade.

Furthermore she said that there is a one-year time in grade requirement for GS positions.

She said that sometimes they didn't always observe that requirement. She that just because they may have helped someone else like that didn't mean that I could ask them to help me that way. She said that when I crossed over something she called FWS, I think that means Wage Grade (WG), to GS that I picked up a whole new set of rules. She said that it didn't matter whether I liked it or not, I still had to abide by them. She said that it would a different ball game if my name hadn't appeared because my qualifications hadn't been updated. However, she told me, the only reason I wasn't picked was because I hadn't been in my present GS position for a year. She said that when that was up I could apply for all the jobs that I wanted, but that I could still only qualify for the ones that were one step above my current position as a GS-05. She said that my civilian business didn't count. She also said that she didn't know why another of the other bases out there would deem me qualified and eligible.

I told Tammy about all this and she said that she would have Jerry Stevens contact me.

-----Original Message-----
From: McGrew Daniel L WG-12 97 LG/LGMCA
[mailto:Daniel.McGrew@altus.af.mil]
Sent: Tuesday, July 30, 2002 4:14 PM
To: 'AFGE Local 2586, AFL-CIO'
Subject: RE: Daniel L. McGrew - Jobs (Help)

The rules also say that you can be granted equivalent GS experience by how much money you are paid. That's a form of safe status. Plus, my WG pay should equate over to the equivalent higher GS pay grade for eligibility requirements. I have the equivalent GS experience per Title 5, Ch. 1, Part 300, Sec. 300.602, (b) Service in positions not subject to the General Schedule (GS) is credited at the equivalent GS grade by comparing the candidate's rate of basic pay with the representative rate (as defined in Sec. 351.203 of this chapter) of the GS position in effect when the non-GS service was performed. The equivalent GS grade is the GS grade with a representative rate that equals the candidate's rate of basic pay. When the candidate's rate of basic pay falls between the representative rates of two GS grades, the non-GS service is credited at the higher grade.

Unless, I'm reading this wrong my old WG experience gives me the creditable, federal service time-in-grade that I need for this job.

Is there another way to read this?

Dan

Tammy responded that same day and told me that she was not an expert on the GS pay system. She had cc'd the email to Jerry, but asked me to contact him anyway.

-----Original Message-----
From: McGrew Daniel L WG-12 97 LG/LGMCA
[mailto:Daniel.McGrew@altus.af.mil]
Sent: Tuesday, July 30, 2002 8:58 PM
To: 'AFGE Local 2586, AFL-CIO'
Subject: RE: Daniel L. McGrew - Jobs (Help)

I appreciate your help. I'm not a GS expert either, that's why I need your help. I never even thought that I'd ever be a GS employee.

Anyway, thanks for forwarding my message.

I sure hope that I interpreted that correctly. If I did then my nomination should have been considered.

Thanks,

Dan

Tuesday, July 30, 2002 (From our illustrious AFGE Union president)

Tammy asked me if I had gotten an email from Mr. Stevens. She said that I needed to contact him immediately. She said that if I were unlawfully denied a position for which I was qualified and eligible then that would be an MSPB appeal problem. She said that she would be more than happy to help me prepare an appeal for the MSPB.

As you can see from this point the union will only represent you when you have done all the work and discovered the wrong-doing for them. Then they might help you.

Friday, August 2, 2002 (Finally a response from the personnel at Randolph AFB)

I have gotten tired of waiting for everyone to do nothing to help me. I emailed the call center at AFPC, Randolph AFB, TX. I had also talked to them on the telephone. They had gotten my email and called to get more details. Ms Kathleen Reese responded and with an explanation of how time-in-grade (TIG) affected GS and WG positions. She said that all my federal service was creditable toward the positions that I had applied for. She said that I also had the experience for the positions (GS-0335-11 & GS-0335-09 target 11) that I had nominated myself for. She said that it too late to do anything about it though because they had already picked someone. She said that since they messed up they would give me priority consideration in accordance with AF Manual 36-203, para. 2.23… that book says, "The priority consideration will be for any position similar to that for which proper consideration was omitted (i.e., same grade and/or same target grade) and for which the employee is qualified. The employee will be given one priority consideration for each instance of omission. The employee will be referred to the selecting supervisor before referral of candidates from other sources that are not entitled to higher priority consideration. Management retains the right to select or nonselect the employee."

She said that since they messed up and skipped me for two announcements that they would give me two priority considerations. One for a GS9 and one for a GS11 spot. She apologized for the inconvenience and thanked me for letting them know about it. She said that if I needed any more help to get it from the people at my personnel office.

Hmmm… I don't know if that's such a good idea, they are the people who messed me up in the first place.

As you can see from the email traffic, the people at building 52 (Altus AFB, OK Civilian Personnel Office) messed up; I was to be given priority consideration for any similar GS-9 or GS-11 positions that came available. Personnel at Randolph AFB, TX put the priority consideration on my record. Altus AFB, OK opens this exact same GS09/11 position two more times and I was never selected. The first time that they posted the job, nothing was said about physical requirements. However, after the priority placement was placed on my record physical requirements were added to the jobs they posted on the AFPC website. That made me ineligible the following two times the jobs were posted. I was retired because of my injury on the flight-line made me physically unable to perform the new job that civil service gave me. As you can imagine being considered for higher paying positions which I was most certainly qualified and eligible for never happened. I was retired as a GS-2005-05. That is, a supply technician.

Within this transition I was offered a free service by the Department of Labor. A rehabilitation specialist, Charles Farr, was assigned to help me after the second and once again after my third surgery. I met him once at Burger King, once at Denny's, and once at the unemployment office in Altus, Oklahoma. I filled out a long sheet of paper filled with questions for him. Then I waited and waited for him to assign me some tasks to rehabilitate me and make me more marketable. That never happened. Kim Bailey told me that they worked very, very slow. So, I called and talked to him after the second surgery and suggested that I go to a school to learn more about computers. He said that DOL would not pay for a school over a year long. I looked for and found a way to get A+ and Microsoft certified. I called him and tried to arrange it, but we had problems over how to pay for it. DOL wanted me to pay for the tests and then they would reimburse me. I refused to do that. I explained that I had a wife, five children, and they were cutting my pay by over 33%. On top of all that, they wanted me to pay for all my training and then they would reimburse me. I told Charles that DOL could buy vouchers at a discounted price. He said that he would look into it. He did, I took, and passed the tests. This is the only rehabilitative help that I have ever received from the Department of Labor, other than a very small paycheck ($90 - $110 / month) because I lost my job due to a work related injury. I also lost my Air Force Reserve job.

Without help from DOL I enrolled in college and got a bachelor's (1 year school like Charles had said) and master's (another 1 year school like Charles had said) degree in Information Technology. I did ask Charles and Carol if DOL would pay for my one year at college to get my bachelor's degree. I never got a definitive answer. I have sent a letter to American Education Services (AES) asking them to bill DOL for my college expenses and have not heard anything from either of them about this undertaking at the present time (December 2007). I have sent a letter to Educaid (The people who I borrowed the money from to attend school - December 2007) and asked them please bill the Department of Labor for my rehabilitation. I have not received a response from them either.

13Jul06 - Called ###-###-#### and talked to the DOL referral agency. They told me that I needed to contact the district office in charge of my case. They gave me the number for the Jacksonville, Florida district (###-###-####). I called them and gave them my case number, they said that my case files were in the Dallas, Texas area. I told them that I had sent a letter (snail mail) to the Dallas office asking them to change my address in the month of May. I called the Dallas office (###-###-####) and told a woman named Sharon that I had sent the letter in May. She said that they had not received a letter. I asked her if I could change it over the phone. She said No we can't do that, you will have to submit the request in writing. She gave me the fax number (###-###-####) and told me that I could also do it that way.

Called and spoke with Chris. I told her that I had faxed a request to Jackie Grizzle in Dallas. She said that the transfer had already begun, but was not completed. I told her that I needed something that explained what my condition was. She said that she had a paper from 9-29-06 that stated I had a disability but was able to work. I asked her to fax that to my Aunt Jennifer at 888-755-4898 and she said that she would do it today. I told her thanks and asked her to have a great weekend.

4Aug06 - I called the Jacksonville office to talk to my case worker. I was told, by James, that they would give her the message and she would call me back within 72 hours (business). I explained that I needed to talk to her (Sherry Bogt) about a job that I might get. I explained that I was getting paid $2400/month by DOL for getting hurt on the job in 1998. When I got a job working for a contractor, after two months, they reduced the amount that I was getting paid to $457.00 per month, then when the contract was terminated for that job the amount of pay remained the same. I wanted to ask her if I take this job in Virginia working for eGovernment Works and it pays me $25/hour, which is more than I was making in 1998, and it reduces my DOL pay to $0.00/month, will it stay that way after the contact ends in three months.

4Aug06 - Overpayment of $1076.22. Must payback $50.00 per month for 21.5244 months. Start date: Oct2005   End date: Aug2007

4Aug06 - Mailed two appeals. One for benefit reduction and the other for overpayment dept waiver.

11Aug06 - I spoke with Cynthia, I asked her for the FAX number so that I could fax these papers. She said that all papers would have to go to London, KY anyway so it would be better for me to mail them in. I gave her the details for the TWC decision that sent me a check for $3,150.00, and she said that she would have my case worker call me. I made copies and put them into the mailbox.

14Aug06 - Called DOL, Jacksonville office, and spoke with D. I asked her about making an organization my beneficiary and she said that she didn't know how to do that, but she would have my case worker contact me and tell me how to do it.

13Sep06 - Called to find out if the appeal that I had mailed into DOL, 4Aug06, had been recieved. She said that the computers were down and she couldn't tell, however she would have my case worker give me a call within 72 hours.

15Sep06 - Elaine (DOL) called me about a request that I had made on 17Apr06. My oldest daughter's (Bertha) wanted to add her to his health insurance. So, I filled out a form to get her removed from mine. Elaine said that she could see the form in their system, but it wasn't filled out correctly so nothing was ever done about it. I find it very annoying that no one bothered to call me and let me know that a mistake was made so that I could fix it. At any rate, she said that she was going to send me another form that was already filled out properly. I explained what I wanted to do, she filled the form out, told me that she going to mail it to me, all I would have to do was sign, and return it.

18Sep06 - Sherry called me. I told her that the health insurance problem was taken care of. She expressed her dissatisfaction with the health insurance system. We talked about how applying for and receiving social security benefits would affect the benefits that DOL was providing me.

19Sep06 - I called and explain that I was attempting to compose an email to AFPC about the job at Anderson AFB, Guam. I asked for advice about explaining my disability and asking them for accommodation. She (De) told me that she would send a message to my case worker and have her call me back. Never got a call from her.

19Mar07 - I spoke with Karen, who told me that my new case worker was Jackie Grizzle. I asked her to tell me what I'd have to do to change my mailing address with DOL. She said that I would have to mail it in to US DOL, PO Box 6300, London, KY 40742.

17Apr07 - Jackie Grizzle called me about sending Med Info to OPM. She told me that she couldn't FAX that much information. She asked me for an address to send the information to. I told her that I would ask Carla Stevenson at OPM. Jackie told me that she would call me back.

I called Carla Stevenson [###-###-####] and told her what Jackie Grizzle had told me. I asked for an address to send the information to. She told me to have Jackie Grizzle send the Medical Information to;
Attention: Retirement - Carla Stevenson
Office of Personnel Management
1900 E Street, NW
Washington, DC 20415

4May07 - Carla Stevenson says that she still hasn't gotten the medical evidence package from Jackie at DOL. Carla will call me, the 9th of May after morning mail and let me know if she has gotten it.

25May07 - I called and spoke with the receptionist. I asked her if she any information about an appeal that I filed in my case over a year ago. She said that her computer was still coming up and asked me what number I'd like to have my case worker call me back at. I gave her my cell number ###-###-#### and she repeated it back to me, said good-bye, and hung up.

8Jun07 - I called and spoke with Makeeba at Othepedic Surgeons in Orangeburg, SC. She told me that I would have to send my DOL medical records to the doctor in order for me to get an appointment with them.

I called and spoke with Bobby at DOL and she said that I would have to mail a letter to their Kentucky office telling them giving them the name of my new doctor.

I called Othepedic Surgeons again and spoke with Kathy. She got some of my information and told me that I simply needed to call my DOL case working and tell them this information and have them fax a letter to them saying that Dr. Marrow could work on me. Kathy made an appointment for me on the 21st of June 2007.

I called and spoke with Susie at DOL. She said that I would need to send them a request in writing to change my doctor.

Mailed letter to change doctors to doctor Marrow.

20Jun07 - Cindy from Dr. Marro's office called. She said that she would need written authorization from WC to get me into the appointment with Dr. Marro. I told her that I had already mailed off my request for a letter to do that. She said that she might be able to do it if I had the name and number of a person at DOL that could help her get authorization to treat me. I gave her DOL's Florida number and my case worker Sherry Bogt's name. She asked me to call her back about 1720 hours and she would be able to tell me if they could see me or not.

10Jul07 - I called and spoke with Dawn at the DOL phone bank. I asked her if they had gotten the response from the letter I sent in asking to use Dr. Marro as my physician. She said that she had the request but no one had responded to it yet. She said that she would call in and find out what was going on and get something in the mail to me. I asked her about the lost wages appeal that I sent in August 7th, 2006 (11 months - almost a year ago). She said that she saw it in the computer, but something was wrong because nothing had ever been done about it. She said that legally they only had 90 days to respond to an appeal, but for some reason they hadn't responded to mine. Furthermore, she said that I had filed that appeal and then it came from another DOL division. She said that the other division was supposed to respond before sending it back to them. That hadn't been done, so she was going to check with her superiors and find out what was going back and have my case worker give me a call. She said that my case worker would have to call me within 3 days. I told her that I had heard that before. I said as a matter of fact I had called and spoke with someone about the Dr. Marro issue already and they said that my case worker would call me back and she never did. Dawn told me that if that ever happened again to call back to the phone bank and tell the girl who answered the information about who I spoke with and when I spoke with her and they would help me file a complaint.

Sherry called me back at 1855 hours. She told me that she was sorry about the fact that they had let my case fall through the cracks. She said that she had referred it and when I moved they let it drop. She also said that they had gotten my letter to change doctors; she processed it, and had already put the letter authorizing me to see Dr. Marro into the mail. She said that she didn't think that the seniors were going to overturn the decision to reduce my wages. But she said that she had already sent it to them, it would be assigned to someone, and they would render a decision.

14Jul07 - Got a letter from William Plunkett who works for OWCP/DOL. The letter states that they are NOT allowed to use temporary positions for 'wage earning capacity' decisions. He says that he is unable to determine if my job with Charter Trading was temporary or permanent. The letter asks me to call him at ###-###-####, extension #####. I did that on Saturday and left him a message with my phone number. I also plan to follow-up by calling him on the 16th of July.

17Jul07 - I called and spoke with Ms. Williams, at the telephone help desk, she looked in my file to see if Mr. Punkett had left anything for me. I told her that I had called and left message on his machine for the last two days. She asked me to tell her what a good time for me would be for him to call me. I told her that 12 noon and 3 o'clock would be great. She said that she would give him the message.

19Jul07 - Mr. Plunkett called from ###-###-#### extension: #####. We spoke of my appeal. He told me how inefficient DOL was. He explained that it took years just to learn enough to get around a little and understand the system. He explained that he was attempting to help me. He told me that that DOL was not allowed to use a temporary job as a reasonable reference of wage earning capacity. That would mean that they made a mistake back in 2006. He said that it was possible and told me that a few things had to happen in order to prove that they made a mistake. He explained what the circumstances were and we started talking about my temporary employment at Charter Trading. He said that he would mail me a letter and wanted me to look at it, correct it, and mail it back to him.

21Jul07 - Received the letter from Mr. Plunkett.

23Jul07 - Corrected letter and mailed it back to Mr. Plunkett.

26Jul07 - Called Mr. Plunkett and left a message telling him that I had already mailed the letter back to him.

31Jul07 - Vickie from Dr. Marro's office called me to recheck the appointment that we made for this Thursday. I told her that I hadn't gotten the letter from DOL yet. I told her that I would call DOL and find out what happened to it. I called DOL and spoke with Bobbie. I asked her about the letter. She said that it had been mailed out on the 11th of July 2007. I told her that I hadn't gotten it. She asked me if I wanted her to resend it. I asked her if she could fax it to me. Then, I thought of a better idea. I asked her if she could fax it Dr. Marro's office. She said that she could, but I didn't have the fax number. So, I asked her if I could call her back. She said yes. I called Vickie at Dr. Marro's office again and got the fax number ###-###-####for DOL. I called DOL and gave the information to Bobbie. She said that she would fax it to Dr. Marro's office. I called Vickie at Dr. Marro's office and told her that they were going to fax it to her. She said that she would call me when the fax came through.

2Aug07 - I went to my appointment at Dr. Marro's office. He diagnosed me with Left knee Degenerative Joint Disease (DJD). He gave me a shot of Marcaine and xylocaine with kenalog. He said that it would make my knee feel better for a while. He also said that he was going to prescribe physical therapy for me. He said that someone from his office would call me.

13Aug07 - I called and spoke with an operator and asked her to get a message to William Plunkett, and ask him if he had gotten all of the information that I had mailed back to him. She said that she would give my case worker the message and have her call me back. Sherri called me and asked what I needed. I told her that I had wanted to speak with Mr. Plunkett. She said that next time I called and spoke with an operator I needed to tell her that I wanted to speak or leave a message for a senior. I told her that I had done that. Sherri told me that she would get my message to Mr. Plunkett.

7Sep07 - Dr. Marro's office never called, like he said that they would (on the 2nd of August 2007). I called Dr. Marro's office ###-###-####. I spoke with the receptionist and she said that I had a follow-up appointment on the 13th at 0800. I spoke with Jenny about the physical therapy that Dr. Marro had mentioned last time that we spoke. She said that, my case worker told her, they needed an authorization form from DOL, the nurse would fill it out, fax it back to DOL, and it would be approved. I asked her if she had the form yet. First she said that it was hidden under another piece of paper in my file. Then, she said that someone had just put it on her desk 10 minutes ago. She said that she would get the nurse to fill it out, then she would fax it back to DOL, and she would give me a call when it was done.

21Sep07 - I got a pink notice from HealthFlex in Orangeburg telling me that I was scheduled to have physical therapy done there.

24Sep07 - Kathy at Dr. Marro's office had sent the requests for physical therapy to DOL in FL on Friday. She had expected to get a response back from them over the weekend. However, when I called and spoke with them, at 1015 AM, they were not aware of any requests at all. I spoke with Kathy and she said that she would check into it and would make the appointment with HealthFlex, for me, once she had finally gotten authorization from DOL. I thanked her and said that I would wait for the authorization (even though I have already been waiting for over a month). So, I couldn't get any physical therapy done, I had to return home. A wasted trip.

5Oct07 - I received a letter from DOL (Mr. Plunkett) explaining that they were vacating their March 2006 decision as of 2Oct2007 and that I am entitled to continue receiving benefits at the initial pay rate. They also sent me a form to report my earnings over the past 15 months. I filled it out and sent it back in on 6Oct07.

26Oct07 - I expected to receive a larger amount of money from DOL, since they vacated their erroneous decision and told me that I'm entitled to benefits again. I expect back pay from March 2006 to the present, or at least the return to my normal pay rate. However, I received what they've always paid me, $150.00. I called and spoke with an operator named Dawn. She told me that she would leave a message for my case worker, Sherry Bogt, and that she should call me back sometime before next week Wednesday. I told her that I had sent my employment verification form in on the 4th. I asked if they had gotten it yet. She told me that they had gotten it on the 11th.

30Oct07 - My new case worker (Betsy Cardona) called me back and said that DOL had had a shift of personnel. I'm not certain what that means. At any rate, she told me that it meant that she was my new case worker. I asked her why I hadn't gotten paid more than $150.00 this month. She said that she would have to speak to her supervisor because the senior (Mr. Plunkett) was supposed to do some of the ground work to get the wage calculations for the vacated decision started, but he hadn't done them. So, they were still computing and that she would call me when they had completed everything. I still haven't gotten permission for Dr. Marro to perform the Carpal Tunnel tests that he wanted to do or the physical therapy that he recommended.

(16Nov07) - I called and spoke with an operator named Russia. I asked her if anything had been done on my case. She said that she didn't see anything new. She said that my next payment from them looked like it was going to be around $150.00. I told her that this was my only income and I really needed to get my wages started back to where they were supposed to be. She said that I must be a really skinny man. I told her that I bought $300.00 worth of groceries last month and I was still eating them. She giggled and said that she would send an email to my case worker asking her to call me and let me what had been done. I thanked her and we disconnected.

(19Nov07) - Betsy called me and started explaining to what she was doing with my case. She talked about the job that I had with CMS (Computer Management Systems). She said that they still had to determine how much money I had made with Charter Trading and CMS. I told her that I had already sent all of that information in to DOL copied directly from my W2. She said that they had to verify it with the IRS. Then she talked about determining whether there were overpayments and/or underpayments. So, I am put on hold again. I told her that I was under the impression that all the underpayment and overpayment calculations were a separate issue from restoring my current pay. She said that she would try to get me put back on the periodic rolls. I told her that that would be a nice thing to do before I starve to death. I'm out of oatmeal to now I'm eating all of the oatmeal cookies. I had bought a large bucket of oatmeal cookie dough at Wal-Mart two months ago for just such an emergency. It's a pretty good deal actually, I don't have to add any sugar, it's already sweet. Therefore, taking government efficiency into account I expect my usual $150.00 check on Friday.

(Dec07) I got a letter from DOL saying that they have vacated their decision, the one that they made in March 06. This resulted in a monitory settlement plus restoring my monthly benefits.

I wrote a letter to American Education Services (AES) explaining to them that my rehabilitation specialist had told me to pick something to do and get started doing it. He said that he would get it approved and paid for. I asked them to bill the DOL for my college. They wrote me back and said that they didn't care, that I was still responsible for paying them back.

(8Jan08) I'm writing a letter to DOL explaining what Mr. Charles Farr (rehabilitation specialist) told me and asking them to pay for my rehabilitation expenses.

Basically, Charles told me to find my own program, because they couldn't' find one for me. I found one and now I'm waiting to see if they will pay for it.

Here is one of the letters that I've written to DOL, AES, & US SC 2nd district representative Joe Wilson.

Daniel L. McGrew
Tuesday, January 08, 2008

212 Cannon House Office Building
Washington, DC 20515

Honorable US Congressman Joe Wilson (2nd District of South Carolina),

I am writing to ask you to help me make the DOL pay for my rehabilitation courses at American Intercontinental University (AIU).

Charles Farr was the DOL appointed rehabilitation specialist attempting to help me find a way to become more marketable. He was appointed to help me following two of my three knee surgeries. The first time I met him at the Burger King in Altus, OK. The second time I brought my entire family and we met at Dennys. I also met him once at the Altus employment office.

At every meeting he handed me stacks of papers to fill out. He never made any suggestions what-so-ever and continued to tell me that I needed to be part of the rehabilitation process. He was incessant about prompting me to find my own form of rehabilitation and he assured me that he would find a way to get it approved and have DOL pay for it. Several times he told me to go ahead and start a program. I asked him who was going to pay for it. Every single time he told me that I would have to pay for it first and then he would get the DOL to reimburse me at the completion of the training.

Okay, I enrolled in AIU and completed the first rehabilitation course in 2004 and the second in 2005.

These courses helped me to get two temporary jobs (7 months for the first one [saving DOL $16,800.00] & 2 months for the second one [saving DOL $4,800.00]) saving DOL approximately $21,600.00. That's almost an entire year's pay. I'm still looking for work. This wonderful rehabilitation provided by DOL may save the US government one or two hundred thousand dollars in my lifetime alone. With this information it is in the best interests of the government/DOL to provide rehabilitation for its disabled employees.

I began the courses during the rehabilitation phase under direct prompting from your rehabilitation specialist, Mr. Charles Farr, and have been waiting for them to be approved and paid for.

Therefore I would like to ask DOL to finish approving and pay for the program that Mr. Charles Farr had asked me to engineer and begin. I would also like to be reimbursed for the payments that I have already made (approx. $2,200.00). However, realizing the promising future that DOL has provided me (one of its disabled employees) with I am willing to forgive that $2,200.00 debt.

On a more serious note I would like to advise that AES be paid quickly as DOL's loans for my rehabilitation are still accruing interest.

You may ask why I waited so long. I waited for 20 months to get paid because DOL made an incorrect decision. I concluded that DOL was going to deal with this after they dealt with my pay issue. Since I've heard nothing I assume that you need to be reminded. Please consider this an official reminder.

Most sincerely,

–   Daniel L. McGrew

Awaiting DOL benefits

Cc
American Education Services (AES)
PO Box 2461
Harrisburg, PA 17105-2461
###-###-####
http://www.aessuccess.org

US DOL/Ms Betsy Cardona
U.S. Department of Labor
District Office 16
DFEC Central Mailroom
P.O. Box 8300
London, KY 40742-8300

I have requested that AES bill DOL. They sent me a letter refusing to do that. I am currently awaiting an answer from my district representative Joe Wilson and DOL.

However, with my physical limitations I can't find anyone to hire me. As you can see from the detailed chart below, I've sent resumes to over 1393 employers in 2006 and out of all the resumes that I sent in (1639), it got 37 responses via phone and email. However in the end they all did the same thing. Not a single one of them would hire me.

These statistics are for the 2006 & 2007 years.

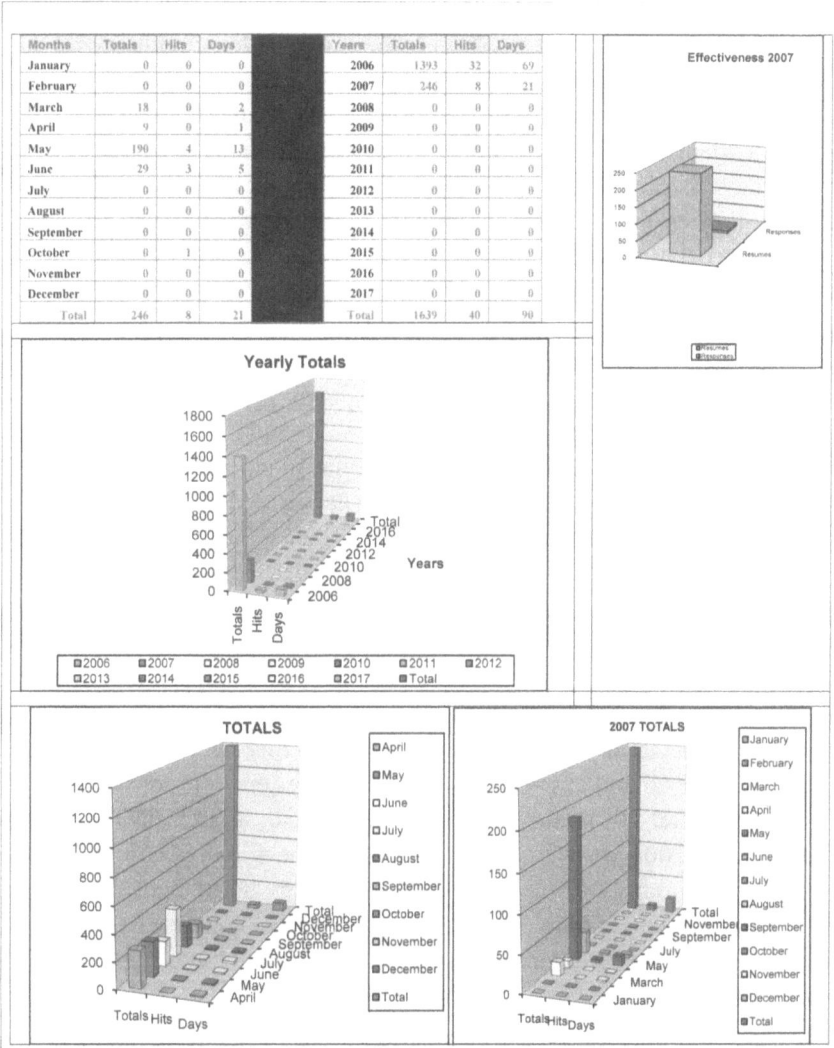

Therefore, I was forced into retirement. In civil service you only have a year from the time that they can you to apply for retirement. So, I applied in March 2007 which was about 9 months from the date when they canned me because I was physically unable to do the new job that they gave me. Kim Bailey told me that they had made a mistake. What she didn't tell me was that there was no way to fix it or that they didn't know how to fix it.

After, they canned me for the supply job; I found a job, off 'Military Hire' and went to Honduras to work as a network administrator. I told my DOL case worker, Carol Morton and rehabilitation specialist, Charles Farr that I was taking that job, because they couldn't find anything for me.

It was a 1 year contract job. Carol and Charles didn't tell me that if you work for someone, in a permanent position, over three months then DOL regards that as your new wage earning capacity. Then they reduce your pay subtracted from that new wage earning capacity figure. In this case, it left me with about $90 to $110 a month. When the contract job ends they are supposed to begin paying you total disability again. However in my case, they screwed up as usual, and continued paying me what they were paying me after my temporary job ended. They just keep paying me $90 to $110 a month. That is, until I finally got thrown out of my house, lights, water, gas turned off, ½ starved to death ect... You can file a paper telling them that you disagree with their decision.

Reconsideration is supposed to be a speedy process, but in my case they lost my paperwork, as usual. It took 20 months (March 2006 to November 2007). My total monthly income during these months was $150.00 +/- a few dollars, $388.00 from the department of Veteran Affairs, and $10.00 in food stamps. Not much money when they were supposed to be paying me over $2,000.00 per month. I had to beg and borrow to get by. My wife couldn't take it so she separated from me until I could start making more money.

In my 20 month wait I had other problems with DOL. When I called and asked for a status, they would tell me that their seniors are working on it. What they really mean is that they are waiting for you to fall off the edge of the Earth and stop calling and writing letters to them.

Finally after 20 months, GOD helped me out, and the DOL vacated their March 2006 decision. They also paid me for the months of pay subtracted from my income. That does not get my house back or help me with any of the punishing, stressful events that have coursed throughout my life in the past 20 months. However, thanks to GOD, I am safe and warm at the present time.

(22Jan08) I wrote a letter asking DOL,ccing my congressional district representative Joe Wilson, to pay for my rehabilitation costs (AES - American Education Services).

(31Jan08) Almost immediately following the sending of the letter, I got a letter from DOL asking me to get a physical. I believe that they are doing this so that they can stop paying me and don't have to pay for my rehabilitation expenses. I've been on the DOL roles since Dec1987 and they've never, ever insisted that I go to a doctor for a physical, no later than 30 days of the date of the letter.

Now, all of sudden after I've sent them a letter and asked them to pay for my rehabilitation expenses, they want me to get a physical. I find it very strange and even a little frightening.

(5Feb08) I'm writing another letter to DOL asking them to move the case file for my hands to the Florida region. When I first called and spoke with them the woman who answered the telephone told me since I was here, in SC, then all of my cases would be here also. I read my case numbers to her and she told me that the one for my hands was still in Dallas, Texas. She said that I would have to write them a letter asking them to send my case file for my hands here and let Dr. Marro have a look at them. This is something that I did back on 8Jun07 and it still hasn't been done.

(7Feb08) – Dr. Marro recommended that I have a knee replacement. He said that it would reduce the pain that I feel in my knee. He gave me a pamphlet about knee replacements and how great they are. He also gave me a prescription to get an EMG done to test me again for Carpal Tunnel. I told him that the pain in my left shoulder was getting so bad that I couldn't sleep at night. He told me that could also be caused by Carpal Tunnel syndrome. I told him that I would get an appointment at the Veterans' Administration hospital in Columbia, the Dorn Medial Facility, to get the test done. I have heard nothing about payment and/or repayment for my rehabilitation classes as AIU from either DOL or my US Representative.

I would also like to make it known that I contacted many organizations, via email and web form mail, asking for their assistance with publishing this book. I explained to them that they could help others by helping me illuminate different types of discrimination, especially against people with disabilities, within the federal government. Not a single one of them made an attempt to contact me and render any kind of assistance what-so-ever. I received no responses at all. I'm certain that they help in some way, but they have no flexibility to help people with disabilities in making workplace injustices know to others. Since they do not attempt to illuminate or assist in illumination then they are, perhaps unintentionally, helping to hide discrimination and other difficulties that disabled people have within their employment. Here is a comprehensive list of the organizations who state that their purpose in life is to help people with disabilities.

Organization Contacted for publishing help	Response	Date Contacted	Contact e-mail	Website
	None			
Advocacy Center for Persons with Disabilities, Inc (Florida)	None	28-Sep-07	ADAP@BAMA.UA.EDU, adap@adap.ua.edu	http://www.adap.net, http://www.uicap.org
Disability Law Center (Alaska)	None	28-Sep-07	webmaster@ndrn.org, press@ndrn.org, info@ndrn.org, webmaster@ndrn.org, webmaster@ndrn.org	http://www.ndrn.org
Advocacy Center (Louisiana)	None	28-Sep-07	akcap@alaska.com	http://home.gci.net~alaskacap/
Advocacy Incorporated (Texas)	None	28-Sep-07	akpa@dcak.org	http://www.dicak.org/
AFGE	None	28-Sep-07	comments@afge.org	http://www.afge.org/Index.cfm/Page=ContactAFGE
Alabama Disabilities Advocacy Program (ADAP)	None	28-Sep-07	webmail (http://www.acdl.com/contact.html), center@uadisabilitylaw.org	http://www.acdl.com
Arizona Center for Disability Law	None	28-Sep-07	panda@azdisabilityrights.org	http://www.azdisabilityrights.org
C.A.R.E.S, Inc. (Maine)	None	28-Sep-07	lrdrr@pai-ca.org	http://www.rehab.calwonet.gov/cap/default.htm
CAPUP (Delaware)	None	28-Sep-07	publicaffairs@dor.ca.gov, begininfo@dor.ca.gov, toainfo@dor.ca.gov, crdinnol@dor.ca.gov, publicaffairs@dor.ca.gov, wdainfo@dor.ca.gov	http://www.pai-ca.org
Client Assistance Program - Department of Rehabilitation (California)	None	28-Sep-07	rlcmail@thelegalcenter.org	http://www.thelegalcenter.org
Client Assistance Program (Alaska)	None	28-Sep-07	nancy.zierberg@pss.state.ct.us, paulette.amoro@po.state.ct.us	http://www.ct.gov/opapd/site/default.asp
Community Legal Aid Society, Inc (Delaware)	None	28-Sep-07	capup@magpage.com	capup@magpage.com
Comprehensive Advocacy, Inc (Idaho)	None	28-Sep-07	elaineuc@doctaal.org	http://www.declan.org
Dept of Employment, Training, & Rehabilitation - Client Assistance Program (Nevada)	None	28-Sep-07	jbrown@uls-dc.org, sbernstein@uls-dc.org, sallen@uls-dc.org, tjohnson@uls-dc.org, svega@uls-dc.org	http://www.uls-dc.org
Disability Law Center, Inc (Massachusetts)	None	28-Sep-07	Low tech - No email, webmaster@advocacycenter.org	http://www.advocacycenter.org
Disability Rights Center - Protect and Advocacy System	None	28-Sep-07	No contact information at all (Software advertisement)	http://www.theOmbudsman.com
Disability Rights Center (Arkansas)	None	28-Sep-07	info@thegao.org, mmoore@thegao.org, jballey@thegao.org, kbailey@thegao.org, nganimohre@thegao.org, rjackson@thegao.org, jholland@thegao.org, eholston@thegao.org, rdevine@thegao.org, mmcall@thegao.org, jnorris@thegao.org, antonio@thegao.org, dlebbel@thegao.org, cthomas@thegao.org	http://www.thegao.org
Disability Rights Center (Maine)	None	28-Sep-07	info@hawaiidisabilityrights.org	http://www.hawaiidisabilityrights.org
Disability Rights Center of Kansas	None	28-Sep-07	coadinc@cableone.net, co-adinc@qwest.net, co-ad@moscow.com	http://users.moscow.com/co-ad
Disability Rights Network of Pennsylvania	None	28-Sep-07	Page cannot be found	http://dhs.state.il.us/ors/cap
Equip for Equality (Illinois)	None	28-Sep-07	contactus@equipforequality.org	http://www.equipforequality.org
Georgia Advocacy Office	None	28-Sep-07	rgallagher@lpas.in.gov	http://www.in.gov/ipas
Hawaii Disability Rights Center	None	28-Sep-07	div.disabilities@iowa.gov	http://www.state.ia.us/government/dhr/pd/client_assit_program
Illinois DHS (CAP program)	None	28-Sep-07	info@ipna.org	http://www.ipna.org
Indiana Protection and Advocacy Services	None	28-Sep-07	Low tech, no email	http://drckansas.org/default.asp
Iowa Protection and Advocacy Services, Inc.	None	28-Sep-07	Vickil. Stagg@ky.gov	http://kycap.ky.gov/
Kentucky Client Assistance Program	None	28-Sep-07	Has a link for contact for, but it doesn't work	http://www.kypa.net/drupal/?q=taxonomy/term/107
Kentucky Protection and Advocacy	None	28-Sep-07	AdvocacyCenter@AdvocacyLA.org	http://www.advocacyla.org/contact.php

Organization		Date	Email	URL
Maryland State Dept of Education - Division of Rehabilitation Services	None	28-Sep-07		http://www.careersnc.org/
Massachusetts Office on Disability - Client Assistance Program	None	28-Sep-07		http://www.dreme.org/
Michigan Protection & Advocacy Service, Inc	None	28-Sep-07		http://www.dors.state.md.us/DORS/ProgramServices/cap
Minnesota's Protection & Advocacy System	None	28-Sep-07	Page cannot be found	http://www.mdclbalto.org/
Mississippi P&A	None	28-Sep-07		http://www.mass.gov/mod/ClientAssistance.html
Missouri Society for Disabilities	None	28-Sep-07		http://www.dc.org.org/
Missouri Protection & Advocacy Services	None	28-Sep-07		http://www.mpas.org/HomePage.asp
Montana Advocacy Program	None	28-Sep-07	mndlc@mtadmnlegal.org	http://www.mndlc.org/RTF2.cfm?pagename=Contact%20MDLC&email=3&subpage=How%20to%20reach%20us
National Disability Rights Network	None	28-Sep-07	Low tech, no email	http://www.mississippiicap.com/
Nebraska Advocacy Services	None	28-Sep-07	Low tech, no email	Spa advertisement (http://www.mapia.com/)
Nebraska Client Assistance Program	None	28-Sep-07		http://www.mosadvocacy.org/
Nevada Disability Advocacy & Law Center - System for Individuals with Disabilities	None	28-Sep-07		http://www.mtadv.org/
New Jersey Protection and Advocacy, Inc	None	28-Sep-07	victoria.rasmussen@cap.ne.gov	http://www.cap.state.ne.us/
New Mexico P & A	None	28-Sep-07		http://www.nebraskaadvocacyservices.org/
New York State Commission on Quality of Care and Advocacy for Persons with Disabilities	None	28-Sep-07		http://dtt.state.nv.us/rehab/reh_cap.htm
North Carolina DHS - Division of Vocational Rehabilitation	None	28-Sep-07		http://www.ndalc.org/index_files/Page406_files/Page406.htm
North Carolina Legal Assistance	None	28-Sep-07		http://www.nh.gov/disability/caphomepage.html
North Dakota Client Assistance Program	None	28-Sep-07		http://www.drcnh.org/
North Dakota Protection & Advocacy Project	None	28-Sep-07	advocate@njpanda.org	http://www.njpanda.org/contactus.htm
Office of Protection and Advocacy (Connecticut)	None	28-Sep-07		http://www.nmpanda.org/index2.html
Ohio Legal Rights Service	None	28-Sep-07	Low tech - No email, webmaster@rpqcapd.state.ny.us	http://www.cqc.state.ny.us/contact.htm
Oklahoma Disability Law Center, Inc., Protection & Advocacy for Persons with Disabilities	None	28-Sep-07	NCCAP@ncmail.net, divrinfo@dvr.state.nc.us	http://dvr.dhhs.state.nc.us/DVR/CAP/caphome.htm
Oklahoma Office of handicapped Concerns - CAP	None	28-Sep-07	dansllp@cluelatorpng.com	http://www.cladisabilitylaw.org/
Oregon Advocacy Center	None	28-Sep-07	cap@state.nd.us	http://www.nd.gov/cap/contact.html
P&A MDCLBalto (Maryland)	None	28-Sep-07	panda@nd.us	http://www.ndpanda.org/
Pennsylvania Client Assistance Program	None	28-Sep-07	Low-Tech - No email, Webmaster@otrs.state.oh.us	http://olrs.ohio.gov/ASP/olrs_Contact.asp
Persons with Disabilities - Client Assistance Program (Iowa)	None	28-Sep-07	capinfo@state.ok.us	http://www.obc.ok.gov/cap.htm
Protection and Advocacy for People with Disabilities, Inc. (South Carolina)	None	28-Sep-07	wu.la.dvrdlc.org	http://www.oklahomadisabilitylaw.org/
Protection and Advocacy, Inc (California)	None	28-Sep-07	Web form only	http://www.oradvocacy.org/rafiam.php
Rhode Island Disability Law Center	None	28-Sep-07	info@equalemployment.org	http://www.nqualemployment.org/#Contact%20Information
South Carolina Client Assistance Program	None	28-Sep-07	intake@drnpa.org, drnpa-litga@drnpa.org, drnpa-phila@drnpa.org, drnpa-pgh@drnpa.org	http://drnpa.org/contact
South Dakota Advocacy Services	None	28-Sep-07	info@ridlc.org	http://www.ridlc.org/home%20page.htm
State of New Hampshire Governor's Commission on Disability - Client Assistance Program	None	28-Sep-07	Law tech, no email	http://www.govoepp.state.sc.us/cap/contact.htm
Tennessee CAP & P&A programs	None	28-Sep-07	info@protectionandadvocacy.sc.org & fwm.mail	http://www.protectionandadvocacy.sc.org/
The Legal Center (Colorado)	None	28-Sep-07	sdav@sdadvocacy.com	http://www.sdadvocacy.com/contact.asp

The Ombudsman (CAP - Georgia)	None	28-Sep-07	Page cannot be found	http://www.tpuinc.org
Universal Legal Services (CAP - Washington DC)	None	28-Sep-07	info@advocacyinc.org	http://www.advocacyinc.org/contact.cfm
Utah's Protection & Advocacy Agency - Disability Law Center	None	28-Sep-07	adiusitabradinksvn@disabilitylawcenter.org, allisondraper@disabilitylawcenter.org, dananderson@disabilitylawcenter.org, jamiepeterson@disabilitylawcenter.org, kittywionari@disabilitylawcenter.org, marylawcentermotes@disabilitylawcenter.org, robynbrickov@disabilitylawcenter.org, sherinewton@disabilitylawcenter.org	http://www.disabilitylawcenter.org/contact.php
Vermont - CAP	None	28-Sep-07	Low tech, no email	http://www.dad.state.vt.us/DVR/cap.htm
Vermont Protection & Advocacy	None	28-Sep-07	nstanton@vtpa.org, tina@vtpa.org, merry@vtpa.org, liz@vtpa.org, jocelyn@vtpa.org, donna@vtpa.org, bthomas@vtpa.org	http://www.vtpi.org/Contact_Us.html
Virginia Office for Protection and Advocacy	None	28-Sep-07	general.vopa@vopa.virginia.gov	http://www.vopa.state.va.us/
Washington - CAP	None	28-Sep-07	Page cannot be found	http://www.capseattle.org/
Washington Protection & Advocacy System	None	28-Sep-07	wpas@wpas-rights.org	http://www.wpas-rights.org/contact_wpas.htm
West Virginia Advocates	None	28-Sep-07	wvainfo@wvadvocates.org	http://www.wvadvocates.org/contactus.htm
Wisconsin Dept of Workforce Development - Client Assistance Program	None	28-Sep-07	Web form only	http://www.dwd.state.wi.us/mail/asp/mailtoAuto_web.asp?WhoTo=dwddvr
Wisconsin Disability Rights	None	28-Sep-07	Low tech, no email	http://www.disabilityrightswi.org/contact.php
Wyoming Protection & Advocacy System, Inc	None	28-Sep-07	wypanda@vcn.com	http://wypanda.vcn.com/

I write in my diaries all the time. That is correct, I said diaries. I have multiple diaries. This is from my aircraft diary. The other diaries included are my 'Job Tracking' ,' Bob Bagg 1998', 'Denise Stuff 1998', 'Graphic Work History', 'Left Knee Trouble', 'Pie Chart Work History', and 'Regular Home' diaries. I am still writing on my diaries. I hope to get one of two more of them published one day. I hope that they will help people, especially with disabilities.

My Resume

(Program Manager) COVER LETTER

I retired from the Air Force reserves in 2003 and Federal Civil Service in 2006.

I've worked as a data switching networks manager, system administrator, system engineer in charge of network/computer security, avionics sensor system specialist, licensed practical nurse, secure communications specialist, and a communications/navigations specialist.

I have been responsible for $265 million dollars worth of equipment and more than 9 employees at once.

I have provided solutions for the following situations;

A project to upgrade all of the servers and increase their numbers at Soto Cano AB, was began a year before I arrived. I studied the purchase and began making plans to implement the upgrades (Win 2K to Win 2K3 server). Our base had stopped making backups a year before I arrived. I learned that a 136T tape library had been ordered with LTO1 drives. Building tables and charts for presentations I convinced the acting project manager to let me talk to J6 and the DELL sales team. By tracking our growth trend I realized that the LTO1 drives would be too slow to backup our current data according to the back tables provided by an IA team. It would take days to perform a single full backup. So, I spoke with our purchasing office, J6, the PM, and the DELL sales team and since the purchase had already been make they couldn't help me. However, the 136T had not been built and nothing had been shipped yet, so I suggested that they withhold 3 of the 24 servers we had ordered and upgrade the LTO1 drives to LTO3 drives. The idea was accepted and I handled all the communication aspects of the deal. With this new configuration our base was able to make its first tape backups in over a year, pass a green team evaluation, and a SAV. I've designed and implemented proposals for coup sites, disaster recovery/ backup plans (warm and off-site), hardware and software (Vmware) laboratories. I did all this in coordination with Information Assurance (Michael Broady) and our configuration management (Robert Bennett) managers, making certain that all proposals were complied with DISA guidance. DOD Laptops were allegedly stolen and allegedly used to steal US communications bandwidth. I selected members for an investigative team to go to Tegucigalpa, Honduras. I provided technical support by telephone and assisted in securing the results of the investigation for the Army. The team was sent to image hard drives that were in the custody of the Honduran police and bring the images back to Soto Cano AB for the Army (J8).

I designed and implemented a proposal to relocate the network operations center (NOC). I designed disaster recovery plans and negotiated procedures with off-site commanders to implement equipment and data storage procedures.

I upgraded all 12 of the servers at Soto Cano AB from MS Windows 2000 servers to MS Windows 2k3 professional servers. After that project was completed I added 24 more servers. All 36 servers had MS Windows 2k3 server installed by the time I was promoted to System Engineer in charge of network and computer security (A period of six and ½ months).

I have setup and loaded images into Cisco, C1600, C2900, C3500, & C3600 switches.

I have repaired computers and networks for the military, friends, and family members for over 20 years. I have coordinated efforts with several on-line services (America On-Line, CompuServe, Prodigy, MSN, DISA, and GNN).

I can use my computer experience to help your company. I can install/ configure hardware and software. I can do upgrades on hardware and software. I can teach other employees how to do these things.

Training employees always makes a company more valuable and independent.

(Information Technology) COVER LETTER

I retired from the Air Force reserves in 2003 and Federal Civil Service in 2006.

I've worked as a data switching networks manager, system administrator, system engineer in charge of network/computer security, avionics sensor system specialist, licensed practical nurse, secure communications specialist, and a communications/navigations specialist.

I have been responsible for $265 million dollars worth of equipment and more than 9 employees at once.

I have expertise in the following operating systems;

• DOS 5+	○ Windows XP Professional	▪ Mepis
• DOS6+	○ Windows Vista Ultimate	▪ Debian (Etch)
• Windows 3.1	○ Windows Vista Home	▪ Solaris 1, 2, 6, & 8
• Windows '95	○ Exchange Server 5.5	
• Windows '98	○ Exchange Server 2003	
• NT 3.5	○ Windows 2003 Server	
• NT 4.0	○ Red Hat 8.0	
• Windows 2000	○ Debian (Sarge)	
• XP Home		

and other operating systems.

I have used a large variety of application software expertise;

❖ Norton anti-virus	➤ Norton Utilities
❖ IIS	➤ McAfee Antivirus
❖ Word Perfect 6.0a	➤ Grisoft AVG
❖ Corel Word Perfect Suite 8	➤ Microsoft Office '97
❖ Quicken	➤ Microsoft Office 2000 Professional
❖ Quick Books	➤ Microsoft Office 2002 Business Edition
❖ Paintshop Pro 6, 7, & 9	➤ Microsoft Office XP Professional
❖ Veritas BU SW	➤ Symantec Raptor/Enterprise FW
❖ Microsoft Office 2003 Professional	➤ Net Beans (Java)
❖ Visual Studios	➤ SQL Server 2000
❖ SQL Server 2005	➤ DELL OpenManage
❖ Partition Magic	

and many others.

I have expertise with the following DELL equipment;

⊥ SAN EMC CX300	⊥ PowerVault 128T
⊥ PowerEdge 6300	⊥ PowerVault 136T
⊥ PowerEdge 6400	⊥ Optiplex GX100
⊥ PowerEdge 2650	⊥ Optiplex GX110
⊥ PowerEdge 2850	⊥ Precision 490

and others

I upgraded all 12 of the servers at Soto Cano AB from MS Windows 2000 servers to MS Windows 2k3 professional servers. After that project was completed I added 24 more servers. All 36 servers had MS Windows 2k3 server installed by the time I was promoted to System Engineer in charge of network and computer security (A period of six and ½ months).

I have loaded images into Cisco, C1600, C2900, C3500, & C3600 switches.

I have installed and configured Linksys wireless routers and NICs.

I have repaired computers and networks for the military, friends, and family members for over 20 years. I have coordinated efforts with several on-line services (America On-Line, CompuServe, Prodigy, MSN, DISA, and GNN).

I can use my computer experience to help your company. I can install/ configure hardware and software. I can do upgrades on hardware and software. I can teach other employees how to do these things.

Training employees always makes a company more valuable and independent.

RESUME

Name: Daniel Leroy McGrew

Education: Graduate Degree

Branch of Service: Air Force (Retired - 2003)

Highest Military Pay Grade: E-6 (Non Commissioned Officer)

Security Clearance: Secret

Availability Date: 3/21/07

Salary Requirement: 75000 /yr

Acceptable Types of Work:

 Full Time   Permanent   Contract

Information Technology Specialist

Daniel L McGrew
181 Lakeway Drive
Saint Matthews, SC 29135
Home Phone: (512) ###-####
danix@mcgrew-fam.net

Resume Last Updated: 1/1/07

JOB INTEREST
Information Technology, Computer, Computer consultant

PERSONAL INTERESTS
Computers, network design, security, education (home-schooling), laser & cryptography hardware & software theory and application.

OBJECTIVE
Information technology consulting, upgrading older (legacy) technology
to new standards. Research and development.

EXPERIENCE
25Sep2006 – 21Nov06: Dell Desktop Support
Computer Management Systems (CMS)
Ft. Sill, OK
Provide complete infrastructural desktop support for Federal Employees
utilizing MS Windows XP Pro, Office 2003 Pro, and Windows 2000.
Responsible for the proper administration and maintenance of 5 DELL,
windows based servers. Perform hardware break/fix. Image Dell PCs,
utilizing Symantec Ghost software. Ensure printers, network and or local
printers are re-assigned to correct users. Verify operation capabilities;
access to the internet/intranet, and e-mail. Equipment covered includes
Contractor and Government Furnished Equipment (GFE) Dell GX-270
Desktops, D800 Laptops, GX-260 Desktop, C840 Laptops, and Tier
2 Unit NCS technologies. I am competent in GUI and command-line
operation, able to map network drives, add network printers, able to add
shortcuts to the desktop. Utilize strong communication, leadership, organi
zational and customer service skills.
Hours per week: 40
Reason for leaving: Two month contract ended
Supervisor's names:
De Brown
Phone: ###-###-####

13Feb2006 – 7Mar2006: System Engineer (Network Security)
Charter Trading (Harris Communications)
Soto Cano Air Base, Honduras
Report directly to the site program manager. Primarily responsible for
the security of 800 Windows XP Professional workstations, 34 Windows
2003 servers, 2 Solaris servers, and over 1000 user accounts at Soto Cano
AB in Honduras. Provide end-user training for LAN and off-the-shelf
applications, including approved specialized applications. Advise program
manager, J6, and staff on security systems-related matters and functions as
the primary source of security information on local technical capabilities
with considerations for applicable DISA guidance pertaining to DOD and
NSA instructions. Perform network scanning and regular upgrades on all
major systems, as required. Perform LAN impact studies for new software

and hardware. Research system security problems, build proposals, attend meetings, discover most convenient network service downtimes for customers, and submit proposals. Provide technical support for system administrators in the performance of their duties and responsibilities.
Hours per week: 40
Reason for leaving: Contract ended.
Supervisor's Names:
Lee Tucker
Phone: 011- ###-###-####
Michael Broady
Phone: 011-###-###-####

1Aug 2005 – 13Feb2006: Data Switching Networks Manager
Charter Trading (Harris Communications)
Soto Cano Air Base, Honduras
Report directly to the site program manager. Supervise 6 system administrators. Primarily responsible for administration of 800 computers, 34 Windows 2003 servers, and over 1000 user accounts at Soto Cano AB in Honduras. Provide end-user training for LAN and off-the-shelf applications, including approved specialized applications. Advise program manager, J6, and staff on technical systems-related matters and functions as the primary source of information on local technical capabilities. Perform troubleshooting and regular upgrades on all major systems, as required. Install, update, and configure Symantec firewall running on Solaris operating system. Direct teams to install, update, and configure security products such as Symantec Enterprise firewall version 8 running on windows 2003 server and Blue Coat 800 proxy server. Track, co-ordinate efforts to maintain hardware and software support agreements and software licenses up-to-date and effective. Perform LAN impact studies for new software and hardware and provide the harvested information to other department heads during scheduled meetings to assure zero impact on our network's resources and its users. I've registered on the Cisco and General Electric websites to download appropriate updates for the switches that we had at Soto Cano AB in Honduras. I read DISA emails about required updates, searched the Cisco & GE websites for information concerning the updates. Downloaded the updates to the appropriate location within our CM library and loaded the ios on Cisco switches (2900 & 3500) & KG-100s. I've updated the ios on some switches when the memory was sufficient, at other times when it was not, I deleted the old ios, loaded the new ios, and rebooted the switch. I've also monitored and troubleshot switches via Solarwinds Network

Monitoring System. We made extensive use of the VLAN technology incorporated in the switches. I have used e-Eye Retina network scanning tools to scan networks. I've researched network/server/workstation vulnerabilities, built and presented proposal solutions, and helped monitor and incorporate the solutions. Reported findings and coordinated solution status with Army J6 and Defense Information Security Agency (DISA). We also had an internal update server (SUS updated to WSUS). I've also designed proposals for, and setup Symantec Enterprise Firewall. I worked with SouthCom purchasing office to straighten out support agreements. I've instigated, tracked, and co-ordinated the purchase and delivery of a Blue Coat proxy server. I also designed proposals for, upgraded its software, and set it up.

Beginning number of servers managed: 12 Dell PowerEdge
Ending number of servers managed: 36 Dell PowerEdge
Hours per week: 40
Reason for leaving: Promoted to System Engineer (Network Security)
Supervisor's Names:
Lee Tucker
Phone: 011- ###-###-####
Michael Broady
Phone: 011-###-###-####

1) 2005 - Passed Army Green Team evaluation with seven correctable defects
2) 2005 - Pass Army SAV with zero defects
3) 2006 - First tape backups performed since the DELL 128T Tape Library broke in 2004
4) 2006 - First disaster recovery plans built
5) 2005 - External DNS structure change to build a true DMZ

30Oct 2001 - 1Jul 2005: Supply Specialist (GS-2005-05-00)
Civil Service (United States Air Force) (Bldg 225)
Altus AFB Oklahoma 73571 ###-###-####
Provided supply support for production, repair, and other operations for assigned aircraft. Maintained accounts and records, completed individual transactions, screened reference files, conducted data searches, and distributed output files. Performed document control work involved in the processing of supply transactions. Provided assistance to customers and other organizations. Provided quality customer support.
Hours per week: 40
Reason for leaving: Increase in workload beyond my physical ability.

Supervisor's Name:
Woodrow W. Wilson
Phone: ###-###-####

1) 20Feb2001 Suggestion Cash Award
2) 7Nov2001 Suggestion Cash Award
3) 19May2002 Performance Award
4) 19May2002 Time Off Award
5) 1Jun2003 Performance Award
6) 1Jun2003 Time Off Award
7) 28Jul2003 Time Off Award
8) 5May2004 Suggestion Cash Award
9) 1Jun2004 Performance Award
10) 3Jun2004 Time Off Award

28Sep1998 - 28Oct2001: Integrated Electronics Systems Mechanic (WG-2610-12-05)
Civil Service (United States Air Force) (Hanger 285)
Altus AFB Oklahoma 73571 ###-###-####
Perform various tasks to maintain aircraft (C-141, C-5, C-17) radio/INS/ instruments and autopilot for communications/navigations. Including, but not limited to, UHF, VHF, HF, GPS, IFF, TACAN, INS, FSAS, GPS/ INS, L-Band SATcomm, and VOR/LOC. These tasks include, but are not limited to, testing, trouble-shooting, installing components, checking/ repairing wiring,
alignments, and final check-out procedures.
Hours per week: 40
Reason for leaving: ACL tear moving a C-141 generator through a hanger door.
Supervisor's Name:
Arnold Garner
Phone: ###-###-####

1) 10Jun1998 Suggestion Cash Award
2) 9Oct1998 Suggestion Cash Award
3) 12Nov1998 Suggestion Cash Award
4) 14Sep1999 Suggestion Cash Award
5) 22Nov1999 Suggestion Cash Award
6) 14Jan2000 Suggestion Cash Award
7) 1Jun2000 Performance Award
8) 26Jun2000 Suggestion Cash Award

9) 25Jul2000 Suggestion Cash Award

21Oct1999 – 11Sep2003: Cryptographic Systems Maintenance Specialist TSgt
United States Air Force Reserves (35 Combat Communications Squadron)
Tinker AFB Oklahoma
Performed various tasks to maintain small IBM computers, Teletype machines,
Multiplexers, and other secure/unsecured communications/computer equipment. Manage all computer installation, maintenance and modification; primarily responsible for administration of all computers, servers, and user accounts at the 507th Air Refueling Wing, Tinker AFB, OK. Provide end-user training for LAN and off-the-shelf applications, including approved specialized applications. Advise commander, NCOIC, and staff on technical systems-related matters and functions as the primary source of information on local technical capabilities. Perform troubleshooting and regular upgrades on all major systems, as required. Install, update, and configure Symantec firewall running on Solaris and Windows operating systems. Direct teams to install, update, and configure information assurance products such as Symantec antivirus and firewall appliances. Track, co-ordinate efforts to maintain hardware and software support agreements and software licenses up-to-date and effective. Perform LAN impact studies for new software and hardware. Maintenance for this equipment included, but was not limited to, testing, trouble-shooting, installing components, checking/repairing inter-equipment wiring, alignments, and final check-out procedures. I configured operating systems and software applications (DOS, Solaris, & Windows) to machine, user, and Air Force specifications. Worked to verbal and/or written specifications using blueprints, wiring diagrams, and sketches
to maintain the systems in peak operating condition.
Hours per week: (One weekend per month [16 hrs X 12 months = 192 hrs]) + One annual tour [2 wks = 80 hrs] = 272 hrs per year ÷ 52 wks = 5.23 hrs per week.
Reason for leaving: Retired in 2003
Supervisor's Name:
Anna Amos

Additional Duties:
   o   Safety NCO

o   PMEL NCO
o   Training NCO

Military Awards and Decorations
Air Force Commendation Medal
Air Force Achievement Medal
AF Outstanding Unit Award
AF Good Conduct Medal
Air Reserve Forces Meritorious Service MDL
National Defense Service Medal
AF Longevity Service Award Ribbon
NCO Prof. Mil. Educ. Grad. Ribbon
Air Force Training Ribbon

1Sep1997 to 1May06: Information Technology Consultant
Family Computers (Tipton, Oklahoma ###-###-####)
Perform various tasks to maintain small IBM computers. Operate and
consult for a 6 computer LAN with one dial-in. Utilize MS Windows
Server 2003, XP Pro, XP Home, Office 2000, and XP. Design and
implement webpage deployment for customers. Perform testing and
approval via XP Pro IIS, via no-ip.com. Maintenance for this equipment
and software included, but was not limited to, testing, trouble-shooting,
purchasing components, tracking components, installing components,
checking/repairing inter-equipment wiring, alignments, and final
check-out procedures. I configured operating systems and software
applications (DOS, Solaris, & Windows) to machine, user, and Company
specifications. Worked to verbal and/or written specifications using
blueprints, wiring diagrams, and sketches to maintain the systems in peak
and secure operating condition.
Hours per week: 40
Reason for leaving: Temporarily moved to SC in order assist dad and
uncle with Vietnam veteran's administration claims.
Supervisor's Name:
Daniel Leroy McGrew Phone: ###-###-####

October 1993 to September 1997 Aircraft Communications/
Navigations Specialist, SSgt
United States Air Force Reserves (315th Air Lift Wing 315th
Component Repair Squadron)
Charleston AFB, SC
Repair HF, VHF, UHF, ADF, VOR, IFF radios. Repair GPS system, SKE

system, color weather radar system. (In-shop) When configured for C-141, C-5, and C-17 aircraft. Additional Duty: I taught computer hardware (Basic and Advanced) at the Charleston Air Force Base 315th MXS Computer Learning Center. I also taught application software courses such as; Word 6.0 for Windows (Basic, Intermediate,& Advanced), Windows 3.1 (Basic & Advanced), Windows '95 (Basic & Advanced), Excel(Basic & Advanced), and PowerPoint (Basic & Advanced), at the Computer Learning Center for the 315th MXS Airlift Wing,.Charleston AFB. I have run a computer bulletin board (PowerBBS for Windows '95) and have expertise in DOS 5+, DOS6+, Windows 3.1, Windows '95, and a wide variety of other operating systems.

Hours per week: 5.23 (One weekend per month [16 hrs X 12 months = 192 hrs] + One annual tour [2 wks = 80 hrs] = 272 hrs per year ÷ 52 wks = 5.23 hrs per week.

Reason for leaving: Moved to Oklahoma for employment with AFPC's federal civil service.

Supervisor's Name:
MSgt. Steve Bruhn. Phone: Unknown

October 1995 to March 1996
Hallmark Health Centers Midland Parkway Summerville, SC
Nurse (LPN) Examined residents, reported and documented findings to doctors and other nursing staff. Co-ordinated care with doctors, facilities, and families. Administered medications, treatments, and feedings to residents. Made rounds, examined residents, monitored progress with medical treatment, and reported all results to physicians. Trained new nurses on staff in proper procedures and guidelines for facility care. Ordered medications, treatment supplies, feeding supplies, and diagnostic supplies. My other duties included purchasing/Installing tape back-up drives, memory chips (SIMMS), and printer sharing devices for our computer (LAN/WAN) network. Used Windows 3.1, '95, and NT.

Hours per week: 40

Reason for leaving: Moved to Oklahoma for employment with AFPC's federal civil service.

Supervisor's Name:
Ms. Harrington. Phone: Unknown.

September 1990 to October1992 Cryptographic Systems Maintenance Specialist SSgt
United States Air Force Reserves 924th Fighter Wing - 924th Secure Communications Squadron

Bergstrom AFB, TX 76530
Repaired teletypes, KY-58s, KG-84s, secure/unsecure computer networks (NT 3.5), small computers, 80386s, 80486s, Pentiums, multiplexers, taught various types of security programs (COMSEC, OPSEC, ect…) to other airmen. Installed radios at bombing range in South Texas, installed all associated wiring for radios. Awarded five skill level and was entered into seven level training. Carefully evaluated and analyzed our unit's computer equipment, to ensure that our needs and requirements were met. Some of my other tasks included, but were not limited to, testing, trouble-shooting, installing components, checking/repairing inter-equipment wiring, alignments, and final check-out procedures. Working to verbal and/or written specifications using blueprints, wiring diagrams, and sketches to maintain the mentioned systems in peak operating condition. While, simultaneously ensuring individual and system wide security remained intact. Prepared recommendations and reports of our computer systems, so that accurate decisions could be made. I was the 924th Secure Communications (Crypto) Shop Chief.

Additional Duties:
- o Safety NCO
- o Security NCO
- o Awards & Decorations NCO
- o Equipment Custodian
- o CAMS (Computer Automated Maintenance) NCO
- o PMEL NCO
- o TO NCO

Hours per week: 5.23 (One weekend per month [16 hrs X 12 months = 192 hrs] + One annual tour [2 wks = 80 hrs] = 272 hrs per year ÷ 52 wks = 5.23 hrs per week.
Reason for leaving: Discovered that my dad had a brain tumor. I moved to SC to assist mom with caring for him.
Supervisor's Name:
MSgt. Donna Pruitt. Phone: Unknown.

September 1987 to October 1991 Avionics Sensor Systems Specialist SrA
USAF 35th & 37th Tactical Fighter Wings Component Repair Squadron
George AFB, CA
Repaired TISEO (Target Identification System Electo-Optical) equipment and associated cockpit equipment. Went to TISEO FTD, at Seymore

Johnson AFB. Cross-utilization training to work on Airborne Visual Tape Recorders, Gun cameras (KB-25), Radar cameras, and associated cockpit equipment. Shop TMDE, avionics AGE, shop Technical orders, periodic maintenance inspections. Setup shop equipment into CAMS computer when it first came on-line at George AFB. Continued seven level upgrade training. (In-shop & Flight-line, F-4 (E&G aircraft)).

Additional Duties:
- o   Safety NCO
- o   Security NCO
- o   Awards & Decorations NCO
- o   Equipment Custodian
- o   CAMS (Computer Automated Maintenance) NCO
- o   PMEL NCO
- o   TO NCO

Hours per week: 40
Reason for leaving: 4 year enlistment completed.
Supervisor's Name:
MSgt. Stanly Gamble. Phone: Unknown
MSgt. Gene Wilson   Phone : Unknown

January 1986 to September 1987 Avionics Sensor System Specialist USAF Reserves 924th Tactical Fighter Wing 924th Tactical Fighter Squadron SrA
Bergstrom AFB, TX USA
Repaired PAVE spike pods, and associated cockpit equipment required for PAVE spike operation. Operational checks of system, troubleshooting systems, training others, making suggestions on AF form 22, and performed scheduled inspections. Awarded five skill level and entered upgrade training for seven level. (In-shop, F-4 (C&D aircraft)).
Hours per week: 5.23 (One weekend per month [16 hrs X 12 months = 192 hrs] + One annual tour [2 wks = 80 hrs] = 272 hrs per year ÷ 52 wks = 5.23 hrs per week.
Reason for leaving: Assessed to active duty.
Supervisor's Name:
MSgt. Simmons. Phone: Unknown.

EDUCATION
07/13/2004 – 6/01/2005:
American Intercontinental University
5550 Prairie Stone Pkwy

Hoffman Estates, IL 60192

Master's Degree
Major: Information Technology
Minor: Information Security
Graduate July 2005
GPA 3.90

Information Systems ITS610 6
7/11/2004 8/14/2004
Enterprise Network Design ITN620 6
8/29/2004 10/2/2004
Object Oriented Programming ITP630 6
10/3/2004 11/6/2004
Database Design and Implementation ITD640 6
11/14/2004 12/18/2004
Introduction to Information Security ITS650 6
1/2/2005 2/5/2005
Cryptography Concepts ITS660 6
2/13/2005 3/19/2005
Special Topics in Network Security ITS670 6
3/20/2005 4/23/2005

06/01/2003 - 07/12/2004:
American Intercontinental University
5550 Prairie Stone Pkwy
Hoffman Estates, IL 60192

Bachelor's Degree
Major: Information Technology
Minor: Computer Technology
Dean's List: Junior and senior years.
Graduate July 2004
GPA 3.98 Summa Cum Laude

Introduction to Information Technology ITB300 10 6/8/2003 7/12/2003
Network Operating Systems ITN310 10
7/20/2003 8/23/2003
Network O/S Administration ITN320 10
8/24/2003 9/27/2003
Data Modeling and Design ITD340 10

10/12/2003 11/15/2003
Database Administration ITD400 10
11/16/2003 12/20/2003
Beginning Programming ITP410 10
1/4/2004 2/7/2004
Advanced Programming ITP420 10
2/8/2004 3/13/2004
Web Applications ITP430 10
3/21/2004 4/24/2004
Advanced Network O/S Administration ITN330 10
4/25/2004 5/29/2004
Strategic Management ITB460 10
6/6/2004 7/10/2004

01/01/1996 - 01/01/1997:
Community College of the Air Force
130 West Maxwell Blvd
Maxwell AFB, AL 36112-6613

Associate's Degree
Major: Aircraft Maintenance Technology
Minor: Computer Technology
Degree program consists of a minimum of 64 semester hours with requirements
typically as follows: Semester Hours
Technical Education 24
Leadership, Management, and Military Studies 6
Physical Education 4
General Education 15
Oral Communication 3
Written Communication 3
Mathematics 3
Social Science 3
Humanities 3
Program Elective 15
Total 64

Leadership, management, and military studies; physical education; general education; and program elective requirements have all been met.

01/01/1997 - 01/01/1998:

Community College of the Air Force
130 West Maxwell Blvd
 Maxwell AFB, AL 36112-6613

Associate's Degree
Major: Electrical / Electronic Technology
Minor: Computer Technology
Degree program consists of a minimum of 64 semester hours with requirements
typically as follows: Semester Hours
Technical Education 24
Leadership, Management, and Military Studies 6
Physical Education 4
General Education 15
Oral Communication 3
Written Communication 3
Mathematics 3
Social Science 3
Humanities 3
Program Elective 15
Total 64

Leadership, management, and military studies; physical education; general education; and program elective requirements have all been met.

I held the journeyman (five) level in the 32252B, 45550A, & 30656 AFSC at time of program completion.

I held the journeyman (five & seven) levels in the 32272B, 45570A, & 30676AFSC at time of program completion.

SKILLS
A+ Certified Professional, Type 80+ wpm.

ADDITIONAL INFORMATION
I can do almost anything with a computer. For the FULL story, check here
--
http://danix.no-ip.info/Resume/index.htm
30+% Disabled Vet

DISABILITY SELF IDENTIFICATION
No lifting more than 25 lbs
No squatting
No bending
No crawling
No climbing

Location Preferences:

Any location – as long as relocation expenses are paid by employer
I am willing to consider other locations in the U.S.

X1 & X2 - are a/craft that I worked on. However, the workload was rather intense at the time, and I did not arrive at the opportunity to document the a/craft tail numbers.

Rode the truck - These words carry special meaning. Anyplace that these words are mentioned indicate that I rode the truck for a minimum of 3 hours. I have ridden the truck for as many as five (5) hours. This at the demand of my supervisors that I stop wandering.

** The terms endearing, when used in this document, are intended to be used with full (Edgar Allen Poe-like) irony. Sarcasm.

*** All of the proper tools, tech data, and equipment were available and used for all of the jobs mentioned in this a/craft history notebook, alias a/craft diary.

v - Retired Col. Bradley (Civil service commander - director of maintenance), the AFGE Union president, and the AFGE chief union steward (Harold Church) all received copies of the first part of this diary. Their copies were taken by Mr. Bradley's secretary, accidentally on purpose. Their copies date from the beginning of this a/craft diary to 15January1998.

***** - Dawn Depew and Tammy Romero have a courtesy copy, opinions excluded, of my a/craft diary, dating from February 23, 1998 to March 13, 1998.

vvv - a/craft that are mentioned more than once per day. This is because, I worked on the a/craft. I helped launch it. The same a/craft returned. I worked on it some more.

- Jobs performed in the ISO docks. These jobs will be counted separately on the graphs.

+++ - the majority of the "æ½¼" designations are my personal opinions, and cannot be used against me for anything what-so-ever. My opinions are my personal property and are to be used only with their owner's (Daniel Leroy McGrew's) permission. In all cases, the use of my opinions, are subject to my desires only.

- Therefore, I have at least four sources of information for each story. I have not written the names of all the sources. Some sources gave me permission to use their names and some didn't. The ones who did are mentioned. The ones who didn't are not. With the knowledge that a member of management's secretary accidentally got her hands on a portion of my diary and copied some it. I continue to try to leave out people's names who request that they not be mentioned in my diary.

++***++ = - The spirit of the exceptions will prevail.

* - Green form or form indicates a 'Duty status report' form. My bosses continued to demand that I bring them these forms. The doctors continued to tell me that they don't know how to fill them out and don't want to learn. My supervisors are telling me to do a job (get these forms filled out by medical professionals) for them (that takes hours and sometimes days), but they are not willing to pay me for it. I don't get time off or money to compensate me for it. When they forget to give me one of the forms. They fuss at me and I have to jump through the hoops to get it done after the fact. Believe me, this is a pain.

1 - About he and Arnie being left in the dark

2 - The parrots are silent, for the moment. Probably saving their energy.

3 – I cannot remember the name or the number that she gave me to call.

4 – Tony is the gentleman in the CPO lobby area. If someone does not answer a telephone, it rings around to his desk.

5 – The initials WC stand for Workers' Compensation.

Extra Special Accomplishments list in A/C diary II

Î - I have put in 18 AFTO 22s. 12 AFTO 22s have been approved by their major commands. 4 were approved, but down-graded to routine. 2 have been disapproved.

Ï - 4 AFTO 22s and AF form 1000s have been approved by their major commands, technical representatives, and Depots.

Đ - Helped ISO/HSC do one time inspection (OTI) on all C-141B engine mounts. We did 11 a/craft in one day. That's 44 engines.

Ñ - Volunteered to stay over 2 hours to help jack an a/craft in hanger 435. I volunteered for just about everything that came along

Ò - People helped with AFTO 22 filling. James Atkins, Quine, and Cecilio.

Let it be known that this entire diary was put into small green notebooks and later typed into a computer at home. No government computers were used. No government computers were harmed or otherwise endangered in the making of this diary. This diary is not to be used to bring harm or endanger any federal employees active and/or retired including me.

.

www.ingramcontent.com/pod-product-compliance
Lightning Source LLC
Chambersburg PA
CBHW061353280526
45784CB00001B/235